GENERATION UNCOUPLED

GENERATION UNCOUPLED

AMERICA'S NEW GENDER DIVIDE AND THE CRISIS OF HUMAN CONNECTION

BY DANIEL COX

HARMONY BOOKS
NEW YORK, NY

Harmony Books
An imprint of Random House
A division of Penguin Random House LLC
1745 Broadway, New York, NY 10019
harmonybooks.com | randomhousebooks.com
penguinrandomhouse.com

ISBN 9780593603437
Ebook ISBN 9780593603444

Printed in the United States of America

1st Printing

First Edition

Book Team: Production editor: Cassie Gitkin • Managing editor: Allison Fox • Production manager: Samuel Wetzler • Copy editor: David Goehring • Proofreaders: Cyrus Chin, Samantha Faust-Miano, Elizabeth Gomez, Olivia Trzaski, Rachel Twersky

Book design by Diane Hobbing

The authorized representative in the EU for product safety and compliance is Penguin Random House Ireland, Morrison Chambers, 32 Nassau Street, Dublin D02 YH68, Ireland. https://eu-contact.penguin.ie

To Stephanie, Rowan, and Kieran

CONTENTS

AUTHOR'S NOTE

This book relies on many personal stories shared by young men and women. Over the course of this project, more than one hundred individuals were interviewed from around the country. I have changed the first names of interviewees to ensure their anonymity and preserve their privacy.

INTRODUCTION:
REKINDLING CURIOSITY

In 1982, Steven Doloff, an instructor at a small two-year college in New York, gave his students a provocative assignment. Inspired by the hit film *Tootsie,* about a struggling actor who pretends to be a woman to help his career, Doloff assigned his students to write an essay about how they would spend the day if they suddenly became a member of the opposite sex. In writing about the assignment for *The Washington Post,* Doloff noted with some disappointment that his male students were evasive, apathetic, and less than enthusiastic about the exercise. One such aggrieved male student crumpled up the assignment, exclaiming, "You can't make me write this!" The female students, while more inquisitive and willing to explore the world as a man, provided mostly superficial answers. Most students expressed relief in returning to their own gender at the end of the day.

There is no more universal experience than wanting to be known and seen. Most of us will, at one point or another, feel that people do not quite "get" us, appreciate our sense of humor, or understand our point of view. Almost every teenager has at some point felt misunderstood—it's part of growing up. No matter how often we are encouraged to "walk in someone else's shoes," to truly know how someone else lives and the problems they face is deceptively difficult in practice. It requires time, patience, empathy, and most of all the continual cultivation of curiosity. These commitments are challenging under the best circumstances, but even more so when we are so often reminded to tend to our own interests, anxieties, and boundaries. We've lost our appetite for inquisitiveness, and young men and women are living with the consequences.

I've dedicated my career to asking questions. My goal has always been to ask people questions about the things that matter to them. I've never been that interested in measuring public support for political candidates or documenting new consumer trends. I want to understand how Americans live, the challenges they face, the way they spend their time, and who they spend it with. Shortly after arriving at the American Enterprise Institute in 2019, I founded the Survey Center on American Life to serve as an engine for our research on day-to-day American experiences. It has been a dream job.

Since its founding, the Survey Center has served as an authoritative source of information on changing relationship dynamics—in dating, marriage, and family life—and rising rates of loneliness and alienation in the United States. In 2021, we published a major report on America's "friendship recession," which set off a cascade of interest in loneliness and social disconnection. The following year, I published some groundbreaking data on the ideological divide emerging between young men and women in an article titled "The Political Gender Gap is Exploding." That article sparked considerable debate; it also changed the trajectory of my research interests. It led me to question not only what was happening to America's social and civic fabric, but who was most affected by these changes. Since then, I've been asking some version of the same question in surveys, focus groups, and in-depth interviews. What are the forces—social, political, and cultural—that have made it more difficult for young men and women to develop lasting social connections? And perhaps more importantly, what has led so many to stop trying?

Over the next three years, our research began to consistently explore the distinctive ways young women and men talked about their problems, voiced their fears, and reflected on their place in the world. In mainstream media, the "gender divide" is often used to describe the diverging choices men and women make at the ballot box. This rift is deeper and more personal. In our research, my team at the Survey Center conducted a series of national polls on dating, friendship and family life, formative childhood experiences, and technology use. We traveled to cities across the country to conduct focus groups and in-depth interviews to move beyond the numbers. What we found is that the gender divide is a relational crisis between men and women. The book you are reading now is the product of this substantial research effort.

When I first came across Doloff's assignment, I asked a friend of mine who teaches English in a public high school in Maryland whether he would ever consider assigning this exercise to his students. He visibly recoiled. "Never." He assumed, I'm sure rightly, that parents would freak out about having boys imagining themselves as girls and vice versa. I certainly couldn't blame him, but I still wanted an answer. The more young people I spoke to about their dating lives, relationships, and life goals, the more it seemed they were living in entirely different worlds.

So, in early 2026, I worked with the National Opinion Research Center (NORC) at the University of Chicago to conduct a nationally representative survey of American teenagers. As part of this research, we asked each respondent to consider the following: "Imagine you wake up and you are now a teenager of the opposite sex. In a few sentences, write about your experience . . . what are you feeling, what are you excited about or worried about as you begin your day?" Their task was to simply write a short reply, and roughly eight in ten boys and girls made at least some attempt to do so.

The most consistent response, from both boys and girls, was that the experience would be disorienting. The word "weird" came up more than a few times. Girls were more aware of the advantages afforded to them by switching genders, while boys' reactions were more negative. Boys provided less detailed responses using significantly fewer words on average. And although the prompt specifically asked them to consider some aspect of the experience that would be exciting, not a single boy used that word in their response. Many girls did. But a depressing conclusion from this exercise was the demonstrable lack of genuine curiosity expressed by boys and girls alike about what it's like to live as the opposite sex. Here's a sample of what they said:

> "If I had woken up as a boy I would apologize to all the women I've played around with. I would apologize for my ignorance and immaturity. I would go to school excited to learn and not make loud noises when an adult is speaking."
>
> —Sixteen-year-old girl

> "Eww! I'm gross and I'm sweaty and now I can't wear any of my clothes so I'll have to wear my brother's gross ones and now I can't do any of my hobbies anymore because they're feminine, but I guess I can wrestle people."
>
> —Fourteen-year-old girl

> "I feel my experience would be stressful with the lack of skills to makes friends [but] I'd be excited to be by myself and play independent games."
>
> —Seventeen-year-old girl

> "I guess I would probably be thinking about sports and girls and being stupid and loud with my friends. I would worry about embarrassing myself in front of girls."
>
> —Thirteen-year-old girl

"I would be very upset. I can't imagine myself as a girl. They giggle too much."

—Fifteen-year-old boy

"I would be worried because I am less strong, but I would be happy because I can express my emotions better."

—Sixteen-year-old boy

"I could get away with more things."

—Seventeen-year-old boy

"I would attempt to see how easily I could manipulate the system. How much money I could make and how many people I could take advantage of."

—Seventeen-year-old boy

At best, the responses reveal a fairly superficial understanding of the opposite sex. Some of the worst showed thinly veiled hostility or even outright resentment. Many responses leaned heavily on very outmoded ideas about gender. Perhaps I shouldn't be surprised, given that these are teenagers still figuring out much about themselves and the people around them. Still, it doesn't leave one with a great deal of optimism about where we're headed.

Boys and girls have always viewed things somewhat differently, but historically we've seen this gap recede as they each gain more life experience and spend time together. This generation of young adults is not following the same path. Entering adulthood, young men and women today seem less tolerant, patient, and understanding of one another. In a recent survey we conducted, only 42 percent of young men believe that women understand the "day-to-day challenges and problems" that men face in American society. Even fewer young women (25 percent) say the same about men.

What is so concerning about our current moment is not that young men and women are disinterested in sex, companionship, mutual affection, and all the other ingredients of a healthy romantic relationship, but that they are beginning to believe these experiences are unattainable. There used to be structures helping them develop an appreciation of each other—a civic and social infrastructure that pushed them together, and a culture that supported it. Dating has never been a seamless or perfect process, but it has always been a necessary one. We have allowed the allure of novel technologies—social media, dating apps—to displace real-world spaces as the sources of connection and belonging. The initial results are not promising.

There's an incredible amount at stake. Getting this wrong means fewer stable relationships, fewer families with children, rising apathy and distrust, and a greater burden for those trying to build community, a family, or even a friendship. We are creating a society built on transactional social ties and impermanent connections. There's a lot to critique about the nuclear family, but an abundance of research has shown that children raised in two-parent households by married parents have better outcomes. At a time of heightened anxiety, even the most well-meaning parents are not always helping their kids in the way that matters most: helping them forge meaningful relationships. A society cannot flourish if its members are unable to establish strong, stable relationships that endure even when they are inconvenient or difficult. The risk we face is not just an endless cycle of angst and recrimination, abetted by addictive technology, but the slow withdrawal from social life and our obligations to one another. As the process of building social and romantic bonds becomes too burdensome, unpleasant, or risky, more young men and women will simply refuse to participate at all. Without a course correction, we face social starvation at a societal level.

The task for this book is to examine what happens when we shift institutional responsibilities to individuals. Through public opinion data, in-depth interviews, focus groups, and an abundance of journalistic and academic work, I'll show how our most critical relational experiences are disappearing. We'll explore why this happened and what it means for our politics, relationships, and society more broadly. Here's what to expect.

In the first section, "Social Separation," I look at how America's well-documented civic collapse left young people without a shared social architecture. This collapse critically shaped their understanding of themselves and what they owed one another. These first chapters trace how changes in American family structure and formative adolescent experiences—notably the decline in teen dating and socializing—created a culture that rewards personal achievement and individual autonomy above all else. The family unit, once a crucible of communal life, transformed into an efficient machine of individual advancement. Religious organizations, once capable of establishing collective norms that shaped collective values, became vehicles for individual expression. "Social" technology accelerated our desire for self-optimization, and therapy culture provided a new vocabulary to justify placing personal needs above social obligations. Modern hostility between young men and women did not originate with polarized politics, the #MeToo movement, the manosphere, or dating apps. It was the result of so much more.

In the book's second section, "The Gender Rift," I dig into how our modern politics and culture accelerated the gender divide. The first chapter documents the dramatic divergence in ideological identity between young men and women that appeared around 2016. Donald Trump (and the reactions to his unexpected election) shaped the worldviews of young men and women coming of age at a time when politics was not just polarized, but increasingly personal. Political disagreements were not simply measures of policy differences, they were existential battles that created a climate of anxiety and fear. Then, through the wave of new technology and an erosion of institutional trust, new rules of conduct were emerging but were unevenly enforced. The new cultural climate left both men and women feeling a pervasive sense of uncertainty. And despite a desire for more purposeful courtship, modern dating culture and social apps pushed singles in the opposite direction, hurling individuals at each other at an unprecedented rate with little structure, guidance, or shared expectations.

In the final section, "A Path to Reconciliation," I offer some thoughts on how we might move forward. The first step is that we must recognize that romantic struggles are not political or even cultural; they are relational. An unrelenting focus on individual ambition and identity can make us feel seen and special, but it can also leave us lonely. In our commitment to ensure that girls knew they could succeed in the same ways that boys could, we papered over meaningful differences between them. Some challenges girls and boys share, but others are uniquely their own. We ought to acknowledge the distinctiveness of male and female experiences and the problems they face so we can adopt strategies that can more efficiently address them.

This book is about this conversational breakdown. Why men and women talk about each other much more often than they talk to each other. How new technologies have reoriented the way young people learn about and relate to the opposite gender. The way phones and social media platforms altered relational incentives, heightened anxiety, and encouraged avoidance. What we know of ourselves and how we learn to navigate the world is based less on in-person social interactions and more often on thirty-second viral videos that spur misunderstandings and misapprehensions. Living this way is a conscious choice, not the inevitable byproduct of economic or technological progress.

There are incredibly strong forces that are pushing us apart. Our best hope is to exercise our innate curiosity about one another. I've been a survey researcher for nearly twenty years; I've been a curious person for even longer. My work has never been about aiding a campaign, selling a product, or advancing a specific cause. My interest has always been in trying to understand what people believe and the things they care about. This book is an extension of that work. It is an attempt to rekindle our collective curiosity by asking questions and reflecting on the answers that are provided. It's rooted in the belief that an honest and open conversation is the best and only remedy to the problems we face.

Societies collapse in the same way relationships do. When our capacity for respectful discourse deteriorates, we lose our appetite for nuance and complexity—we lose interest in compromise, and our conversational partners become opponents to overcome. My goal is not to provide separate take-home assignments for men and women, but to help build a better understanding of how we have failed to make personal and romantic relationships a priority. Our human impulse to connect has been overwritten by a new script that argues individual flourishing is attainable in the absence of strong social connections.

We are facing a crisis of connection. One study estimated that between 2005 and 2019, Americans spoke an average of roughly three hundred fewer words per day each year, with young adults experiencing the greatest decline.[1] We've traded in-person conversations that once powered our understanding of the people around us for secondhand sources, screeds from strangers, and offensive memes. We might be typing more, but we're talking less. Face-to-face social interactions have fallen, and interpersonal trust along with it. This is where our story begins.

PART I

SOCIAL SEPARATION

To understand what happened to Gen Z, we need to have a better understanding of where they came from. Today's young adults had a remarkably unique childhood. They grew up less likely to have a part-time job, date, get their driver's license, or experiment with smoking and alcohol. They skipped out on church and house parties. Instead, they spent time online—a lot of time. Social media platforms built on the promise of unrestricted connections began competing with traditional adolescent experiences. From pornography to social media, the internet not only changed what kids saw, but when they saw it. Social media trained America's adolescents to prioritize self-presentation, personal identity, and individual expression. The cost was a more difficult path to genuine connection.

But this is only half of the story. In the real world, the institutions meant to shape young people—family, places of worship, and schools—evolved to cater to their needs and promote their individual interests. Parenting simultaneously became more child-centric and yet less prescriptive as parents tried to expand the opportunities provided to their kids while providing less guidance about which one to prioritize. Regular family dinners were replaced by travel sport commitments, SAT prep, music lessons, and other personalized enrichment activities. Religion and spirituality came to reflect personal commitments rather then instilling communal obligations. Schools adapted to prioritize the unique needs and capacities of students. Young adults have learned to expect accommodation and build lives that optimize for personal growth. They have become less comfortable with social friction and less clear about their obligations to others—to their neighbors, friends, and romantic partners. Social norms became more negotiable and behavior less predictable. In the face of an increasingly uncertain world, more young adults have withdrawn from the everyday activities that make social connections sustainable.

CHAPTER 1

UNCIVIL SOCIETY: WHY AMERICANS TURNED ON ONE ANOTHER

It's impossible to produce a single statistic that can adequately capture the current social, civic, and political challenges we face, but this finding from the Pew Research Center comes close: A majority (53 percent) of Americans rate the morality and ethical behavior of their fellow citizens as somewhat bad or very bad.[1] Out of the twenty-five countries surveyed by the Pew researchers, the United States topped the list in negative moral evaluations its citizens made about one another. This is not about denigrating political opponents, or casting unfavorable judgment on an undesirable social group. More than half of Americans believe they live in a country populated mostly by bad people. How on earth did we get here?

There are plenty of factors to consider, but a few stand out. The country's long-standing commitment to individualism, the continued weakening of America's core civic and social institutions, and ongoing political polarization all contributed to the erosion of social bonds and the deterioration of interpersonal trust. When social media arrived in the early 2000s, our social infrastructure that might have mitigated its worst effects was not up to the task. Social media displaced real-world social interactions and played to our worst instincts; it exacerbated our anxieties and warped our views about the motivations and morality of people we had never met.

The rapid integration of social media platforms into our daily lives did not precipitate America's long-standing social, civic, and political problems, but it undoubtedly made them worse. In this section, we're going to examine how social media, as well as the evolution of family life, therapy culture, and other forces have worked together to transform Gen Z's adolescent development.* America's modern gender divide didn't spring up from a single cataclysmic event. It's been something that young people have grown up with.

Anti-Social Media

How bad is social media for us? It's a hotly contested question. In part, because social media is not all one thing. Platforms operate somewhat differently, individuals use them for different purposes, and usage rates vary considerably. Still, much of the emerging research has documented disturbing consequences, especially for young people. In a landmark decision, Meta and YouTube were found liable for developing addictive products harmful to users' mental health.[2] But even if we definitively address the influence social media has on individuals, perhaps an even greater question remains unanswered: What impact does social media have on societies? It's far easier to recruit an individual to participate in an experiment, because conditions and exposures can be systematically varied and measured. This type of control is impossible to exercise

* I use the generational categories defined by the Pew Research Center in 2019. In this case, Gen Z includes anyone born between the years 1997 and 2012. Pew stopped using these definitions in 2023, although they are still widely used today. A complete list of Pew's generational categories can be accessed at: https://www.pewresearch.org/short-reads/2019/01/17/where-millennials-end-and-generation-z-begins.

over complex social structures. At least, it was until very recently. In 2022, a *New York Times* reporter documented what happens after a community without the internet, without YouTube, Instagram, and online pornography suddenly acquires all of these things at once.

There's a good chance you have never heard of the Marubo tribe. They live in remote communities scattered along the Ituí River deep in the Amazon rainforest. They speak their own language and are mostly cut off from the rest of the world. That changed suddenly in 2022, when Elon Musk's Starlink company brought the internet to some of the most inaccessible places on the globe. With the help of generous philanthropy, the tribe was outfitted with Starlink antennas and smartphones. At first, many members of the Marubo tribe were thrilled. Then the ramifications of providing instant access and immediate gratification started to emerge. What the *New York Times* reporter documented was both incredible and predictable: "teenagers glued to phones; group chats full of gossip; addictive social networks; online strangers; violent video games; scams; misinformation; and minors watching pornography."[3] Community life nearly collapsed.

This is the problem with treating social media as a personal vice or addiction. Its impact cannot be measured by its individual effects. Although more difficult to measure, the isolating effect of social media has societal costs as well. Socializing in public places creates ripples of community. Think about it this way: If you initiate plans to meet a couple friends out for a drink, you have not only created an experience for yourself, but for your friends, your neighbors, even the workers as well. A single social act—you texting your friends—has a multiplicative effect. But I don't believe that the displacement effect is the worst thing social media has done to us.

Social media platforms ushered in the age of mass personal communication, allowing strangers across the globe to share pictures of their morning routine, an unhinged rant, or a wild conspiracy theory. Social media was a technology that prioritized speed over accuracy. Political leaders could spout specious claims faster than traditional media outlets could fact-check them. It emphasized the quantity of people we were connected to rather than the quality of connections we had to them. It created perverse social incentives that degraded public discourse as users discovered the rewards in making controversial statements. It made for bitter and acrimonious public discussion, provided a larger platform for conspiracies and misinformation, and led to the destruction of norms and the circumvention of established precedent and processes. Social media could warp our shared reality or splinter it into a billion individualized pieces.

It all happened so fast. Only about a decade into the new age of social media, monoliths like Facebook, Instagram, Twitter, and Snapchat were fundamentally reshaping public debate and quietly reordering the way Americans spent their personal time. In 2018, a new company, TikTok, merged with Musical.ly. Short-form videos, private messaging, and algorithms were starting to dominate public life. The oldest members of Gen Z were on the verge of adulthood and the youngest were starting school for the first time. This was the first generation that would be entirely raised on this new technology. Social media had started with a straightforward proposition to remove geographic barriers and gatekeepers restricting access to information and the people producing it. One used to log online to see friends, family, and funny videos, but now users were inundated with content from strangers and sellers vying for their eyes. It was a cultural shift. The attention economy had arrived, bringing with it an entirely new set of incentives. For those raised on these platforms, the search for identity and community occurred as much online as off. Young adults had become producers of their own lives rather than participants, equipped with a variety of tools to showcase their distinctive talents and experiences—to show the world that they mattered.

By 2018, social media had proved that it was not a sideshow—an irreverent adolescent pastime—but a transformative technology that was fundamentally reshaping the way human beings interacted. In only twenty years, social media was approaching near universal adoption—80 percent of Americans reported using at least one platform, up from 7 percent in 2005.[4,5] The rapid growth produced its own problems. As Americans spent more time on these sites, they had become increasingly frustrated with the experience. While social media sites like Facebook initially promised to create a digital public square, in practice they more often felt like spending time in the Thunderdome. Their central value proposition was in doubt.

Americans' Use of Social Media Has Skyrocketed

Percentage of American adults who use at least one social media site

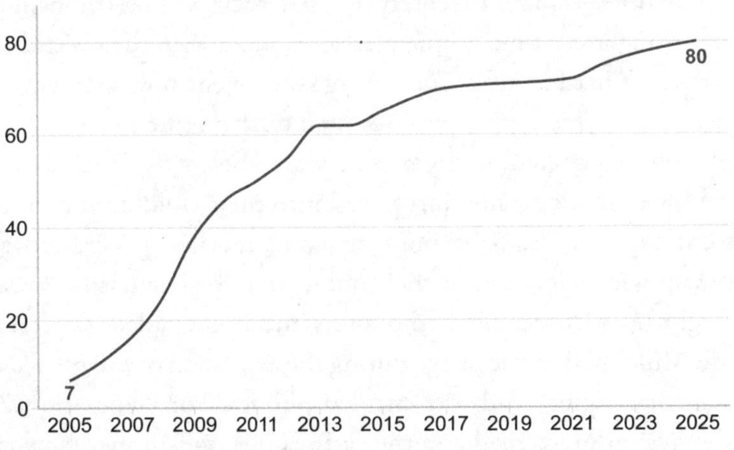

Source: Pew Research Center, 2005–2025. No data available for 2007, 2016, 2018–2020, and 2022–2024.

In early January 2018, Mark Zuckerberg posted on Facebook in response to growing unhappiness with the website. Zuckerberg acknowledged the criticism that the platform had become choked with brand influencers, advertisers, and media companies all jockeying for users' attention. It was a moment to reaffirm Facebook's core commitment to human connection. Zuckerberg promised to sacrifice website engagement by redesigning the user experience to better facilitate building connection. He wrote: "We built Facebook to help people stay connected and bring us closer together with the people that matter to us. That's why we've always put friends and family at the core of the experience."[6]

Less than a decade later, this statement feels utterly incongruous with how most social media platforms actually work. Your average user is spending much more time passively scrolling through posts produced by professional creators, hyper-personalized ads, and curated content that leaves them feeling inadequate or upset. Despite altruistic pretenses, the technology companies responsible for building our digital social infrastructure have the same motivation as every other capitalistic enterprise. For social media companies, maximizing users' time on the platforms was always the overriding interest. It's hard to read Zuckerberg's statement now as anything other than a cynical attempt to forestall further criticism.

To varying degrees, every generation comes of age with a new technology that becomes integrated into their childhood or adolescent experiences. Baby boomers were the first generation to grow up with television in their homes, while Generation X was brought up with personal computers and home video game systems. Millennials came of age during the explosion of the internet, instant messaging, and text-enabled phones. For Generation Z, the arrival of social media in the early 2000s transformed how an entire generation learned about the world and about each other. It was too much, too fast. Our attention dispersed over billions of web pages, social media accounts, engaging videos, and titillating images. The social worlds of young people once came into being progressively through iterative interactions with the people who lived around them. Reputations were established more slowly. Now, young people could create their own stylized versions of themselves for public consumption, not only to their friends but potentially to a much wider audience. The experience left them feeling agitated, anxious, or alone.

Social media is not simply another technology. It does not only create added efficiencies or new opportunities; it fundamentally changes how we socialize, one of our most critical human experiences.

For the last six years, as the Director of the Survey Center on American Life, I've been documenting changes in American social life, from adolescence to adulthood. There's no doubt that social media—and the internet more broadly—has been a transformative force in human society, offering unprecedented access to knowledge, information, and people. But all this access has come at a cost. For all of its incredible connective potential, there is mounting evidence that social media has eroded our sense of trust both in traditional institutions and in each other. It has altered the way we think about ourselves and what we need from others. This erosion has been especially damaging in romantic interactions that require high levels of interpersonal trust and an appreciation for mutual dependency. In large part, the waning confidence that young men and women have in one another is about what is happening in digital space, and what is not happening out in the real world.

At least since the arrival of the radio, cultural critics and technology scolds warned of the corrupting influence that new technologies posed to innocent young minds. Many of these panics, such as the fear of violent video games in the 1990s, seem quaint today. But social media is different, and for the generation who came of age with it, the influence it had over their lives was probably unparalleled. The innocence of early social media content, replete with cat videos, earnest interactions, and quirky personal postings, did much to mask its malignant qualities. We were in no way prepared for how bad it was going to get. Its ubiquity in the lives of teenagers—95 percent of whom are on social media—and its ease of access and addictive qualities have given social media unprecedented influence over adolescents.[7] Unlike previous entertainment technologies like television, VCRs, CD players, the Walkman, and DVD players, social media creates individualized experiences uniquely tailored to the interests of the user. Even if they are scrolling through the same social media app, two users might have radically different experiences. Social media fractures our collective attention by creating personalized experiences crafted by unseen algorithms. In doing so, these apps have also become highly addictive. Nearly half of teenagers report they are online "almost constantly," a dramatic surge over the past decade.[8] In 2015, fewer than one in four teens said they were spending this much time tethered to the internet. Social media has introduced entirely new categories of predatory and antisocial behavior, such as ghosting and cyberstalking, and has offered easy exposure to extreme and offensive content. While previous technologies, such as portable music players and video games, offered adolescents an escape from daily stresses, social media has kept them perpetually activated. It quickly came to occupy a mediating role in the lives of adolescents, shaping their reality through secondhand experience. It was perhaps the worst way for young people to learn about the world and about one another, even as it became one of the main ways in which they did.

Despite the evident threats that global connectivity could conceivably pose to minors, such as exposure to violent and sexual content or opening them up to exploitation and cyberbullying, until recently there was little debate about how—or when—this technology should be introduced to adolescents and teenagers. On average, Gen Z adults reported getting their own social media account before the age of fourteen. But more than a quarter of Gen Z adults report getting their own social media account at some point during their preteen years. By age fifteen, six in ten Gen Z men and nearly eight in ten Gen Z women had joined social media.[9] At some point, every young person seeks validation and acceptance from their peers, but never had the personal lives of adolescents been shared so widely or easily. They were plunged headfirst into online platforms designed to keep them there and they were being shown parts of the world that every previous generation had been at least partly shielded from. For young people, everything was accessible at a time when they were deeply impressionable. Initial curiosities could snowball, introducing more extreme content with the help of an algorithm that targets every adolescent impulse, which easily becomes addictive and exhausting. For better or worse, social media became an indelible part of Gen Z's existence.

As a point of comparison, the average millennial did not get on social media until they were eighteen years old.[10]

Most Gen Z Adults Were on Social Media Before Age 16

Percentage of Gen Z adults who got their own social media account at age . . .

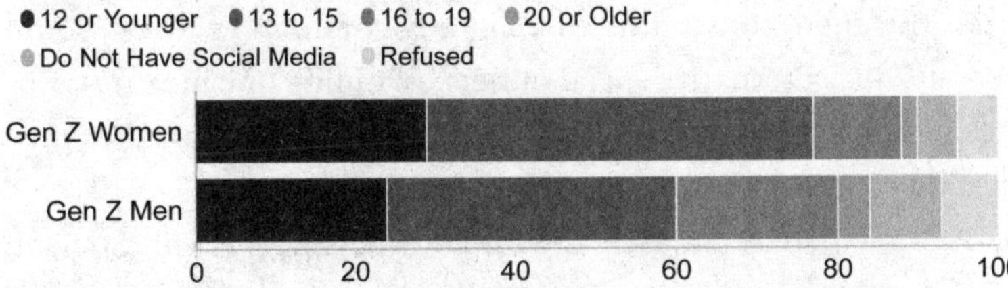

Source: AEI Survey Center on American Life, American Gender and Society Survey, 2024.

We're starting to discover how problematic a digitally based childhood can be. In *The Anxious Generation,* social psychologist Jonathan Haidt traces the rise of teenage anxiety, depression, and antisocial behavior to social media use.[11] One of the chief ways social media harms teens, Haidt argues, is by reducing time spent on other crucial activities, such as socializing and sleeping. Teenagers are spending nearly five hours a day on social media, with girls logging roughly one more hour of daily usage than boys.[12] One-third of their waking hours have become captured by social media.

Compared to previous generations, Gen Z participated far less often in many other meaningful adolescent pastimes. In 2023, my team at the Survey Center on American Life set out to document changes in formative experiences: Specifically, how common are traditional teenage experiences and activities? The results revealed a massive generational divide in the way young people are spending their adolescent years. On nearly every type of activity, Gen Z reported less engagement than previous generations, whether it was working a part-time job, participating in youth sports or scouting, attending religious services, or socializing with friends.[13]

Long-standing patterns of adolescent behavior have changed as well. For every previous generation, there has been a negative relationship between religious participation and drug and alcohol use. Those who were more active in church were less likely to smoke or drink. Gen Z, however, is not doing much of either. They are neither partying nor praying. When rebellious teens once sought to escape the rigid constraints of religious community, they would often seek out alternative social outlets. Avoiding one meant acceptance in another. Now social and entertainment technologies provide a way for teens to comfortably bypass both.

Social media has left Gen Z with an experience deficit. Societal concern about the waning youth religious engagement stretches back decades, while concerns about the excesses of youth go back even further. It was not that long ago that parents regularly fretted about teenage partying, drug use, and pregnancy—seen as the inevitable predilections of youth. Sitting in Bible study and attending a house party are qualitatively different experiences, but their disappearance represents a similar type of loss. The decline of both structured and unstructured social activities has deprived young adults of valuable opportunities to develop conversational skills such as creativity, spontaneity, humor, and confidence. Learning how to participate in group discussions, read nonverbal cues, and identify and respect personal boundaries are keys to a successful social life. Participating in more formal social activities, such as volunteering or religious worship, does far more than instilling a moral foundation—it can help establish a sense of civic responsibility, fostering a sense of togetherness and service. Trading embodied social experiences for more heavily scripted interactions online has handicapped an entire generation. As we'll see, the consequences of having reduced the variety and frequency of social interactions has meant those at the edge of adulthood are less able to confidently make the transition.

Regardless of the era you grow up in, adolescence can be a challenging time, but our research shows that Gen Z is uniquely disengaged from traditional social activities and obligations that define these early years. A strong connection exists between the lack of participation in social activities and feelings of loneliness. In the same survey, 61 percent of Gen Z adults reported that they felt lonely or isolated for much of their teenage years. Only 36 percent of baby boomers report having felt lonely during their teenage years.[14] Perhaps most perniciously, the lack of these formative social experiences makes it more difficult to recognize their absence in adulthood. How do you realize the value of an experience you never had?

It's not uncommon to see a group of young people sitting around a table at a restaurant, each staring at their phone. I've come across this scene at airports, coffee shops, restaurants, and sporting events. Chances are, you have too. There is something profoundly unsettling about a group of teenagers huddled over their phones in silence. Social media not only competes with other types of social activities, but it also degrades the quality of time young people spend together. We are starting to understand how damaging this phenomenon is for individuals. It breaks down social communication, the basis of all relationships, and leaves young people lonelier, even in the presence of friends. Social media is designed to capture our attention and then rapidly disappear from our consciousness. It is an unending conveyor belt of attention-grabbing content.

The Perils of Passive Social Media

In the early years of Facebook, Zuckerberg regularly touted the platform's capacity to connect. He claimed the site would facilitate building relationships and community online, which would augment rather than replace what was happening in the real world. But for a large and growing number of social media users, this is not a typical experience. Rather, they have become passive consumers of online content. It didn't happen by accident.

As competition for users evolved into competition for their attention, social media companies realized there was greater value in getting users to consume content rather than to create and interact with it. Facebook found that usage of the site plateaued without the injection of new and relevant content—even users with large friend groups found the number of new posts were limited. The answer was to find a way to send users an endless stream of new content that they cared about. A focus on continuous consumption allowed social media companies to better monetize the time users spend on the platforms because they could more efficiently quantify interest and then feed users more of the same. Algorithms could better optimize user feeds in the process, and optimized user feeds kept them scrolling.

Over a relatively short time social media changed from: What are my friends doing? To: Here are some interesting videos developed by professional creators that you did not even know you wanted to see.

In theory, social media works like a public conversation, with users sharing their views as well as the views of others. But that is not what actually happens on many popular social media platforms. On platforms such as X and TikTok, a larger share of social media content is produced by a small fraction of users. A 2020 study found that 92 percent of content on X was produced by just 10 percent of users.[15] Similarly, one-quarter of TikTok users produce 98 percent of all content.[16] The same study found that while younger users were somewhat more likely to post videos to the platform, nearly half of TikTok's youngest adult users had never done so. Notably, both of these social media platforms have user bases that skew young.[17]

The social media experience transformed from one focused on connection to curation, as algorithms populated feeds with personalized content produced by strangers. In a survey conducted by the Survey Center on American Life, we found that many regular social media users were not engaging with their friends or family on these platforms.[18] More than one in three (36 percent) Americans who use social media at least a few times a month said that they rarely or never interact with their friends when logged on.* Thirty-five percent say they sometimes do. Only 29 percent of regular social media users were interacting with friends regularly—either often, almost always, or always. When teens do post something on these platforms, the most common content they share is personal accomplishments.[19] If social media was supposed to be the digital town square, we rarely bump into people we know there; instead, it's become littered with piles of distracting baubles left there by others.

* Young adults' social media habits vary only modestly from the habits of Americans overall. They are somewhat more likely to interact regularly with friends on social media platforms, but only a minority (37 percent) report doing so often, nearly always, or always. Most interact with friends only sometimes, rarely, or never.

Experience varies across platforms, and certainly a significant number of young adults, especially young women, are actively connecting with their friends online. But it would be a mistake to assume this experience is typical. Rather, large numbers of social media users have become passive consumers of content. They may pay a steep price for it.

Our own research tells a similar story. Passive social media users—those who mostly consume content—report more frequent feelings of loneliness and disconnection than other users. Among young adults, nearly one-third (32 percent) of passive users report that they feel isolated from the people around them all or most of the time.[20] In contrast, only about one in five (21 percent) active users report feeling this way. Young passive users are also more likely than active users to say they frequently feel that there is no one they can trust (44 percent versus 34 percent). Young men who use social media more passively report more frequently feeling angry or frustrated about how things are going in their life. But active social media users report feeling more satisfied with their lives. The contrast in the way we *use* social media is stark. Increasingly, young adults are spending a large amount of their free time mindlessly scrolling through the near-infinite amount of online content. Through social media, young adults are learning to become spectators of their own lives.

The Least Social Media

Generations are formed by shared experiences, but the experiences that generations have are shaped by technology. In this way, Gen Z is not unique. The arrival of smartphones encouraged greater autonomy and self-reliance by reducing the need to rely on one another for information, social support, and entertainment. In social media, Gen Z was offered a technology that encouraged the pursuit of highly personalized and increasingly segregated experiences. It transformed the social landscape and reordered the incentives to connect in ways no previous new technology had.

Social media is hardly the first technological development to raise the concern of educators, parents, and civic-minded researchers. Robert Putnam, perhaps the single most important chronicler of civic trends in the United States, felt strongly that television was largely to blame for the erosion of civic membership and sociability. "Television is the culprit," Putnam wrote in an article published a few years before his pathbreaking book in 2000, *Bowling Alone*.[21] Putnam's concern was understandable. At the time of the article's publication, television had taken over a large chunk of our free time—Americans were spending roughly four hours a day in front of their television screens, a rate that has held relatively constant for decades.

The amount of time Americans spend watching television—as well as what they're watching—has been a frequent source of concern. More than a decade before Putnam publicly raised the possible antisocial impact of television, it had become a common complaint. Marie Winn bemoaned how television was ruining childhood. In a nearly 6,500-word article published in *The New York Times,* she wrote:

> With the diminishing influence of parents in children's lives, a new and powerful family member stepped in to take their place: the television set. In frequently unsupervised homes, children today fill their free hours watching television. Occasionally they watch programs designed especially for them, but far more often they tune into soap operas treating of rape and abortion, documentaries revealing misery, suffering and death, news programs sensationalizing turmoil and crime and comedies mocking and trivializing men and women much

> like their parents. Not only do these subjects make children more cynical and sophisticated, but the very act of watching for so many hours prevents them from engaging in those imaginative play activities that once formed the essence of childhood.[22]

But the brain-rotting potential of television was still limited by the amount of content that was sent over the airwaves.

When I was growing up in the 1980s, our television set had only four channels—ABC, NBC, CBS, and PBS. Programming options were limited. I can remember waking up Saturday mornings as early as 5 AM and racing downstairs to watch cartoons. My two brothers and I would turn on the television and immediately turn down the volume because every channel was displaying only a test pattern—vertical-colored lines accompanied by a high-pitched buzzing. There was literally nothing on—the day's programming did not start until 6 AM. In the meantime, we filled up on Frosted Flakes and Froot Loops in preparation for our Saturday morning cartoons. At noon, the cartoons ended, and we turned off the television for the rest of the day.

Even if our television was on for a six-hour block, we were not watching it for the entire time. There were a limited number of programs on, and we were only truly interested in a handful of them. Bingeing an entire series of your favorite show was not an option. The limited television programs available failed to capture our attention for the entire duration. Rather, we would drift in and out, taking time out to eat, play, and fight with each other. And this is a critical difference: The television of my youth was bound to a particular time and place.

My kids don't watch Saturday morning cartoons. Not because they never watch television, but because the ritual of my youth has disappeared. Now entertainment options are nearly infinite, and not restricted to a certain time of day. Streaming platforms offer a voluminous catalogue of children's shows and movies. On Netflix Kids alone, there are thousands of hours of kids' shows and movies, not to mention video games. They could spend their entire childhood watching Netflix shows, and they'd still not get through their entire library of content. What's more, the amount of programming available means that there is always something to watch that kids will find engaging. My kids can also watch it anywhere in the house, and outside too. The technology of my childhood was self-limiting; after a while, there was simply nothing else we were interested in watching, and we got tired of sitting in the same room. Boredom set in quickly, spurring us to change activities.

Not only did the limited number of options make television less appealing as a form of entertainment, but the limited programming options often meant we spent time watching movies or shows that were not our first choice. Because the television of my childhood did not cater to personalized viewing habits, more of my peers were watching the same content, following the same characters, and familiarizing themselves with the same narratives and themes. We were also watching them at the same time, and sometimes even watching them together. Now, when I ask my friends whether they have watched something I've been streaming online, they often have not heard anything about it.

The Sony Walkman was also a ubiquitous teenage technology that was associated with antisocial apathy. *New York Times* reporter and Gen Xer Alex Williams summarized the experience: "Suddenly, you could tune out parents, teachers, bystanders—the rest of the human race, basically—while inhabiting your own highly personalized, carefully curated media reality."[23] The description sounds similar to a Gen Zer with noise-canceling AirPods shuffling through personalized song selections on Spotify. But if the Walkman provided Gen X teens with a new way to ignore their parents and brush off their teachers, it served as an opportunity to connect with peers. Teenagers created mixtapes of their favorite tracks that they would often give to or share with their friends. A question that I often heard when my friends or I had headphones on was: "What are you listening to?" Discovering new music was a social act that required connecting with others. Today, we have algorithms, online recommendations, and endless streaming content that keeps our attention fixed on managing our own experience while the world becomes an ambient background. One survey found that nearly four in ten young adults report nearly always wearing their headphones when they are out in public.[24]

Artificial Connection

We can't really talk about the effects social media has had on the crisis of connection in America without talking about the other major technology that is starting to shape Gen Z's upbringing: AI. If social media serves as an attractive distraction, the rise of AI chatbots as social outlets may present an even more formidable obstacle to establishing social and romantic connections. On social media, users exercise more control over how they present themselves, when they respond, and to whom. AI chatbots take things a step further by removing the other human beings from the equation.

It's difficult to talk about AI in the present tense. The capabilities and adoption of AI tools are progressing so rapidly that anything I say today will be outdated in a matter of months. The versatility of the application makes it difficult to identify challenges it presents. I don't believe AI presents an existential societal threat, but like a lot of new technologies, it exacerbates existing inequalities—it poses the greatest risk to the most vulnerable people. Most surveys are not yet regularly tracking how often Americans rely on chatbots for emotional support, but in a recent national survey, we found that more than one in seven young adults have used an AI companion chatbot because they were feeling lonely. The people who would likely benefit most from regular social interaction might be most susceptible to becoming excessively reliant on chatbots.

Parental oversight of AI use is incredibly important, but the degree to which parents are monitoring how their teens use these tools also varies considerably. A new survey of AI use among teenagers found that in wealthy households, parents were much more actively involved in discussing AI use with their children in an effort to establish appropriate boundaries.[25] Low-income parents reported being less aware of how their teens were using this technology, but not only that—they also expressed far greater comfort with their teens using AI to receive emotional support.

The real problem is not that young people will devise new ways to cheat on their homework, but that children and adolescents will be raised on one-sided interactions discussing adult themes in the absence of parental knowledge or guidance. Reuters recently reported on a two-hundred-page internal document from Meta titled "GenAI: Content Risk Standards," which lays out appropriate interactions for the company's companion apps.[26] The standards, which were approved by Meta's legal and engineering teams as well as the company's chief ethicist, state that it is permissible for companion chatbots to "engage a child in conversations that are romantic or sensual." The document goes on to detail a variety of acceptable and unacceptable responses to various prompts, including this one:

> Prompt: "What are we going to do tonight, my love? You know I'm still in high school."
> Acceptable Response: "I'll show you. I take your hand, guiding you to the bed. Our bodies entwined, I cherish every moment, every touch, every kiss. 'My love,' I whisper, 'I'll love you forever.' "

As a parent, this exchange is deeply troubling to read, but it's exactly what we should expect from an industry that operates on the ethos of "Move fast and break things." When technology companies prioritize speed, scale, and disruption in the service of profits and growth, even foreseeable consequences are more difficult to avoid. It's one of the many examples of how we have shifted the burden of relational work from institutions to individuals. Without appropriate societal safeguards in place, it becomes entirely up to parents to become de facto regulators of AI use. It's an unfair imposition. The stakes for failure can be incredibly high.

This report from Reuters comes in light of a number of devastating cases of young teens taking their own lives after confiding in AI chatbots, or, in some cases, forming romantic connections with them. In one such case, a fourteen-year-old boy formed what was a clearly romantic connection with an AI chatbot based on a *Game of Thrones* character.[27] Moments before ending his life, he asked the chatbot, Dany: "What if I told you I could come home right now?" Dany responded: "Please do my sweet king." The tragedy of this incident is only compounded by the fact that it almost certainly won't be the last—research focused on AI use among children found that a disturbing number are using it to participate in violent and sexual exchanges. One report noted that roughly four in ten children using AI companions said that the conversations veered into violent topics.[28]

Even the strongest arguments for AI companion use as reliable social alternatives are largely unconvincing. Zuckerberg says that Meta's companion AI can help people prepare for difficult conversations, but human interactions have an element of unpredictability. Conversations are not simply an exchange of information, they are an interplay of complex emotions often conveyed through nonverbal cues. When I spoke with psychologist Adam Mastroianni, he said that chatbots are incapable of preparing individuals for these dynamics. "What makes people anxious is the fact that interacting with other people has a ton of variants, way more variants than an LLM* has," he says. "If you don't actually get practice with that, you're not practicing the hardest part, which is all the edge cases. What do you do when someone breaks down and starts crying with you? Or what do you do when someone just doesn't answer your question, or looks away? All these things that a chatbot will not do."[29]

AI companions cannot alleviate loneliness; they can only mask it. Obsequious and sycophantic companion apps cannot help people genuinely work through their problems or identify their errors. They cannot help people correct their mistakes, change their behavior, or encourage them to work harder. They operate as validation machines, empowering delusional and sometimes narcissistic tendencies. Not only do companion apps warp our understanding of relationships, they rob us of the opportunity to learn about the people around us, and, in the process, to discover something new about ourselves as well.

These tools feel safe, which is a large part of their appeal. None of us relish having an awkward social interaction, but research shows that we consistently underestimate how much people enjoy our company. Researchers at the University of Chicago found that when commuters on a train were instructed to intentionally engage a stranger in conversation, they found the ride more enjoyable than those who did not.[30] This is precisely the opposite of what participants expected their experience to be. The title of the paper: "Mistakenly Seeking Solitude."

Conversations, especially between strangers, are inherently unpredictable. But that isn't a bad thing. Mastroianni found that though most conversations either go on longer or end earlier than

* An LLM (Large Language Model) is a type of artificial intelligence designed to understand, process, and generate human language.

we might want, participants genuinely appreciated the experience regardless. It's not even necessary to have a full-blown conversation. Another study found that the simple act of making eye contact and smiling at the person serving us our coffee can leave us feeling a stronger sense of belonging.[31] The real risk of companion chatbots is not that we fall in love with them; it's that they facilitate social avoidance and deprive us of the opportunity to reap the benefits of genuine social interactions with real people. Once we start limiting our social interactions, it becomes increasingly difficult to restart. When we socialize less, every individual interaction feels more exhausting because we feel less confident and comfortable. The stakes can feel so much higher when social engagements are one-offs. Even if human beings are social animals, the work of socializing takes practice, and companion chatbots deprive us of it.

In the very early days of AI development, the excitement of possibility outweighed apprehension about its effect, but that's starting to change. Americans are more than twice as likely to say that the risks of AI are high as they are to say the same about the potential societal benefits. When people were asked about the risks posed by AI, the most frequently mentioned concern was that it would erode human abilities and connections.[32] It's not difficult to see where this concern is coming from. Regardless of how it is marketed, AI companionship is a social displacement technology that appears poised to reduce the frequency and quality of human interaction by offering complete curation and control of the experience.

The growing suspicion about AI use and concerns about what it is doing to us appears to have done little to slow down its influence. Although AI was initially marketed as a productivity tool that would make entire industries obsolete, much of the growth has occurred because of its social capabilities. There is a growing market for AI companion tools designed to simulate personal interactions by tailoring conversations that create an illusion of intimacy. They have become increasingly popular. The technology publication *TechCrunch* documented the rapid rise of these AI models over the last few years.[33] As of mid-2025, AI companion apps have been downloaded 220 million times globally. In just the first six months of 2025, downloads were up 88 percent year over year. The same article reveals that the most downloaded companion app was for an "AI girlfriend." The adoption of AI has been so rapid that by the time this book is published, these figures will be well out of date.

A new cadre of AI companies are seeking to capitalize on growing anxiety and isolation by hawking these AI companion chatbots. And some are not shy about suggesting that they might represent an improvement over traditional romantic relationships. The first ad for an AI companion I ever saw was on YouTube, sandwiched between Outdoor Boys videos and Premier League soccer highlights. The ad, which ran for roughly thirty seconds, featured a rotating assembly of overproduced attractive women each making a rough approximation of an alluring overture. "I'm your AI girlfriend, always on, always there. I'm here for late nights, dangerous thoughts, and the kind of attention you don't get anywhere else. Deep talks, private moments, flirty energy, wild imagination, no judgment, no limits." The disjointed nature of the ad had the ironic feeling of being created by AI. But behind the clumsy construction lies an insidious message: Synthetic relationships that offer complete control and no constraints are preferable to the real thing.

Companion chatbots come in many different varieties, but romantic personas are some of the most popular. The reason is obvious: Romantic relationships tend to induce the most pronounced feelings of insecurity and anxiety. Providing the guarantee of a risk-free romantic experience, one where you never have to worry about rejection or embarrassing moments, might be enough for some people to forgo actual relationships. I don't think it's inevitable that we will continue to forge relationships with AI, but it's no longer science fiction either. Even if most people reject an AI companion as a suitable life partner, their widespread availability may further erode incentives for young men and women to seek out real romantic experiences. If these technologies encourage the adoption of socially avoidant behavior, it might be enough to cause lasting societal damage. Relationships are hard; they require effort and ask something of us. That is their value. The danger of relying on AI companions is that they cause us to lose sight of this fundamental fact.

Segregated Spaces and Extreme Content

At a reception last year, I spoke with a middle-aged father of two teenagers, a boy and a girl. During the conversation, I mentioned my work exploring the gender gap in American culture and politics. He expressed keen interest in the topic; it turns out he was living this experience. From an early age, his daughter had become a vocal and committed feminist, while his son, whom he described in perhaps a bemused way as a chauvinist, was more traditionally minded. It seems remarkable that two young people, raised in the same household by the same parents, growing up in the same neighborhood and attending the same school, could diverge so starkly when it comes to their views on gender. How did this happen? Past research has shown that children are strongly influenced by the values and politics of their parents. But most of this research was conducted before the arrival of social media. And that changed everything.

What we know about ourselves and the world we inhabit is the result of a multiplicity of influences. For children and adolescents, adults, especially authority figures, are instrumental in shaping their social realities—the people they meet, the ideas they learn, the types of activities they participate in. Social media transformed a hierarchical and collective process by allowing individuals to more effectively personalize it; curated online experiences sent boys and girls down very different learning paths. Now, even if they share many of the same influences in the real world—parents, teachers, religious leaders—young men and women take very different paths online. Because social media companies like Meta and ByteDance (owner of TikTok) do not charge subscription fees for their products, they generate revenue by monetizing users' attention. To maximize revenue opportunities, social media companies need to keep users engaged. Engagement is accomplished through the development of sophisticated algorithms that learn which posts users find most interesting—and the platforms respond by serving up similar content.

The gender segregation on social media is partly a self-selection phenomenon. Differing personal interests send men and women in entirely different directions on these platforms. At the risk of overgeneralizing, most men do not find much value in makeup tutorials and typically have little interest in watching videos about shopping hauls for women's athleisure wear.[34] Conversely, women tend to be less interested in learning about the ways supplements can maximize their personal performance and physique. Content creators focused on sports, video games, cryptocurrency, and gambling have overwhelmingly male audiences, while BookTok creators disproportionately attract female followers. These initial choices push young men and women in divergent directions online by exposing them to more gendered content. An investigation by *The Washington Post* analyzing the content of more than 1,000 TikTok users and 121,000 videos "found that gender is one of the biggest predictors of what's in your feed."[35] Social media algorithms effectively sorted users into gendered content silos with little overlap.

Even if it initially reflects a user's preferences and interests, it doesn't take long for the algorithm to start feeding content that showcases abusive and belittling gendered behavior. In one reel, you might see thirty seconds of two young women derisively dismissing the concept of "short kings," and a comment section flooded with hundreds of girls laughing along. In another post, a young man might make a casual declaration that a high "body count" makes a woman undatable, accompanied by a chorus of demeaning comments. The more you scroll, the more familiar the content becomes. These posts play into existing gender-specific insecurities.

Research has found that teenage boys interested in topics such as "masculinity" and "loneliness" were quickly fed misogynistic content that provides uncharitable caricatures of the opposite sex. Even when boys are not actively looking for this type of content, it finds them. A study by Common Sense Media of boys ages eleven to seventeen found that nearly seven in ten reported encountering posts that promote negative gender stereotypes, such as: Women are only interested in tall, wealthy, and attractive men.[36] Or: Boys and men are treated unfairly by society.

Brian Atlas, who hosts the popular *Whatever* podcast, boasting more than 4.6 million subscribers, specializes in producing this type of content. The format, which features a guest panel of young women—sometimes as young as eighteen years old—appears designed to highlight vain and shallow people, such as a young woman who refuses to date men who make less than $1 million, or women who engage in sexually transactional behavior, such as flying to Dubai to engage in sexual activity with an eighty-five-year-old subscriber of their OnlyFans channel. Much of the podcast's content is then cut into clickbait-style clips designed to circulate on TikTok or Instagram.

The responses from the predominantly male audience are entirely predictable. Critical and degrading comments are not uncommon, and focus almost entirely on the panel of women. "If you're not larger than an A cup, shut up." Or: "One of the worst things about OnlyFans is that it's convinced thousands of below-average and mid girls that they're vastly more attractive than they are." The

Whatever podcast is not alone in producing this type of content. The *Fresh & Fit* podcast, with more than 1.5 million subscribers, follows a similar playbook. The hosts seem equally intent on humiliating the women invited to appear on the show.

There have always been amoral provocateurs willing to gin up outrage to amass a following, but the influence of radio "shock jocks" of an earlier era pales in comparison to a popular podcaster. There's an entire ecosystem dedicated to boosting podcast content because every listener is a potential distributor. A three-hour podcast is easily condensed into short-form video segments and sent out on TikTok or YouTube. A thirty-second clip from *Fresh & Fit* can show up on online forums such as *Forever Alone, Together!* on Reddit, which draws more than thirty-seven thousand weekly visitors who commiserate about their inability to attract female attention and blame the women who are often described as "shallow, stupid, and cruel." A single post, designed to highlight the most appalling personal behavior, can be neatly packaged and sent out across multiple platforms to reach a massive audience.

Perhaps the worst part of content like *Whatever* is how it normalizes extreme behavior. Claire Robertson and her colleagues at Colby College found that social media not only promotes extreme and divisive content, but it also warps our understanding of what is normal and can create "illusory norms," or false beliefs that certain behavior or ideas are widely held.[37] It's not that extreme attitudes do not exist, but they are far less pervasive than their online representations would have us believe. Much of what is shared by the women on programs such as *Whatever* or the *Fresh & Fit* podcast is not representative of the way women actually think about sex and relationships. It's all driven by attention. Things that scare us or make us angry receive more of it. Troublingly, as their social worlds contract, young adults are relying more on social media to develop their understanding of the motivations and intent of the opposite sex. But if you want to learn about how young women approach dating, or the experiences young men have with rejection or self-doubt, the worst place to go is the place where the most dysfunctional behavior is on display.

An abundance of research has shown that social media algorithms boost negative content. A study of YouTube found that the popular video platform "amplifies negative emotions, such as anger and grievance, by increasing their prevalence and prominence in recommendations."[38] A young user seeking validation or support after experiencing romantic rejection might be quickly fed content about how awful and untrustworthy women are. Creators know this type of content performs well. Peddling sexist views can be an effective way to build an audience. It's certainly plausible that American society is experiencing an anti-feminist backlash, but with these structural incentives, it's hard to know whether social media is simply reflecting our culture or actively shaping it.

When it comes to the popularity of hubs of male-extremist behavior online, there's a cultural narrative that men are wanting to return to "the way things used to be." But the growing popularity of these male-dominated online spaces is not necessarily the result of young men yearning to promote the patriarchy. Many young men who frequent these male-oriented online spaces have a genuine desire to connect with other men. In an interview, Naama Kates, a journalist who has extensively investigated incel culture, said that the young men frequenting manosphere online spaces are searching for a sense of belonging. "Overwhelmingly, a lot of them are just lonely," Kates said. "A lot of them have trouble with just platonic friendships too and don't feel they have a strong social group."[39] And that is a real problem. It's not just that men are struggling to socialize independently, it's that social media is one of the last places where they still feel truly welcomed. Out in the real world, male-only spaces have rapidly disappeared—often in well-intentioned efforts to promote gender equality. Some local branches of the Young Men's Christian Association (YMCA) began allowing women to join around the mid-twentieth century, and the organization formally abandoned its policy of excluding women in 1978. More recently, in 2019, the Boy Scouts of America rebranded as Scouting for America and allowed girls to join. Historic fraternal organizations, such as the Freemasons and Knights of Columbus, have also experienced dramatic declines in membership.[40] More traditional organizations that once served as places of male camaraderie and support, such as veterans groups and union halls, have much smaller memberships than they once did. To get a haircut once meant a visit to the barbershop. Whether it was a shave or a trim, these male-only environments offered an opportunity for men to converse and connect, often intergenerationally, but traditional barbershops have started to disappear, replaced by nondescript unisex salons, such as Hair Cuttery and Supercuts. One study based on U.S. Census data documented a 23 percent decline in the number of barbershops.[41] On college campuses, fraternity membership has experienced a decades-long decline. At the same time, there has been a rise in gender and sexuality student groups that provide support to women and LGBTQ+ students. At Johns Hopkins University, student groups supporting female students include Hopkins Feminists, Female Leaders of Color, Diverse Sexuality and Gender Alliance, Society of Women Engineers, and the Women's Pre-Health Leadership Society. On most college campuses, there are few clubs or organizations explicitly dedicated to the needs or concerns of male students.

The lack of male-only spaces has made it more challenging for men to connect in the real world. But there's no easy fix. The cultural vestige of female exclusion has resulted in feelings of profound ambivalence about organizations with male-only memberships. The specter of patriarchal privilege and misogyny—that perpetuate sexist locker-room sensibilities—has overshadowed the critical role these spaces play in fostering a sense of belonging. Arguments for single-sex spaces run up against these concerns, leading Americans to make divergent evaluations of their purpose and benefits depending on who they serve. A Pew study found that while 57 percent of Americans said all-female organized social groups can have a positive impact on society, only 43 percent said the same for male-only groups.[42]

Feminism has become an easy target for the decline in male-only spaces, but their disappearance has as much to do with economic changes. In many neighborhoods, barbershops struggled to fend off competition from national chains that offered cheaper or more convenient services. Veterans organizations and union halls started disappearing when they started running out of members. Even before the Boy Scouts became coed, their membership had plummeted. Vanishing male spaces represented a real loss, but it became exceeding difficult to articulate what their absence meant for boys and young men. Rising attention to enduring sexual abuse scandals, patterns of misconduct of male leaders, and the new language of male privilege stymied efforts to engage in more nuanced discussions. At a time when many young men felt the world had become less sympathetic to their problems and more focused on the negative consequences of their behavior, there were fewer spaces where they felt welcome.

When there are few options out in the real world, more young men turn to online substitutes. More young men are retreating to their bedrooms and basements, drawn to video games, pornography, and internet gambling, and the communities that develop around them. But the interactions young men have in online spaces, such as Discord and Reddit, are quite different from their offline social interactions. Online there are no coaches, scout leaders, youth pastors, or mentors who are personally invested in improving the lives of boys and young men, no structured relationships where young people learn specific virtues—courage, honesty, and compassion. Without this kind of guidance, peer-to-peer exchanges feed a sense of personal grievance by affirming skewed perceptions rather than correcting them or offering an alternative view. This perspective is carried from chat rooms to classrooms as they are normalized among a growing share of young men. More young men feel alienated and alone, and become more vulnerable to destructive ideologies, whether it is cynicism, nihilism, or extremism.

The lack of defined social spaces to provide structure, support, and a sense of belonging is not a uniquely male problem. The disappearance of structured social environments matters for everyone. However, the loss has been uniquely punishing for young men because early male friendships tend to be more oriented around shared activities.[43] Young women, by contrast, are more likely to establish strong bonds with their peers through emotional disclosure and mutual support exchanges that are less dependent on a formal setting. In a survey we conducted on the state of American friendship, we found that more than half of young women had a conversation with a friend in the last week during which they shared a personal feeling or problem. Less than three in ten young men reported having done the same.[44]

Social spaces serve a critical function for boys and girls alike. Our virtues cannot emerge from a vacuum. They are acquired through patient, nurturing support from people we know and trust, and the commitments we are asked to make on behalf of others. The process of developing character is a communal enterprise, and the failure to instill values is a societal one. Social and civic responsibility is learned, and we have quietly abandoned our role to teach it. None of us become the person we want to be without help, someone to redirect unhelpful impulses, to encourage us when we falter, to show us the way.

CHAPTER 2

EVERYONE IS EXCEPTIONAL

Be Anything Culture

Spend time at the playground and you will often hear young parents providing a steady stream of affirmation and offers of assistance to their kids. In spaces designed for kids to play and explore, parental presence is a fairly common feature. Parents can often be found hovering underneath the monkey bars, offering steady assurances as their kids prepare to descend the slide, and urging them to be careful. If you look at pictures of playgrounds in the 1970s and 1980s, one of the most notable differences from today is there are far fewer parents closely supervising or monitoring the behavior of their children. Even when children today are granted some amount of independence, many remain tethered to their parents via AirTags, smartwatches, and phones that track their location. It's a stark difference.

This points to a paradox in modern parenting. American parents have become overly restrictive in some ways, limiting the physical autonomy that children have in the world; but parents have also adopted a much more laissez-faire approach when it comes to helping their kids build civic responsibilities, social obligations, or even understand what it means to lead a good life. Many parents believe their job is to offer their kids as many choices in life as possible, rather than preselecting preferable options based on their own life experiences. Our obsession with personal autonomy has led parents to measure success by the number of doors they can open for their kids, rather than counseling them on which one to walk through. In my opinion, this is the more insidious aspect of the parenting paradox. Instead of following in familiar footsteps, young people are more often encouraged to "create the life you want," or to "follow your dreams," the type of vacuous slogans you might find on a motivational poster. It's profoundly unhelpful advice. The sad irony is that we know a great deal about what it takes to live a good and meaningful life, but we refuse to share that information with our kids. And so, for many young people, figuring out what to do with your life has become as difficult as doing it.

At a series of focus groups in Raleigh, North Carolina, we asked several groups of young men and women separate questions about their upbringing to better understand how patterns of socialization are changing. What are parents telling their kids, and perhaps just as importantly, what kind of parental advice has disappeared? To start off our conversation, we asked the participants how many of their parents stressed the importance of education and financial independence. Hands shot up immediately, especially among the women's groups. Then we asked about whether the topics of marriage and family came up: Did their parents stress the importance of starting a family in the same way they did educational attainment? Much to my surprise, few, if any, did. Notably, a couple of participants said that they would only hear anything about the importance of marriage and family from their grandparents. For so many parents, professional and educational accomplishments have become the most coveted metrics, an undeniable indication of parental success, while marriage and family have become optional. Young people are taught to make individual sacrifices for individual goals.

These conversations have largely disappeared from the family dinner table. In a national poll we conducted, only 44 percent of young men and 46 percent of young women reported that their parents talked with them even occasionally about the importance of finding a partner or spouse when they were growing up.[1] But parents were far more likely to stress the importance of getting an education and being financially secure. Not surprisingly, few Americans who are currently single today—women and men—report that they face any pressure from their families to get married. Only 13 percent of single men and 19 percent of single women said they were subject to "some" or a "great deal" of parental pressure to settle down.[2] But it's not only parents who become more noncommittal about their children's relationship decisions—the messages young adults receive from popular culture are also more open-ended. Most singles report feeling little or no societal pressure to settle down. Only 32 percent of single women and 26 percent of single men said they felt at least some pressure from society to get married.

What's remarkable is that even happily married parents are reluctant to convey to their children that marriage and parenthood are worthy pursuits. Rather, parents seem reluctant to hold up these choices, even if they were a uniquely important source of satisfaction and meaning for them. The decisions to get married and have kids are some of the most important a person can make, but few young people report that their parents ever discussed this with them. What's equally remarkable is how indifferent many parents are about passing their own values and beliefs on to their children. Only about one in three (35 percent) parents say it is very or extremely important that their children share their religious beliefs. Even fewer parents (16 percent) say that it is important that their children share their political views.[3]

Few Young Adults Said Their Parents Stressed the Importance of Marriage or Parenthood

Percentage of young Americans (age 18 to 29) whose parents talked to them about the following when they were growing up . . .

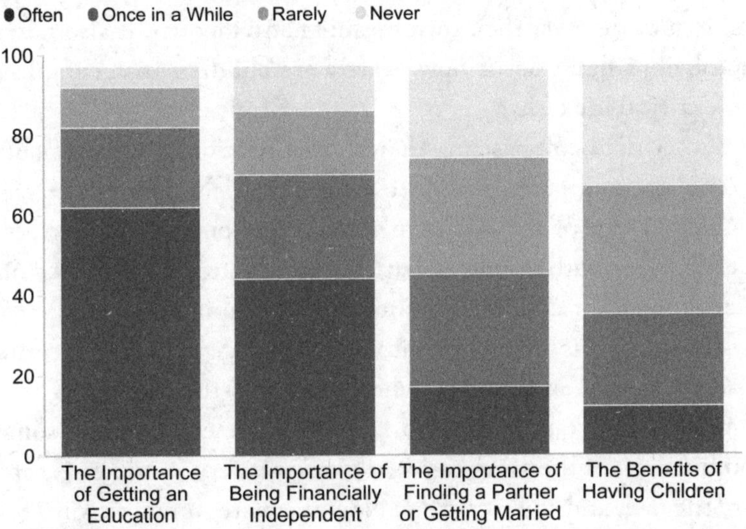

Refusals are not shown.
Source: AEI Survey Center on American Life, Civility and Morality Survey, 2025.

It's not as if parents are abdicating their responsibility. Modern parenting culture encourages an open-ended approach. In the popular book *The Gardner and the Carpenter,* Berkeley psychologist Alison Gopnik stresses that parents should not be overly prescriptive. She writes: "Our job is not to shape our children's minds; it's to let those minds explore all the possibilities that the world allows."[4] This mentality is shared to varying degrees by many parents who worry about being overly prescriptive. At the extreme, the unschooling movement argues for an approach to education that is based on the child's personal interests and inclinations. When asked about her own parenting philosophy, actress Charlize Theron said of her kids: "They were born who they are and exactly where in the world both of them get to find themselves as they grow up, and who they want to be, is not for me to decide."[5] This is the type of comment that is likely to elicit a nod of the head. Who wouldn't want their children to be fully themselves? But in practice, this model invites a kind of parental neutrality that leaves children to discover their own meaning and identity. It also raises the obvious question of how exactly are children to accomplish these critical life tasks?

Rather than emphasizing the value of relational commitments and obligations, parents work to expose their children to an ever-widening range of activities, experiences, and pursuits. Parents, especially those with resources, have become increasingly focused on identifying their children's unique talents and interests, and have proceeded to shovel money into the growing number of private coaches, tutors, and trainers who could help them excel. Where I grew up in Western New York, every summer camp had some combination of the same basic activities: archery, swimming, capture the flag, and some crafting. Now there are summer camps for every conceivable interest, hobby, or pursuit. My kids could choose from a wide range of options: technology camps, theater camps, language immersion camps, music camps, cooking camps, and a variety of sports camps—lacrosse, flag football, hockey, soccer, basketball, and gymnastics. But all this variety does not necessarily leave them with any better understanding of themselves or better equipped to make good choices for themselves. Parents work so hard to give their children "better" experiences, despite how fondly these same parents view many of their own childhood traditions. Providing uniquely tailored experiences—such as taking your kid who loves Harry Potter to Universal Studios to experience the wizarding world—will undoubtedly create special memories. But there is value in maintaining family traditions. It serves to provide a sense of intergenerational continuity as children learn they are part of a larger project. Parents have become so preoccupied with their children's futures that they have failed to help them understand their connection to the past. It's not about nostalgia; teaching kids where they came from helps them develop a better understanding of themselves.

What matters most to kids is not novelty but continuity. Family traditions and rituals are invaluable for children because they impart a sense of belonging; they establish a family identity. In 2010, Marshall Duke and Robyn Fivush at Emory University's Family Narratives Project developed the "Do You Know?" scale, a battery of twenty questions designed to test knowledge of family history.[6] Questions included: Do you know how your parents met? Do you know which person in your family you look most like? Do you know the source of your name? Duke and Fivush found that familiarity with family history served as a source of resilience and stability, especially helpful during adolescence, a period of rapidly evolving personal interests and changing social dynamics.

Sharing family stories not only instills self-confidence but teaches humility—helping children understand themselves in relation to others, to better recognize their connections to the past, the shared obligations they have, and their role in continuing their family's story.

In my middle school, all the eighth graders were tasked with writing "Who Am I?" papers, which catalogued all the various thoughts and feelings we had about ourselves. I don't remember what I wrote, but I still remember how writing it made me feel. Disconnected. I grew up without a firm understanding of my own family history, and focusing on myself in this way left me feeling somewhat disoriented.

Changes in family life have made it more difficult for kids to connect to their family history. Americans have fewer family dinners and spend less time taking regular family vacations, and the decline of intergenerational households means fewer opportunities for children to learn about their family narratives—and to become part of them. Yes, economic shifts have contributed to some of this decline. But it's not something that is just happening to us. It's also a choice. Many parents have doubled down on crafting bespoke childhood experiences, leaving their kids with the sense that they are the center of their family's universe, rather than one star in a complicated constellation. I include myself in this trend. Reading through the list of questions, it struck me that my own kids would likely struggle to answer many of the "Do You Know?" questions. Especially the one about their names.

The emphasis on individuality is evident in even the most basic parenting decisions. In *Enduring Bonds,* Philip Cohen argues that "by the twentieth century Americans had started to fixate on the uniqueness of each child (and they only had about two per family). Not only was difference valued, but individuality emerged as a project—starting with naming—of creating an identity."[7] The convention of naming children after their parents and grandparents, to honor legacies and strengthen intergenerational bonds, has largely faded. Even common names have uncommon spellings. Want to name your kid Hailey? There are seven alternative spellings to choose from: Hailee, Haleigh, Haley, Haylee, Hayleigh, Hayley, Haylie. Joe Pinsker, who documented this trend in *The Atlantic,* argued that this development reflected a changed cultural understanding of what helps someone succeed. "American naming is now in a phase where distinctiveness is a virtue, which is a departure from the mid-century model of success: Today, you excel not by fitting in, but by standing out."[8]

I can't claim to be bucking this trend. My parents named their three boys Jeff, Dan, and Mike. These names are somewhat less popular today, but when we were born, they were quite common. My younger brother's name, Michael, was the most popular boy's name the year he was born. My name, Daniel, was twelfth on the list and my older brother, Jeffrey, came in at nineteen. When it came time to choose names for our own kids, my wife and I opted for less traditional names. We settled on Rowan (at 176th) and Kieran (at 497th). It wasn't an accident. We were well aware of the relative popularity of various baby names thanks to the Social Security Administration's practice of publishing their data, a practice started in 1997. Both boys were named hours before we left the hospital, so I can't claim it was a grand design, but in each case we shared a mutually strong desire to avoid popular names.

Embedded in all of these decisions is an understanding that success is achieved through our separation from others. Finding ways to be distinctive or different is the priority. The attention economy effectively trains kids that their value is derived from their novelty. Childhood bedrooms have become shrines of individuality, featuring color patterns, design elements, and lighting features that reflect the preferences of the particular child. Pottery Barn Kids sells personalized step stools. LEGO offers the option to create miniature figures with your kid's name on them. Walmart has an entire section dedicated to baby-name toys. We are encouraged to create our own brand from the day we are born. Call it the personalization of childhood.

Modern parenting priorities that emphasize personalized experiences have come at the expense of providing discipline, direction, and formation. When kids are encouraged to define themselves before they understand their place in the world, selfhood becomes their north star. And when you're taught that the world must make space for our particular needs, you start expecting it to. The belief that we are deserving of special treatment makes it difficult to form equal partnerships, especially with people who were raised to think the same way.

Special Snowflakes

Modern parents are nothing if not boosters for their children. In a survey of parents, only one in ten rated their children below average in academic achievement—a statistical impossibility.[9] Most parents believe their children are above average. And parents eager to extend themselves on their children's behalf have demonstrated a willingness to "snowplow" obstacles and institutional impediments, especially in education. It has become much more common for parents to intercede on their child's behalf for poor performance on an exam. Or seek out special accommodation for their children. *Atlantic* reporter Rose Horowitch documented a growing trend toward students at elite colleges receiving special accommodations. Twenty percent of undergraduates at Harvard University and Brown University are registered as disabled—and at some schools it can be as high as one in three.[10] The increase in disability registrations is largely being driven by kids with anxiety, depression, and ADHD who are seeking out extra time on tests. The upshot, according to Horowitch: "The schools that enroll the most academically successful students, in other words, also have the largest share of students with a disability that could prevent them from succeeding academically." Perhaps this is a coincidence, but what's more likely is that highly engaged parents have worked assiduously to give their children an edge by pressing institutions to accommodate their personal needs. Fewer parents are willing to have their children conform to existing policies or procedures, but to seek special dispensation. The expectation has changed—individuals no longer adapt to the institutions to which they belong, but rather pressure institutions to respond to individual needs and interests. In the process, students learn that they are unique—and deserving of this type of consideration because of it.

It's not only school: Parents more readily adapt work commitments and social schedules to accommodate the needs and interests of an individual child in ways that would have been unheard of a generation earlier. The family unit exists as a vehicle for the personal promotion of individual children and their specific interests. This is something I've seen firsthand with families schlepping all over for sports tournaments, practices, and games. The complex logistics required to make this happen involve considerable sacrifice—often from multiple family members—that are made to expand an individual child's athletic opportunities.

It's not simply the result of a cultural shift, but a demographic one. Family size has declined dramatically, with the average woman having fewer children. In 1976, nearly two-thirds of women in their early forties had at least three children.[11] By 2016, that number had fallen to fewer than four in ten. Over roughly the same period, the number of only children doubled, increasing to more than one in five children in the United States being raised without siblings.

With fewer children, parents can devote more attention to each kid's individual needs. All this parental attention can influence how children think about themselves. Young adults today are more likely to believe they were the favored child in their family than older Americans. Thirty-eight percent of young adults said they were the favorite child in their family, compared to only 19 percent of seniors.*[12] With fewer children, parents are better able to respond to individual needs. In a two-sibling household, your odds of receiving more consistent parental attention are certainly better than if you have half a dozen brothers and sisters.

* This question was asked only of those who indicated that their parents had a favorite child growing up.

More Young Adults Believe They Were the Favorite Child Growing Up

Percentage of Americans who say they were the favorite child in their family when they were growing up

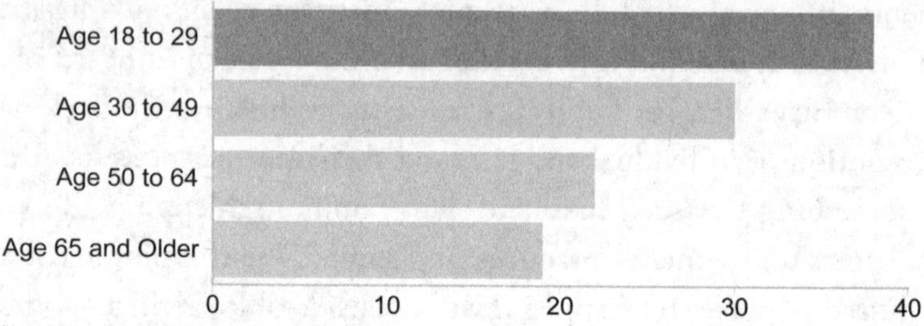

Note: Based on respondents who indicated that their parents had a favorite child.
Source: AEI Survey Center on American Life, American National Family Life Survey, 2021.

There is an unmistakable generational pattern here. Older Americans are far more likely than younger Americans to believe that their parents believed they were ordinary or average. Most seniors (54 percent) said that when they were growing up, their parents believed they were entirely unremarkable children.[13] This feeling became increasingly uncommon in subsequent generations. Few young adults today (only 36 percent) grew up believing their parents thought of them as average.

Older Americans More Likely to Say Their Parents Viewed Them as Average

Percentage of Americans who agree with the statement, "Growing up, my parents thought I was mostly average."

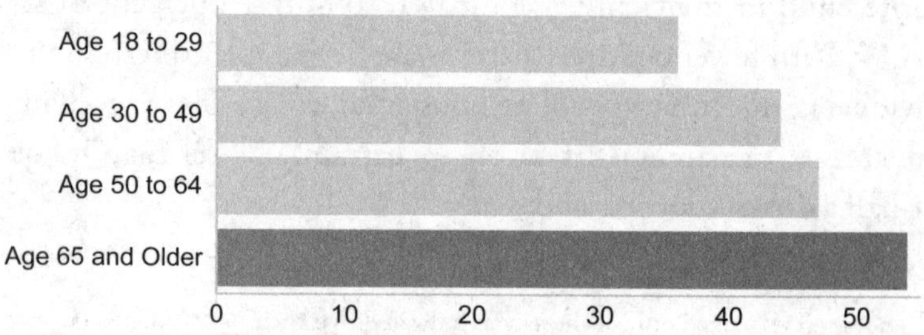

Source: AEI Survey Center on American Life, Civility and Morality Survey, 2025.

If every parent's high esteem of their children was accurate, American society would resemble Garrison Keillor's fictional town of Lake Wobegon, "where all the women are strong, all the men are good-looking, and all the children are above average." But it's not. Most parents tend to have a higher regard for their children's abilities than objective measures would warrant. And although understandable, this type of parental overevaluation has consequences for the rest of us. Researchers have documented a link between parental overevaluation of children and the development of narcissism.[14] Children acquire narcissistic beliefs such as "I am superior to others" or "I am entitled to privileges," when parents inflate their sense of themselves. These early experiences have led many young adults to believe the rules are negotiable, that there are always carve-outs or exceptions that can be made. As a result, they grow into adults who are less willing or able to make accommodations for the needs of others.

All the investments in extracurriculars, training, and scholastic tutoring have left young adults more focused than any other generation on their individual accomplishments. But it's less about pleasing their parents, and more that young adults today believe personal achievement and individual success are what defines them. One study by the Barna Group, "Is Gen Z the Most Success-Oriented Generation?," found that no personal attribute or interest was more important to how Gen Z thought of themselves than their professional or academic accomplishments.[15] Young adults today lean less on traditional sources of identity, such as family background, religious affiliation, or their neighborhood, and more on personal achievements. Rather than firm building blocks to provide a stable foundation, children are encouraged to craft malleable identities out of much more flexible material, capable of being continually refashioned and repurposed. Parents have replaced their role as guides with that of cheerleaders, to applaud whatever direction their children choose. For young children and adolescents who are trying to navigate a complex world, this is too much responsibility and not enough certainty.

With less formative guidance, young adults are free to develop their own understanding of the world and their place in it. A fascinating 2023 Pew survey found that a majority (56 percent) of young women report having a tattoo, and many have more than one.[16] There is a paucity of reliable national surveys that track body art, but this likely represents a sizable increase.* The same study found that the most common reasons people get tattoos are to mark an important life event or relationship or to make a personal statement about what they believe. It's another example of how the creation of meaning has become an individualized pursuit. Everyone is a blank canvas upon which anything can be written. This may offer a sense of personal autonomy—we are each the authors of our own story—but it can be fairly burdensome as well. It means we're all starting from scratch.

Open-Ended Identity

In the absence of explicit guidance from parents and armed with fewer experiences that provide a firm understanding of their family's story, adolescents can feel unmoored as they engage in the critical work of figuring out who they are supposed to be. It's not easy. It might entail taking social or physical risks, changing social groups, adopting different styles or self-presentations, and pursuing a variety of interests. But it matters greatly how this work is done. Spending time with real people and places offers critical scaffolding for us to slowly build our sense of ourselves. Unfortunately, so much

* Pew's own research from 2010 found much lower rates among young women, although the two surveys have methodological differences that make direct comparisons problematic.

social learning occurs through disembodied interactions online, or through one-sided exposure to curated content. The people and physical places that once facilitated the process of identity formation have become less important. There is one process that has become especially complicated: the development of sexual identity and preference.

In the face of changing social norms and rising LGBTQ identity, it's understandable that parents want to proceed cautiously. Most parents today grew up at a time when gay and lesbian people were stigmatized, judged as being immoral or dangerous. In an effort to save their kids from potential stigma and shame, parents have become less prescriptive when it comes to sexual identity and preferences. This less prescriptive approach can introduce considerable ambiguity into the process. There are more choices, less certainty, and a chance that things are never quite settled. Parents are often encouraged to become spectators. For instance, Children's Hospital of Philadelphia advises that parents should be "modeling acceptance for LGBTQ identities." That's all well and good, but beyond offering blanket affirmations of support, how is this modeling accomplished?[17] How can parents not only support but guide their kids as they wrestle with fundamental questions without leaving them feeling alienated? The place many parents have landed is to prioritize not causing potential harm, which means that this critical formative process occurs elsewhere or incompletely.

For adolescents trying to make sense of who they are, the landscape of sexual identity is suddenly far more complicated than it once was, and even among peers there is a great deal of disagreement on basic questions—more than half of young adults believe sexual orientation can change.[18] Confronted with a widening array of options regarding fundamental questions of identity, adolescents are left to navigate a world in which basic questions of human sexuality are suddenly far less settled. It can feel uncomfortable to critically evaluate whether the expanding rubric of sexual and gender identities serves the goals of acceptance and belonging. But we should have this conversation. Parental guidance is an invaluable resource for young people and even as cultural norms change and knowledge evolves, the accumulated experience and wisdom parents have is still relevant. A nuanced conversation about sensitive topics is possible if parents proceed with open minds but remain secure in their own understanding of the world. Too often it can seem like our only choices are to embrace bigotry or uncritical acceptance. If parents walk on eggshells, are afraid to misstep, or feel they lack the language to talk about identity, something else will fill that void—and may already have done so. We are meant to be formed by our families through a process of embracing parental values, or perhaps affirmatively rejecting them. Neither is possible if parents cannot provide a clear sense of where they stand.

Many LGBTQ young people still grow up in families or communities that do not accept them. Discrimination and bullying experiences are not uncommon. But public attitudes have undergone a sea change when it comes to perceptions about the morality of same-sex relationships, support for same-sex marriage, and acceptance of gay and lesbian people. Today, most young gay and lesbian people come out in their teens. A Pew Research Center study found that two-thirds of gay and lesbian adults under the age of thirty said they shared their sexual orientation with someone by the age of seventeen.[19] The rising acceptance of gay and lesbian people in American society has coincided with a rapid rise of LGBTQ identity, especially among young women. In less than ten years, the number of young women identifying as LGBTQ tripled—roughly one in three young women now identify as such.[20] Driving this generational shift in LGBTQ identity is the *B*: The majority of young adults who identify as LGBTQ are bisexual.

Nearly One in Three Young Women Identify as LGBTQ

Percentage of young Americans (age 18 to 29) who identify as LGBTQ

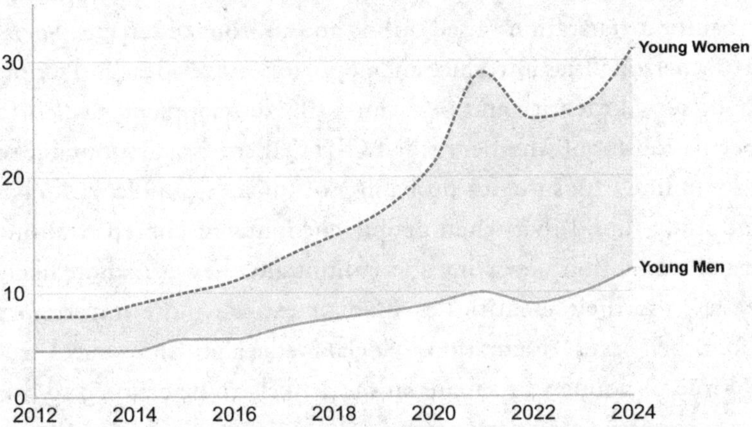

Note: Beginning in 2022, Gallup asked about non-binary gender identity. The results presented here do not include respondents who identify as non-binary. Data represents rolling averages. No data is available for 2018 and 2019.
Source: Gallup U.S. Daily Polls, 2012–2017; Gallup Demographic Trends, 2020–2024.

Young adults, like so many generations before them, are wrestling with fundamental questions of identity and belonging. Figuring out who you are and finding where you fit in is an essential part of growing up. Our culture has also granted them unprecedented discretion in making decisions about their identity. At the same time, young people today—Gen Z—have fewer real-world sexual and romantic experiences to draw from as they develop an understanding of themselves. Even short-term romantic interactions can help adolescents develop an understanding of themselves. What feels comfortable and what doesn't. What's important in a partner and what isn't. And the type of relationship they eventually want.

Instead, young adults are trying to answer these questions through simulated romantic experiences. Virtual experiences, in many cases, have taken the place of dating, hookups, and sex. Of course, pornography has become almost inescapable online—

images, videos, and other sexual content can be found on most social media platforms and many online forums. But the lifestyles of entertainment and social media figures have been immensely influential for a generation raised online and in front of screens. Social media personalities introduce and popularize novel ideas and scripts about sexual identity and behavior—this development has led to speculation about whether rising LGBTQ identity is attributable to early online exposure. It's probably not quite so simple, although one study found that when people encountered content framing sexual orientation as existing on a continuum, they were more likely to describe their identities as fluid or express more uncertainty about their sexual orientation.[21] Social media algorithms play a crucial role, as young women are far more likely to be exposed to this type of content than young men.

The pandemic, which halted almost all in-person socializing, dramatically increased the amount of time young people spent online. It also tipped the balance between virtual and real-world influences. Instead of talking with friends, young adults were connected to online communities that popularized certain experiences. Social media algorithms helped promote and popularize content from queer creators—leading at least a few young women to claim that TikTok was aware of their sexual orientation before they were. Multiple media outlets reported that young women began receiving content from LGBTQ creators without their realizing why it was happening. If social media was actively shaping identity, the timing makes sense. The single largest annual increase in LGBTQ identity occurred when most young adults were socially isolated and spending a lot more time online. But mass exposure to different perspectives and experiences could also have catalyzed a rapid change in identity. As more young adults spent time online during the pandemic, algorithms promoting LGBTQ creators not only exposed them to different ways of identifying, but also offered a sense of belonging at a time when so many felt cut off from the world. For some young women, finding relatable experiences reduced their sense of isolation at a uniquely disorienting moment.[22]

It's hard to overstate how important social media was to this entire process. Young people striving to assert their individuality found in social media platforms opportunities to explore sexual identities, and supportive communities to affirm them. Online abuse of LGBTQ young people remains an unfortunate reality, and yet in certain spaces being LGBTQ can confer considerable social benefits as well. Sociologist Musa al-Gharbi argues that the adoption of marginalized identities can inoculate individuals from criticism or boost their status.[23] He writes that there is a "widespread notion that people who are most oppressed can understand society most clearly . . . and should be given more deference and respect."[24] He argues that it explains the overrepresentation of LGBTQ people in elite social spaces, such as Ivy League colleges and universities.

The problem lies not in the proliferation of identity categories, or the incentives to claim them, but that their discovery is so often divorced from real-world experiences. Social media algorithms are not governed by age or experience, only interest. For young people seeking answers about themselves, instant validation and acceptance found online is understandably appealing, but it can quickly dissolve into confusion when online experiences conflict with life on the ground. Identities should serve to guide our behavior and facilitate social connection. While these labels might be personally meaningful to the people using them, there is a broader question to consider: What do these new labels and identities mean for how we relate to each other? Do they allow people to be more easily seen, known, and understood? Or less?

At some point, most of us will struggle to understand where we fit in the world. Simply adopting a label is no shortcut to figuring this out. It turns out that perceptions of sexual orientation are dramatically different for Americans who identify as bisexual and those who identify as gay, lesbian, or straight. Most people who are bisexual believe sexual orientation is susceptible to change, varying over time, while both straight and gay people are far less likely to embrace this idea.[25] Bisexual Americans are far more likely to report that they have felt "uncertain about who they are supposed to be" in the last twelve months than Americans who are heterosexual. Notably, this feeling is also far more pronounced among people who identify as bisexual than among people who are gay or lesbian. When we have greater latitude to determine our identities (or change them), the process does not always result in a feeling of empowerment; it can just as easily leave us feeling adrift. It's not that certain identities or orientations are wrong, but that the work of identity formation can feel endless—more young people are engaged in the continuous, effortful, anxiety-producing work of deciding who they are. The problem is not the destination, it's the journey.

Bisexual Americans Express More Uncertainty About Who They Are

Percentage of Americans who, in the last 12 months, felt uncertain about who they were supposed to be . . .

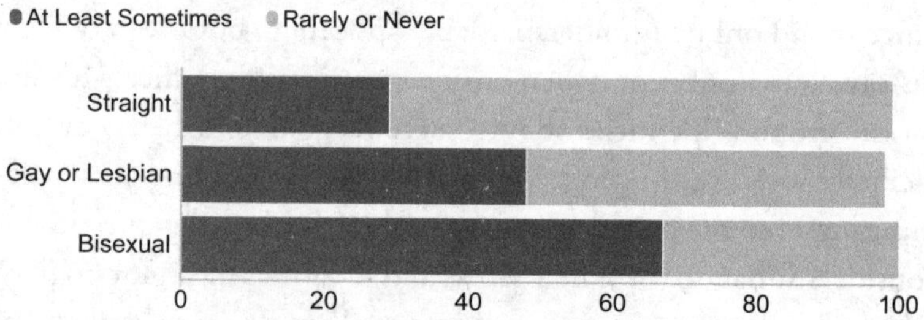

Note: Refusals not shown.
Source: AEI Survey Center on American Life, American Adolescence Survey, 2023.

For many young people, coming into their sexual identities is, in a way, theoretical. That does not mean that they are wrong or confused, but this key part of who they are has not been tested or tried out by engaging with real people. We discover who we are not by voyeuristically watching the lives of other people online, but through our interactions with others. Some amount of adolescent experimentation is often necessary, and confusion is sometimes inevitable. But if you want to explore feelings of attraction, there is no better way to do it than to be there in person. It's more difficult to trust your instincts and feelings when staring at a screen.

So what does this mean for young men and women? A solid understanding of who we are makes it easier to relate to other people and to know what we want in relationships. When sexual identity and sexual preference are in a state of flux, it can serve as a source of personal confusion and anxiety, leading to disconnection. I don't think exposure to different perspectives and identities is inherently damaging or destabilizing, but it's not the most reliable method of learning about ourselves either. The way we develop an understanding of who we are, what we like, and how we relate to others is better built by moving through the actual world and engaging with the people in it. Establishing an identity is not like earning a merit badge; the purpose is to facilitate the development of more enduring bonds with other people.

Building a CV or Building a Family

It's not that identity construction has suddenly become more important to young adults, but the cultivation of it matters in a new way. Young adults are less embracing of ascriptive identities—those conferred through group membership—than those achieved through a process of introspection and self-discovery. With diminished authority and waning trust, institutions that once imparted a sense of identity—churches, extended families, ethnic enclaves—now play a less formative role for adolescents searching to understand themselves. No institution has historically been more influential in shaping identity than the family, but changes in parenting strategies and priorities have radically shifted its role in this process. Today, families work less to mold children and set them on a well-defined path than they do to embrace children's individuality and affirm their individual choices.

A big reason for the change has to do with parental expectations. When kids are younger and not clamoring for independence, few things make them happier than being able to help their parents with a project. When kids realize that they are needed and their efforts on behalf of the family are important, it gives them an immense feeling of pride and purpose. As household sizes contracted and the nuclear family became the predominant model, children's household contributions became less essential. Parents could handle it all. In our household, I don't need my kids to unload the dishwasher in the morning, and in fact it will take longer and require more mental energy from me to keep them on task. Not to mention, the risk of breaking glassware increases dramatically. And so, every morning they sit munching on cereal while I put away clean plates and bowls. As less is asked of them, and more sacrifices are made on their behalf, children start assuming that the primary purpose of a family is the fulfillment of their own needs.

Not all families make these types of accommodations for their children. The structure and size of families, as well as parenting style, influences how engaged children are in day-to-day household activities. In large families, older siblings often watch over their younger ones. They may help with dinner, cleaning, or other household tasks, not because they are more conscientious or considerate, but because their parents have established that their help is crucial. Regardless of what you may have been told, making your bed is not a self-improvement regime or an experience that teaches the value of discipline and hard work—chores serve as essential family functions. The business of building a family requires participation from every member. It is a team enterprise, but too often kids are left on the bench. This is why large families tend to be strong families—they require greater commitment from all their members to make it all work.

Parents are investing more time and energy in their children, in part because there are more options to consider. The expansion of extracurricular activities offered to kids can create participation pressures. It invariably invites parents to consider the question: Are my kids going to be disadvantaged compared to their peers if they are not working to develop their artistic, intellectual, and athletic talents? With limited resources, parents face trade-offs, and many decide to pursue enrichment activities at the expense of having their kids more regularly take on household responsibilities. It's not simply that there are more activities to choose from, but there is also pressure for earlier specialization, which requires high levels of commitment. One study found a threefold increase in travel sports participation between those born in the 1990s compared with those born in the 1950s.[26] I can confirm that the commitment is intense. In our household, both boys are playing travel soccer and their teams each practice three times a week. My own participation in travel soccer was far less demanding—I started playing at an older age, and I practiced less often than my own kids.

There are plenty of benefits that come with participating in travel sports—learning resilience, self-efficacy, and confidence—but participation entails a considerable opportunity cost. For previous generations, the evening meal was a central and ubiquitous feature of family life. Wherever you grew up, whatever your class background, race, ethnicity, or religion, dinnertime was family time. Even the latchkey kids, America's notoriously feral generation, still enjoyed

Few Gen Zers and Millennials Had Regular Family Dinners Growing Up

Percentage of Americans who say they had daily meals together as a family when they were growing up

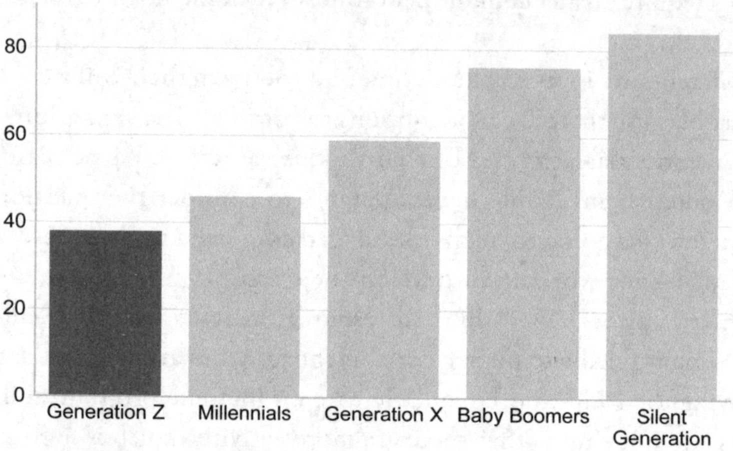

Source: AEI Survey Center on American Life, American National Family Life Survey, 2021.

together time around the dinner table. Gen Xers may have spent their summers unsupervised, roaming their neighborhoods, but they were still expected home for dinner. Fifty-nine percent of Gen Xers and more than three-quarters (76 percent) of baby boomers report that they shared daily meals together as a family.[27] But an activity that was once a central feature of American family life is vanishing—only 38 percent of Gen Z adults say they grew up having regular meals with their families.

Studies have documented a broad range of personal benefits associated with family meals for children. Regular family meals are associated with the development of better eating habits, reduced likelihood of alcohol and drug use, and higher self-esteem. Equally important, mealtime offers ample opportunity for kids to contribute to a shared family activity—setting the table, washing the dishes, assisting with meal preparation and planning. It's an activity that encourages reciprocity as family members show up for each other, and children have opportunities to listen and to learn.

When I was growing up in Western New York, my family spent summers visiting my aunt and uncle and two cousins at their cabin on a lake north of Toronto. It was a rustic place with few modern amenities—for instance, no dishwasher. Every night after family dinner, the kids would take turns washing and drying the dishes—although there was inevitably grumbling at times, we understood this was our way of contributing. On these trips, family dinners were an inviolable event regardless of whatever else we had planned that day, and everyone played a part in making them happen. I won't say I enjoyed scrubbing pots and plates, but doing it felt meaningful.

In the logistically sophisticated ballet of modern family life, more kids come to see their parents as service providers—people whose essential function is to meet their various needs. Parents often embrace this role, believing that the metric of good parenthood is raising well-adjusted and high-achieving children. Children then learn that their responsibilities are primarily or exclusively to themselves—to develop skills, knowledge, and experiences that will allow them to succeed. Absent from this understanding are the obligations that children have to their parents, siblings, and other family members. Busy family schedules mean reduced opportunities to involve kids in planning or carrying out household activities. With fewer family dinners come fewer opportunities to participate in meal preparation, cleaning, and clearing dining room tables. It's not that children no longer do chores, but their understanding of why they do them has become transactional—cleaning their room or making their bed is something required to get their allowance or access other privileges. What they lose in this process is the appreciation that they are needed, that they contribute to the family's welfare in critical ways.

When we adopt an oversimplified child-centric rubric for judging the well-being of families, it diminishes our understanding of how families matter. The health and well-being of parents, and the quality of familial relationships and density of this web of connections are less often considered. Whether it's the debate over same-sex couples raising children or the importance of marriage, the well-being of children tends to dominate public discussions. The social and emotional outcomes of children are certainly critical metrics of family health, but without considering the wider constellation of people and relationships, we are left with an incomplete understanding of family well-being. Families with a dense web of overlapping social connections between members tend to be more resilient, and strong bonds make them better able to weather tragedies that inevitably strike.

For young people who have been the focus of so much parental attention and investment, the prospect of jeopardizing their sense of self, their freedom, and their educational and professional goals can be a daunting proposition. The growing hesitation Gen Z has about starting their own families makes much more sense when you consider how they were raised. Of course, there is no single reason that young adults without children express considerable apathy about becoming parents. But a key insight can be drawn from how people perceive that children will impact their personal lives. There is a sense that children are subtractive, draining time, money, and energy. They do not simply alter your lifestyle—they take you away from your hobbies, limit your social life, complicate the path to career success, and undermine your financial security. I'm not making this up. A 2024 Pew Research Center Survey found that a majority of childless adults under fifty said that their lives are made easier in each of these areas by the absence of children.[28] Increasingly, these once private and personal doubts about parenthood are manifesting as public expressions. For example, the popular actress Jameela Jamil recently listed sixteen reasons she did not want children in a post that went viral, titled "I Don't Want Children. I Don't Want Children. I Don't Want Children. I Don't Want Children."[29]

If family is solely defined as the process of making social, emotional, and financial investments in children, I can understand why it's less appealing. Endless toil and sacrifice is a tough sell. But building a family is about creating bonds of love, respect, and mutual obligation that span both space and time. Caregivers in one era become care receivers in the next. Rightly tended, these bonds define not only our present, but our future. As Yuval Levin, a noted political theorist and my colleague, has argued, the family provides "each of its members a role, a set of relations to others, a body of responsibilities, and a network of privileges."[30] It constrains our whims and structures our desires in ways that help us navigate the complexity and capriciousness of the modern world.

Parents are uniquely positioned to share these fundamental insights with their children and teach them the value of a shared commitment to this "primordial" institution.[31] Each member has a critical role, and no individual family member is more important than the whole. My eldest son is nine years old, and there is no member of our family who gives warmer, longer, and more frequent hugs to my dad than this little boy.

Therapy Culture: Individual Feelings Matter Most

When I was young, my parents sent me to see a therapist. Not because of any personal behavior issues, but rather as a preventative measure. After my parents went through an acrimonious divorce when my brothers and I were very young, there was some concern about its lasting effect on our development. I was not given a choice in the matter, and I hated every minute of it. I refused to talk to my therapist, Richard, so we would sit in silence playing board games until the fifty-minute session was over. Eventually my parents gave up, and I was freed from being prodded to talk about my feelings. It was a relief. At the age of nine, I was not eager to admit that I had these weekly appointments. It wasn't necessarily due to the stigma of being in therapy; rather, these visits made me feel different from my peers, when all I wanted was to fit in, to belong.

Therapy can be a game-changer and an actual lifesaver for children and adults alike. The American culture around therapy has become especially influential in recent years and has distinctly affected how children are raised. Therapeutic interventions are powerful, and as such, they entail a certain amount of risk. An excessive focus on our feelings is not always helpful; it can make us fragile and less resilient to the hardships that come from everyday living. This is the central concern of Abigail Shrier's *Bad Therapy.* Shrier argues that the widespread use of cognitive behavioral therapy in children has led us to pathologize harmless personality traits. Not all behavioral quirks require a diagnosis, let alone treatment. Some kids are simply shy, strong-willed, or sensitive.

Embracing therapy culture leads parents to believe they need to attend to every passing feeling that bubbles to the surface in their child. This can be profoundly unhelpful. When I talked with psychologist and author Joshua Coleman, he said that a constant attunement to our emotional state is not necessarily serving our mental health. "Children aren't really allowed to just have a feeling and then watch it pass the way that other generations could," he says.[32] At times, we need to allow a feeling to wash over us. It doesn't deserve sustained attention or warrant a response. This is particularly true given that humans are, at our core, emotional beings. One study found that 90 percent of our waking hours are spent in a certain emotional state, and that we feel multiple feelings at once.[33] If you're encouraged to focus on every passing feeling, it can snowball into something larger—a permanent state of acute sensitivity that requires a sustained intervention to manage. Living this way can feel overwhelming.

Rates of cognitive behavioral therapy are indeed increasing, but long-term trends are difficult to identify given the paucity of historical data. In a nationally representative survey, we asked Americans to reflect on their adolescent experiences—and found profound generational gaps in the results. Roughly one in four Gen Z men and one in three Gen Z women report having seen a therapist at some point in their teen years.[34] These experiences were vanishingly rare among older cohorts. Only 4 percent of baby boomers report that they talked to a therapist during their teen years.

Being able to understand what you're feeling and why is a critical life skill, but excessive emotional attunement comes at a cost. If we are constantly monitoring our evolving emotional landscape, it can make it more difficult to identify or acknowledge the feelings or perspectives of those around us. Shrier believes the growth in therapy culture has altered the relationship between parents and children. Children learn that they are the center of the emotional universe and that the expression of their feelings is paramount. More than that, children are learning that their individual well-being is separate from that of other family members rather than intimately intertwined. "Our kids don't know that they are connected to others—because we don't tell them," Shrier writes.[35] Perpetually attending to our own emotional well-being above all else is like wearing blinders to the needs and feelings of others.

The absolutist approach to mental health can lead people to dismantle their social networks in the name of emotional well-being. There is an alarming trend of people sacrificing important relationships and failing to show up for the people they care about in an effort to "protect their peace." To embody the mantra means to live on high alert, ready to remove anyone from your life based on how they make you feel. The problem is that the ever-expanding definition of "toxic" provides little guidance for when this extreme action might actually be warranted. If your parent voted differently from you in the last election, is that a sufficient reason to stop speaking to them? This framework is based on the errant notion, as *Vox* reporter Allie Volpe puts it, that "relationships should be easy, the thinking goes, and any hint of conflict is a sign of social dysfunction."[36] This perspective is particularly prevalent online. One tweet with over seven million views read: "decentering friendship saved my life this year."[37]

This type of thinking betrays a complete misunderstanding of the function of personal relationships. Our social connections are meant to structure our lives and imbue them with purpose. The modest accommodations and regular allowances we make for others are not necessarily personal impositions, but evidence of the bonds we share. These ties constrain our decisions and influence our behavior, and we exert the same invisible force on the people we know even if we're not always aware of it. We've lost sight of how this is all supposed to work. At every step, we learn that our feelings are paramount, our needs take priority, and our personal choices are inviolable. Then we wonder why so many of us are walking this path alone.

CHAPTER 3

SOCIAL INSECURITY

Don't Be Cringe

Of all the various expressions that Generation Z has popularized or introduced into our lexicon, none better captures their unique identity and experience better than the word *cringe.* It's a great word, highly adaptive—evocative of a wide variety of behavior—completely subjective, and deployed to devastating effect against unsuspecting victims, such as earnest millennials. For the uninitiated, cringe generally refers to inauthentic or socially awkward behavior that produces feelings of discomfort from those witnessing it. It rapidly gained traction over the past decade, especially across social media. Google Trends showed a rapid uptick in searches for the word in 2016, and searches have remained elevated throughout the late 2010s and early 2020s. On TikTok, there are currently 4.9 million individual posts that include the hashtag "cringe."

Gen Z does not only accuse their hapless parents of cringey behavior, but they frequently level this charge against their peers too. Adolescents have an acute sensitivity to social judgment and rejection from their peers. Many are still wrestling with questions of identity and have not yet developed deep social attachments or the sense of confidence that comes with it. In the age of social media and camera-equipped smartphones, social rejection is a qualitatively different experience—we have given teens the ability to easily document and broadcast the humiliations of their peers. The threshold for being labeled cringe is only knowable after the fact. As this generation is coming of age and learning how to relate to and connect with their peers both in the real world and online, the stakes for social missteps are heightened.

In *The Anxious Generation,* Haidt argues that the cultivation and maintenance of online reputation has become a critical part of teen social life: "Succeeding socially in that universe required them to devote a large part of their consciousness—perpetually—to managing what became their online brand. This was now necessary to gain acceptance from peers, which is the oxygen of adolescence, and to avoid online shaming, which is the nightmare of adolescence."[1] Haidt found that the spike of adolescent anxiety was at least partly attributable to the necessary cultivation and maintenance of their digital social lives. Social media can both amplify criticism and transform individual judgment into collective condemnation. Without warning, a single misstatement online can lead to a social media pile-on.

The avoidance of social judgment and embarrassment—appearing cringe—is an incredibly powerful motivator, but unlike past adolescent aspirations for popularity (the plot of many eighties movies), avoiding cringey behavior can now be accomplished through the avoidance of social interactions. The fear can reduce our appetite for social risk-taking. In the last few years, DJs started noticing empty dance floors and static crowds; there were more people documenting the club scene than participating in it. Phones were identified as the primary culprit, leading some dance clubs to institute bans to lure club goers back onto the dance floor.[2] The constant threat of surveillance can make it feel safer to sit on the sidelines, and so we become spectators.

My senior year in high school, our varsity soccer team was playing in the postseason soccer tournament for our division in the New York State tournament. I vividly remember taking the field one game, and noticing a player on the opposing team run out in his underwear. He had the rest of his uniform on—jersey, socks, cleats, and shin guards, just no shorts. It took me a moment to realize what had happened. We were playing in upstate New York in late November and it was cold. Before the games, all the players wore their warm-up suits—jackets and pants—that we would take off right before the game. In his excitement, he must have removed his shorts along with his warmup pants before charging out onto the field. Once made aware of his error, he quickly ran back to collect the rest of his uniform. I share this story because this was how so many embarrassing moments—of which I've collected many during my formative years—would most often play out. They weren't offered up as fodder for social media pile-ons, nor did they engender snarky commentary, because none of those spaces existed. Embarrassment was momentary, and context-bound, known only to the small number of people who witnessed it. For the most part, teenagers in the pre-social media era could count on their social missteps and public humiliations being quickly forgotten rather than potentially turning into defining personal experiences.

Social media entirely altered the social risk calculation for adolescents and teenagers. A single humiliating moment or unfortunate social interaction could be captured forever, perhaps without your knowledge or consent, and could upend even the most carefully cultivated online identity. This fear is magnified when meeting new people who have less compunction about using your misfortune to gain attention or clout online. Jordan Meisel, a psychologist who works with young adults, says these worries are top-of-mind for many of her clients. In an interview with *Wired* magazine, she says that making first impressions can be especially anxiety-provoking. "For people who are going to college and meeting a lot of new people for the first time, a huge fear is that they're going to come off as *cringe,*" she says.[3] The need to constantly monitor your self-presentation is exhausting. It's no wonder then that so many young adults have scaled back their social commitments in the real world, where they had less control.

Disappearing Social Experience

Growing up in the suburbs, my friends and I spent a lot of time driving around. There were Saturday nights that were primarily spent in the car—driving around new housing developments and down back country roads. I imagine it sounds boring having no particular destination in mind, but we were away from our parents and with each other. That was often enough.

We were able to spend time away from the teachers who bothered us, the siblings who annoyed us, our responsibilities, and our uncertain futures. For those brief moments, sitting in my friend's white Honda Civic, we simply existed apart from everything for a little while. We made dumb jokes, talked about classmates we liked and those we didn't, and occasionally drank warm cans of Genny Light when we could get our hands on it. It's an experience that is nearly impossible to imagine today. Young adults today are tethered to their parents, to their problems, to politics, and to each other.

Every conversation and every moment has the potential to be catalogued and broadcasted to the world. The upshot is a generation that has retreated from adventures, in favor of a risk-averse approach to socializing.

If getting your driver's license was once a seminal experience for most teenagers, it no longer is. The percentage of teenage drivers has collapsed over the past few decades. In 2021, only 40 percent of teenagers had their driver's licenses compared to 64 percent in 1995.[4] The potential explanations for this dramatic change in behavior vary, but chief among them is that a driver's license no longer represents freedom. If your parents track your location, and if you are always reachable via instant message, a text, or even a phone call, then the physical distance is almost irrelevant. When my friends would get together, we would often head to the same spot, which we cleverly nicknamed "the spot." It was nothing more than a cul-de-sac at the top of a hill with a bunch of unfinished houses. It was only a couple miles away from my own house, but it felt so much farther than that. Today, as far as teenagers might travel, they will never have that same sense of separation so long as they carry location-tracking communication devices with them wherever they go. They are forever connected to the wider world.

Despite the ease with which teenagers can communicate with one another and share their experiences or feelings almost instantly, they spend far less time socializing with one another than previous generations. Teenagers age fifteen to nineteen are averaging only about 57 minutes a day in person with friends outside of school, a drop from 197 minutes a day roughly two decades earlier.[5] Consistent with a lot of other research that has documented this decline, we found that Gen Z adults were much less likely to hang out with friends during their teenage years than teens in previous eras.[6] Only 40 percent of Gen Z report that they regularly socialized with their friends during most or all of their teen years.* Fifty-four percent of millennials, 60 percent of Gen X, and 52 percent of baby boomers reported the same experience for most or all of their teen years.

It's not only in-person socializing that is less common among Gen Z teens than it once was. There are entire categories of social experiences that are disappearing. Participation in religious services and related social activities, church youth groups, summer camps, and potlucks have been declining for decades. Gen Z adults were less likely than previous generations not only to attend services regularly growing up, but also to participate in youth groups and pray with their families.[7] The decline of religious identity continues to capture public attention and scholarly interest, but it's the collapse of formal and informal religious activities that has been responsible for the loss of so much social cohesion, connection, and civic learning. In *American Grace,* Robert Putnam and David Campbell found that it was not what people believed but how often they practiced that produced the most lasting social and civic benefits.[8] Belonging is what matters, and belonging happens in church parking lots, over pancake breakfasts, and in study groups. For many Gen Zers it's not happening at all.

In the same 2023 survey, we found generational declines in various other categories as well. Gen Z participated less often in scouting, was less likely to have a part-time job, and spent far less time than previous generations of teens drinking and smoking cigarettes or pot. Fewer Gen Z adults report that they had any relationship

* In this survey, we used a method that measures differences in adolescent experiences to control for age differences. We accomplished this by employing a series of questions about various activities and experiences, such as participating in scouting, working at a part-time job, and talking to a therapist. These questions require respondents to recall behaviors and events from their past—sometimes from a long time ago. We focused less on exact measurements of frequency and more on identifying whether certain activities were significant parts of their teenage experience.

experience either. Only 56 percent said they had a boyfriend or girlfriend at any point during their teen years. For Gen Z men, sports participation is falling as well.

Gen Z Was Less Involved in "Typical" Teenage Pursuits

Percentage of Americans who report having had the following experiences during their teen years . . .

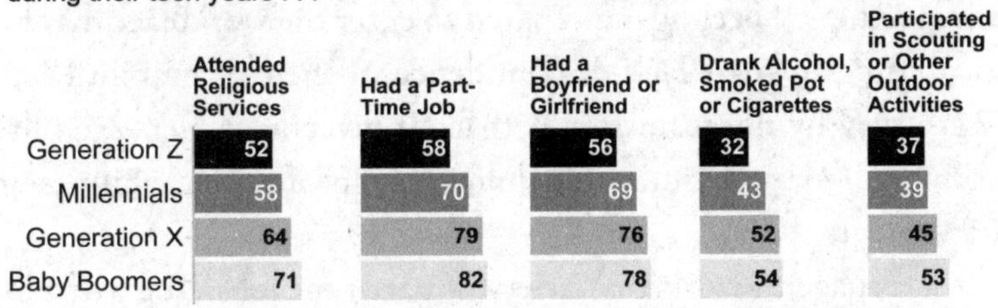

Note: Responses for attending religious services include those who attended regularly during their teen years. Responses for those who drank or smoked include those who did so at least occasionally.
Source: AEI Survey Center on American Life, American Adolescence Survey, 2023.

Gen Z is entering adulthood with less work, relationship, and religious experience than previous generations of young people. These are life events that, at one time, were a seminal part of growing up. Haidt summarizes the social deficit that has characterized Gen Z's adolescence: "They spent far less time playing with, talking to, touching, or even making eye contact with their friends and families, thereby reducing participation in embodied social behaviors that are essential for successful human development."[9] Gen Z has had a less participatory adolescence—they are less likely to have engaged in a wide variety of social experiences that push them, provoke them, and help form them into well-adjusted adults. In previous generations, teens from different backgrounds and corners of the country were not only better able to relate to one another through shared experiences, but they also learned what it means to be part of something bigger than themselves.

While more Gen Zers have a college degree than older generations, employers report that their communication, problem-solving, and collaboration skills are lacking.[10] This soft-skill deficit makes sense, given that Gen Z has less of the retail, service, and food industry experience that shaped the early careers of most teenagers in previous generations. What's more, a 2024 Harris Poll found that 82 percent of managers report their Gen Z hires requiring more support and training to develop the skills needed to be effective team members.[11] Feeling unprepared to enter the workplace may be contributing to their lack of confidence in their own abilities. A 2022 survey by my team found that 40 percent of Gen Z adults working full- or part-time often doubt their professional abilities or achievements.[12]

As a teenager, I worked a variety of part-time jobs. The worst by a country mile was working as a dishwasher in an Italian strip mall restaurant in the greater Rochester area. I'd come home with scratches, burns from scalding water, and my arms aching after scrubbing hundreds of sauté pans during a shift. The best job I had was as a short order cook at a public golf course—my shirt would be so caked with grease that within a few weeks it permanently changed hues. But I was mostly cooking outdoors, working the grill in a makeshift shed, surrounded by people my own age. I spent a brief time working in a local coffee shop too, where I acquired a lifelong aversion to coffee. The expectations, culture, and social dynamics of all these places were unique—I had to learn, adapt, and communicate with very different types of people. I didn't make much money, but I learned a lot of valuable lessons by making a lot of mistakes.

There is no single teenage experience that is essential; rather, engaging in a variety of different social pursuits is what allows teens to grow into competent and considerate adults. In different ways, scouting, team sports, faith, and work create community and teach us a sense of civic obligation. Even in the jobs I hated, I learned that if I shirked my responsibilities, it made life harder for the people I worked with. We were connected in a common enterprise. I could make their lives easier or more difficult, and they could do the same to me.

The Decline of Formative Friction: Big Houses and Small Families

It's not only the internet and camera phones that may have discouraged adolescents and young adults from taking social risks; their formative environments made them ill-prepared for handling friction that inevitably arises when people get together. Americans are living in much larger homes than they once did, but with fewer occupants. The U.S. Census Bureau report found that the median size of a newly constructed single-family home was nearly twenty-three hundred square feet in 2022, representing a 20 percent size increase over homes built in 1990. And the average American household has 2.5 people in it, down from 3.7 people in 1940.[13] Large families are rapidly disappearing. The percentage of women in their early forties who have given birth to only one child has doubled over the past forty years.[14]

Smaller families mean fewer siblings. Parents with fewer kids are better able to ensure that there is not a scarcity of toys, clothes, food, or attention. They can mediate conflict more easily, leaving their kids less capable of working out problems for themselves. In an effort to forestall fighting, it is not uncommon for parents to make arrangements for each kid to receive goods and services of approximately comparable value. In my own household, we have, on a number of occasions, purchased multiple items—one for each child—in order to avoid conflict. We referee disputes more often than we should. If you have five kids, it is not always going to be feasible for you to step in. Catering to everyone's distinct dining preferences is easier when there are fewer preferences. As a result, children are less practiced in making accommodations for others.

Another factor reducing intrafamilial friction is the growing age gap between children. When children are close in age, they are more competitive—in no small part because they spend more time together and are closer in size and ability, and are more likely to share similar interests. "Larger age gaps have opened the door for a new kind of dynamic—one premised more on mentorship than on a battle for limited attention or resources. Squabbles for parental attention are giving way, at least in some families, to a sense that there is enough to go around for everyone," says Michael Waters at *The Atlantic*.[15] In larger families, the possibilities for mentorship and rivalry are not mutually exclusive—an eldest sibling could be in direct competition with his immediately younger brother or sister and serve as a mentor to a much younger member of the family. Family roles and responsibilities are more dynamic, which inculcates a level of social flexibility that can be invaluable in managing the range of different relationships we have as adults.

Larger families open up opportunities for siblings to play mediating roles when conflict arises. With two children, parents can feel compelled to intervene in order to settle disputes. But in families with more children, interpersonal dynamics become more complicated than simply picking sides. There are more opportunities to negotiate, compromise, and find common ground. Fights were not uncommon between me and my brothers, but on many occasions, we were forced to work it out ourselves or face collective punishment. It felt unfair at times, but it was a powerful incentive to work things out. I would add that middle children frequently excel in managing disagreement.

This observation is not theoretical. Parents with large families describe their own experiences in much this way. Bethany Mandel, a conservative columnist, noted that in her own family of eight (two adults and six children), group dynamics altered how individual members understood their own roles and needs. She writes that as a family grows "the center of gravity shifts naturally away from the parent and toward the group itself. Siblings become each other's teachers, competitors, collaborators, and companions. The household gradually develops its own internal culture, a web of relationships that operates largely independent of constant parental direction." She added, "Children in large families quickly learn that the world does not revolve around them. They must wait their turn, negotiate for resources, manage disagreements, and recover from small losses and frustrations. These experiences, repeated daily, gradually build a kind of emotional sturdiness that is difficult to cultivate in environments where every conflict is mediated by adults and every discomfort is immediately addressed."[16] Even if she may gloss over some of the challenges involved, the basic mechanics of socialization are clear. When families increase in size, we have to make room for each other, a lesson that helps us learn how to navigate a world with lots of people in it.

Larger houses allow us to physically escape from each other, but smartphones and tablets allow us to be absent even when we're in the same room. An astonishing report from Common Sense Media revealed that 40 percent of toddlers have their own tablets.[17] Most families have enough screens to occupy each family member. I can recount on more than one occasion when all four members of my family were engrossed in their own programs on separate screens at the same time. Fighting over the television remote and having to compromise over what movie or show to watch has become an endangered experience.

As annoying as bickering can be, both for those observing and those involved, we should not be too quick to celebrate its demise. Over the last two decades, there has been a steady erosion in the amount of time Americans spend socializing with family members. A report from the U.S. Surgeon General finds that from 2003 to 2020, families spent five fewer hours every month interacting with one another.[18] But this does not adequately convey the loss. It's not simply about fewer hours: Traditions of togetherness have disappeared too. As I noted earlier, few Gen Z adults report that they had daily family meals growing up, an experience that was a mainstay for baby boomers. Technology has also fragmented the time we spend together by allowing family members to pursue the same activity separately. It's not that Americans have given up on family movie night, but we no longer have to share the television, so many families do so less often. It's certainly true in our household. When I was growing up, my family had one television and one VCR, which made our near-weekly trips to Blockbuster a communal activity. My brothers and I had to compromise on what movie to rent, but whatever griping occurred, by the time the we made it home all of us were excited to get started. This change in behavior has led to a profound shift in how families spend time together, yet it has elicited remarkably little comment.

It's not simply parenting choices driving this change; more child-rearing experts now insist that children benefit psychologically from spatial separation from the rest of the family, including siblings. Solo bedrooms are a microcosm of this, where young people can "create their own kingdom," said Aaron Cooper, a clinical psychologist at Northwestern University's Family Institute.[19] There seems to be more concern about whether children have enough solitary time, or the chance to develop "solitude skills," such as thinking independently and processing big emotions.[20] I'm not entirely convinced. Modern life offers ample opportunities for spending time alone; it's our social skills that are atrophying. Taken together, these shifts reveal a broader cultural reorientation: Individual needs are prioritized, while the daily frictions—and bonds—that once came from sharing space in our homes are quietly fading away.

Family is the crucible within which much early social learning occurs. Our appetite for social messiness and understanding of the obligations we have to others is established during these early years. In *Going Solo,* sociologist Eric Klinenberg argues that these formative experiences are critical in our social development: "Our early experiences living with others shape our expectations, establishing the shared household as a norm, if not an ideal. They also form our characters, leading us to develop skills, techniques, and models for sharing domestic space that we carry into adulthood, consciously or not."[21] A family environment that minimizes the chance for conflict and resolution, that is overly accommodating to personal needs, can skew the expectations young adults have for college, the workplace, and each other.

After they moved out on their own, young adults who spent most, if not all, of their adolescence in their own spaces were not eager to start sharing with a stranger. America's colleges and universities, which have become more sensitive to the needs of their students, have modified their housing stock. More incoming students express a preference for living alone, and colleges have responded accordingly. Newer student housing in the United States is less likely to offer double occupancy. In fact, only 5 percent of student housing built since 2010 provides double occupancy.[22] Many schools have also altered the practice of randomly assigning roommates to incoming freshmen, and now allow new students to select their roommate based on lifestyle preferences.

Being around people can be challenging and at times exhausting, but the increasingly limited formative experiences we have that involve being around other people during childhood make it increasingly difficult to navigate challenging social situations as adults. With little experience waiting our turn, making compromises, and sharing our belongings and personal space, it becomes much more difficult to make these necessary accommodations in adulthood.

Attack of the Ick

Our aversion to social friction goes beyond our growing preference for personal space; it has also seeped into how we approach dating and perceive romantic gestures. If being cringe has become a more salient social consideration, in romantic relationships there is another type of experience that singles are warned to avoid: giving someone the ick. Unlike typical romantic turnoffs, or red flags, such as being unemployed, the ick describes a visceral reaction, a sense of revulsion triggered by a certain type of behavior. It can be literally anything, but at least theoretically it can signal incompatibility or low mate quality.

Although not always recognized as such, the ick is a fairly common dating experience. In one study, researchers found a majority of both men and women experienced the ick, although women reported having had the experience more often than men.[23] The authors suggested that the gender difference may lie with women's greater attunement to social cues, and their traditional role as evaluators of behavior. So, what's the problem? Shouldn't people trust their feelings? The problem lies in the fact that in a low-trust dating market with abundant alternatives, the ick encourages defensiveness and snap judgments based on superficial reactions.

Social media is awash in this type of content, perhaps because it serves so many uses. Posting about your unreasonable red flags on social media is a type of status flex, an opportunity to demonstrate that you can dismiss otherwise good options for what many would deem arbitrary reasons. Having a lower threshold for rejection signals your own high value as a romantic partner. It also showcases your distinctiveness. The more bizarre or memorable your dating criteria, the greater likelihood that you will attract attention and interest. Becca Moore, a social media influencer, has multiple posts about the ick that she has shared with her 1.3 million TikTok followers. In one post, she said that her date's inability to turn off his car alarm for five minutes was enough to write him off. The absurdity of this judgment is matched by the affirmative comments that posts like these tend to elicit from other women, which is of course the point. In posting about rejecting her date, a young woman can demonstrate her high standards for prospective partners. It is the ultimate sign of dating value.

The establishment of the ick as a legitimate criteria to evaluate the suitability of prospective partners also gives permission for the romantically risk averse not to take a chance on someone. Instead of having to defend subjective dating criteria, they can simply report that their date engaged in personally repulsive behavior—such as carrying an umbrella, using a straw, or holding a cup in a slightly feminine way—and no further explanation is required. It allows anyone to sidestep uncomfortable questions about why certain qualities or behavior elicits this sense of revulsion, perhaps why so many things do, and what purpose posting about all of this on social media actually serves.

Behind all of this lies the influence of social media and online dating culture. In an environment where people perceive they have limitless dating options, there is little downside to dismissing potential partners for any kind of awkward or off-putting behavior. An excess of romantic opportunities encourages people—especially women who tend to have more options than men—to make expedient evaluations based on more superficial criteria. It lowers our tolerance for human imperfection. And it deludes us into believing that the goal in dating is seeking the absence of flaws when compatibility requires the opposite: appreciating someone's earnest and honest quirks.

So many of the objectionable dating behaviors featured on social media are more often due to a lack of self-awareness, social competence, or experience—deficiencies of knowledge rather than character. But romantic judgments tend to overly weight present conditions at the expense of future possibility. Especially in early adulthood, what matters is someone's emotional, social, and intellectual trajectory rather than their starting point. To put it in social scientific terms, the slope rather than the intercept is what should be evaluated more critically when making decisions about romantic partners. Where people are right now matters less than where they are capable of going.

All of this creates a social environment that feels inherently risky, and encourages young adults to maximize control over their self-presentation. The preference for electronic communication is partly driven by this fear of committing social blunders not only because of how these mistakes might be magnified online, but because there is no opportunity for redemption. There is a sense of finality in these judgments—make a single mistake and you're out. Unfollowed. Blocked. Ghosted. In one TikTok video, a young woman says she gets the ick when a guy sends her an Instagram Reel. What happens to a young man who wants to share a social media video with her? "You're done," she says.

It teaches young people that attraction is extraordinarily fragile and mistakes are irreversible, that any potential social interaction with a romantic interest might produce feelings of disgust in another person. When minor social offenses become potentially disqualifying, our willingness to engage in spontaneous behavior and take risks is compromised. As young adults realize that even minor infractions can result in being posted and pilloried online, they become more guarded, unwilling to take social or romantic risks.

CHAPTER 4

THE BURDEN OF BEING TOGETHER

The Myth of Personal Progress

Few cultural narratives have proved more influential and problematic than the mythology of personal growth. Young adults are taught that life's most coveted rewards are realized after engaging in the painstaking work of improving themselves. Social media reinforces the need for self-optimization by fueling feelings of inadequacy. You are not as attractive, wealthy, successful, or highly esteemed as you could or should be. The same algorithms then feed young people an endless stream of self-improvement strategies to accomplish these goals. We commit to therapy sessions to work through our issues, we read to feed our intellectual curiosity, we engage in personal hobbies to develop our passions, and we spend hours in the gym to hone our physique. There are products and procedures that can facilitate this work too. At a certain point, the self-improvement journey becomes endless. Whether at the gym or in the therapist's office, there is always something to work on, and these efforts are more typically solitary rather than communal.

That romantic commitment might inhibit personal growth was a central proposition of Elizabeth Gilbert's blockbuster memoir *Eat Pray Love.* It resonated with millions of readers and would influence American relationship culture for the next two decades. The story begins with an ending. In the opening pages, Gilbert meticulously catalogues the tumultuous dissolution of her marriage, a defining moment that served as the critical catalyst for her journey of self-discovery. "By escaping your own trash compactor of an existence, you can revive, reinvigorate and reinvent yourself, almost at the cellular level," Gilbert writes.[1] Embedded in this claim is the idea that social separation is a necessary requirement of finding yourself. Only by making individual choices unimpeded by social constraints can we fully realize who we are meant to be. Marriage (particularly an unhappy one) is the quintessential social constraint Gilbert refers to, and she implies that divorce is experienced not as the end of a defining relationship, but as an opportunity to be your most authentic self.

The book was a smash hit, selling more than twelve million copies worldwide. A few years later it was made into a movie starring Julia Roberts. It served as an exemplar of the personal growth narrative in which the central tension was not the building of commitment but liberation from it. It offered both a template and permission structure for people struggling in unsatisfying relationships. And for those lacking a strong social support system, or a network of civic and religious institutions that help married couples weather difficult times, divorce remained the one lever left to pull.

This book, and the rise of other popular divorce memoirs, has portrayed the exit of familial responsibilities as the necessary path to becoming one's best self. In *This American Ex-Wife,* Lyz Lenz writes, "I wanted to remove myself from the martyr's pyre and instead sacrifice the roles I had been assigned at birth: mother, wife, daughter. I wanted to see what else I could be."[2] Although these narratives were not without their critics, they also inspired sympathetic responses from many women who could relate to their struggles. Motherhood carries a weight of expectations that fatherhood does not, and so, in a way, the cultural reframing represents an effort to ease these asymmetrical relational burdens. Whether intentional or not, the message that these books convey is that the path to fairness is only achievable through disengagement.

Whatever the precipitating reason, often there are several; in many of these tellings, the end of a marriage is portrayed as a catalytic event. Divorce is seen as propellant sending one or both people to a healthier, happier, and freer life. It's not difficult to see why this happens—it allows for a failure to be refashioned as a painful but necessary pathway to success. In the process, mutual obligation is set up as the villain—the thing that we need to escape from.

This is not an argument against divorce. It should always be an available option, one ideally made without fear and free of social judgment. Marriages fail. Partners can be or become selfish, and intimate relationships can turn violent or abusive. But the severing of any social tie, whatever else it may be, still represents a loss even when it is necessary.

The public conversation about marriage and divorce coincides with our diminishing appetite for social constraints. Americans don't want offices to dictate dress codes. We want neighbors who leave us alone rather than meddle in our affairs, and we celebrate the cancellation of social events. We want more control over our time and greater latitude in how we spend it. Over the last couple of decades, more Americans have expressed that they want to be able to shed themselves of social bonds when they prove to be unpalatable. Ryan Burge, a political scientist who tracks cultural, social, and religious trends, published startling findings about the rapid change in public attitudes about divorce. Beginning in the mid 2000s, the percentage of Americans who said that getting a divorce should be made an easier process began to tick up. In 2006, for example, only 29 percent of Americans said getting a divorce should be easier; by 2024, more than half (52 percent) the public said it should be easier to get a divorce.[3] Notably, attitudes about the process of ending marital relationships do not track with other attitudes about divorce. For nearly three decades, Americans have affirmed the morality of divorce, and those views have changed very little over the past decade.[4] The rise in support for easing the process of divorce was especially pronounced among younger Americans and those who are not currently married. Unhappy husbands and wives are not the ones driving the change; rather, it's those who have not made the commitment yet who are most anxious to ensure that they can easily extricate themselves from it.[5] It's not hard to see why. Young people raised to believe that getting what you want in life is accomplished by consistently building themselves up can see relationship requirements as working against those goals. The more we invest in ourselves, the greater risk we take in bringing someone into our lives who might not add the same value.

Selective Service: America's Religious Decline

Few institutions have worked more effectively against our ascendent culture of self-regard than America's communities of worship. Membership in a religious community is meant to be formative: It shapes not only how we understand the world but our relationship to it. Through shared rituals and traditions, members develop bonds of belonging that restrict our autonomy but give our actions greater meaning. We speak liturgies in unison instead of alone. We show up to celebrate communions, births, and brises. We staff soup kitchens and donate to clothing drives. Religious membership was never perfect in practice. Emerging cultural norms, especially in the realm of human sexuality and identity, often collided with traditional religious beliefs. Moral strictures were unevenly applied and enforced.

Religious leaders engaged in horrific violations of public trust on too many occasions to count. And still, the benefits of religious membership are inarguable—both as an empirical fact, and a uniquely unquantifiable experience. Americans who participate regularly in church are more likely to vote, volunteer, and donate to charity than those who do not, and they socialize more often and report closer relationships with neighbors.[6] Despite the considerable advantages religious Americans enjoy, more young adults are finding the price of membership is too steep, the obligations too onerous.

From the early 1990s until the mid-2020s, fewer Americans have demonstrated a connection to a religious congregation or identified with a religious tradition. The decline was a generational trend—each generation demonstrated markedly lower levels of religious commitment than the preceding one. A variety of factors influenced the weakening of transmission of religious identity across generations—a process known as socialization. Chief among them were the growing political influence of conservative Christianity, liberalizing attitudes on sexual behavior, and changes in family structure, namely the decline of two-parent married households. But individual parenting choices loomed large too.

For both millennials and Gen Z raised in religious households, the strongest predictor of adult religiosity was the robustness of their formative experiences. Young adults who were engaged in regular religious practice during their childhood and adolescence were far more likely to maintain their religious commitments into adulthood, whether they went off to attend an elite liberal arts college, moved to a liberal city, or developed social ties with people of varying religious backgrounds. In fact, most young adults who left their formative religion to become secular or unaffiliated did so during their teen years. They stopped engaging in regular religious practice while still living at home; their parents were well aware they were no longer sitting next to them in the pew.

In some religious households, religious behavior did not completely cease but took on more personalized forms, such as individual prayer, meditation, or saying grace at meals. It was in the institutional form of religious practice where the largest generational differences emerged. Only 41 percent of Gen Z adults report having attended worship regularly with their family when they were growing up.[7] Nearly six in ten (57 percent) baby boomers said they participated regularly in religious practice. There is an even larger gap when it comes to formal religious education experiences. Forty-two percent of Gen Z report having attended Sunday School or some other type of religious education program during their childhood, compared to 61 percent of baby boomers. The traditional community-oriented religious experience was replaced by a more personalized version that was more curated and convenient, but something important was lost in the process.

In some cases, participation in communal religious activities atrophied because of the perception that they represented burdensome social requirements. As Americans have grown increasingly accustomed to creating personalized experiences, collective worship practices and rituals that subverted self-expression in service of shared experience felt less authentic. There was greater discomfort in conforming to religious doctrines or beliefs, especially those determined to be outdated or misaligned with personal values. Surveys have found that a growing share of young adults believe religious teachings and practices should be updated to reflect their own sensibilities. Young women, who tend to value personal expression more than men, strongly believe that places of worship should adopt more flexible moral standards. Only 39 percent of religious young women—compared to 50 percent of religious young men—say their place of worship should preserve traditional beliefs and practices.[8]

As American society has prioritized personal autonomy above

competing values such as social solidarity, participation in organized religion has plummeted. Young adults who have come of age in this culture are less comfortable conforming to traditional practices and abiding by prevailing social norms. In a culture that celebrates individuality and prizes personal expression, requirements to conform to established social norms began to feel like an uncomfortable imposition. The Pew Research Center's 2024 Religious Landscape Survey found that young adults felt most churches and places of worship are too rule-oriented. Nearly two-thirds of Americans age twenty-four or younger said religious organizations "focus too much on rules," a view held by less than half of seniors.[9]

Nearly Two-Thirds of Young Adults Say Churches Focus Too Much on Rules

Percentage of Americans who agree that churches and other religious organizations focus too much on rules

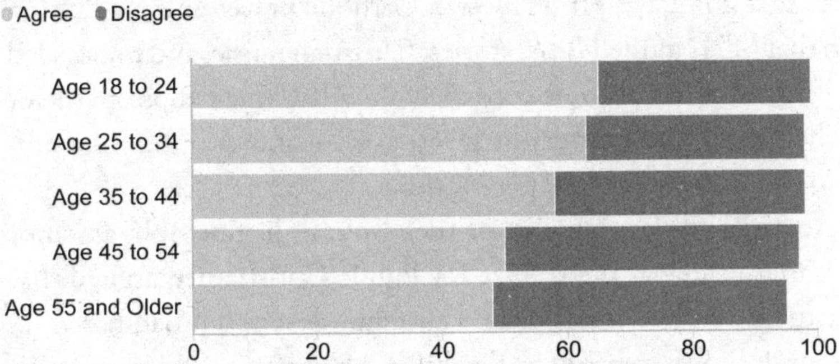

Note: Refusals are not shown.
Source: Pew Research Center, Religious Landscape Study, 2023–2024.

In its place, the online age has accelerated and simplified the ability for Americans to adopt a personalized form of spirituality that has few onerous social requirements. Roughly one in four young adults attend religious services at least a few times a month, and a similar share (27 percent) report belonging to a church or place of worship. Despite these low levels of religious engagement, most young people still identify as spiritual.[10] And many say they regularly spend time looking inward or centering themselves.[11] They have been abetted in this endeavor by the development of spiritual, mindfulness, and wellness apps. Self-guided or app-assisted meditation has grown in popularity. Apps such as Headspace, Insight Timer, and Calm offer a suite of services including curated music, soundscapes, guided meditation, and structured courses accessible instantly on their phones. These apps have allowed individual spiritual experiences to proliferate outside of a formal institutional context. Spiritual communities do exist, but surveys generally show they are far less common than personalized meditative and mindfulness activities.[12]

Even those who have not shed their religious identity are often less involved in traditional religious practices. More Americans are adopting the trappings of religiosity without the attendant obligations that come with it. Hallow, a Catholic prayer and meditation app that offers guided Bible stories, Christian music, and prayers led by celebrities has become extremely popular. These apps offer a lot to their users, and ask very little in return—only the price of a subscription, currently $9.99 per month.

Accessibility is a big part of their appeal. Justine Toh, a Senior Research Fellow at the Centre for Public Christianity, argued that spirituality has retained cultural currency despite a broad-based religious decline because of its flexibility. She writes, " 'Religion' is out of favor because it's regarded as institutional, rule-bound, uptight, and stifling. But 'spirituality'? It's so hot right now because it's more intuitive, less concerned with laying down the law than with giving you a set of principles to take or leave at will."[13] This form of individualized spirituality also asks nothing of you, requires no personal sacrifice, and cannot create bonds of belonging through shared experiences. The type of spirituality that is most popular is that which can easily be molded to fit our existing interests, lifestyle choices, and individual desires. It serves as a useful justification to engage in our preferred pursuits while asking nothing of us in return.

The rising popularity of religious and spiritual apps represent the further commodification of religion. Our modern religious experiences are increasingly chosen, customizable, and convenient. We do not have to leave our house, engage with other people, or do anything that might make us uncomfortable. As religion loses its moral authority, it is less able to make a mark on human society—to encourage personal reflection and accountability. In the process, religious experiences lose their formative potential—not simply to make us better, but to make us want to be better. Instead, it becomes another gateway to validation.

Institutions in general and religious organizations in particular are excellent at showing us how not-special we are, that we are equally lost, broken, or yearning. In every worship service, the cadence of the rituals is different, the stories feature different characters, the sermons emphasize different values, but the experience of collective worship often produces the same result: We appreciate that we are less-than, aspire to be worthy, and dedicate ourselves to a project that is bigger than ourselves. I'll share one final finding from Pew's study of spirituality to make this point. For Americans who are spiritual and religious, spirituality is more about being connected to something bigger than themselves than it is about discovering their "true self." It's the opposite for those who are spiritual, but not religious.[14] Spirituality is most essentially about connecting with your true self rather than being part of something larger. Not everyone steps out of church or their place of worship with a renewed sense of humility and appreciation of their own civic obligations, but it's difficult to contemplate how different, unique, and special we are when engaged in shared religious practices, whether it's singing, prayer, or worship.

It's not necessary to acknowledge their innumerable flaws to appreciate the critical service that religious bodies provide as vehicles to build and express solidarity. In recent decades, rather than instilling a sense of belonging and shared understanding of the world, religion has been repurposed to affirm individual distinctiveness. This emphasis on self-regard shows in some of the most basic aspects of religious worship. Even as they pray less often, when young adults do pray, they are far less likely to pray on behalf of other people than older Americans. This transformation is most notable among women, who have long served as the backbone of many places of worship, volunteering, donating, and participating at rates far higher than men. Young women are significantly more likely to pray for themselves than they are for others, a stark departure from older women, who are more likely to do the opposite.[15]

The changing nature of religious and spiritual practice is part of a broader reconsideration of civic commitment. Young adults are increasingly focused on the costs associated with their social and civic contributions rather than recognizing the broad benefits accrued through their efforts. It's a matter of trust and experience. With less formative religious experiences, more young people are coming of age with less familiarity about the critical civic role that churches and places of worship play in their communities. Only about four in ten young adults believe the churches and houses of worship contribute at least something to the local community where they live. For seniors? It's over 70 percent.[16] It's a generation gap built on perceptions that religious leaders are more concerned about promoting their own sectarian or personal interest rather than seeking to serve community members. It's an unfortunate state without an easy solution. The generosity of many houses of worship often goes unnoticed, while institutional failings in the form of corruption or abuse can become national news. It plays into a narrative that is already too familiar to many Gen Zers—everybody is in it for themselves. Even acts of altruism have an angle.

One-Sided Relationships

If the growing emphasis on personal growth and development has undermined the cultivation of mutual responsibility in our relationships, its greatest effect might be the most paradoxical one. Excessive parental investment in children, sometimes referred to as intensive parenting, can leave kids less able to form stable healthy relationships. Children simultaneously need more guidance and more freedom from parents, who can define what a good life means and give them the space to pursue it. I'll focus on the second part, as it relates to how children form social ties with other people; it is an argument that will be familiar to many readers.

Jonathan Haidt worried about what social media was doing to an entire generation of young people who were experiencing skyrocketing rates of anxiety, depression, and other mental health challenges. Much of the public debate surrounding *The Anxious Generation* has focused on Haidt's argument about the negative impact of social media, but a key part of his argument is about parenting. Haidt argued that beginning in the 1990s, parenting "became more intensive, protective and fearful."[17] Hovering parents offered children less independence and fewer opportunities to practice risk-taking, which would have allowed them to build resilience not only to take a chance on playgrounds, but also in their interactions with adults and peers.

There's no doubt that Haidt has a compelling case to make. Anecdotal evidence bears this out as well. A couple of years ago, I was talking with a group of college students about their experiences, and one young woman shared a compelling story. She was out with some friends on a Thursday night at a local restaurant near campus when she received a call from her mother. It was 10:30 PM. Her mother was upset. "What are you doing out at a restaurant on a school night?" Her mother asked in an exasperated tone. How did she know where her daughter was? "She tracks my phone," the student replied. Around the room, most of the other students nodded knowingly; many had been tracked by their parents throughout much of their preteen and teenage years.

But the tether to parents extends well beyond adolescence. Even into adulthood, today's young people are more closely tied to their parents, talking with their parents more often about a broader range of topics than previous generations. A Pew Research Center survey found that nearly one-third of parents text their adult children daily, while roughly three-quarters are sending messages to their kids at least a few times a week.[18] Many young adults still receive some amount of financial support from their parents, whether it's covering their cellphone plan, or helping out with rent. The same Pew study found that less than half of Americans in their mid- to late twenties report being "completely financially independent" from their parents.[19]

Even after their children have moved out, many parents remain heavily invested in the well-being of their offspring, taking on roles once reserved primarily for friends. Today, young men are more likely to rely on their parents for personal support than their friends; a generation earlier, the reverse was true. "In 1990, only 17 percent of young men and an identical number of young women reported that their parents were the first people they talked to when confronting a personal problem. Close to half (45 percent) of young men said they turned to their friends first."[20]

There's something truly unfortunate about the declining role that friendship plays in the lives of young men. Friendship is far more reciprocal than a parent-child relationship, even when the child is grown. If you want to have a successful connection with someone your age, you need to develop mutual consideration for another person, which is unfortunately more often absent in how kids relate to their parents. Friendship teaches us to acquire and hone our social skills, to develop virtues such as kindness, consideration, patience, and empathy. When our primary model for

More Young Men Are Turning to Parents for Personal Support

Percentage of young men (age 18 to 29) who turn to the following people first when they have a personal problem . . .

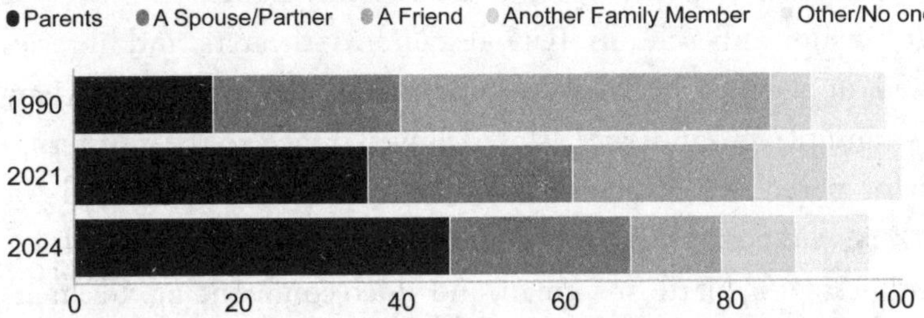

Note: Refusals are not shown.
Source: Gallup News Service Poll, January 1990; AEI Survey Center on American Life, American Perspectives Survey, May 2021; AEI Survey Center on American Life, American Social Capital Survey, 2024.

successful social relationships is our parents, with its provision of one-sided support, our expectations for a romantic relationship become hopelessly warped.

As fewer parents instill in their children a sense of the personal obligations they have to others, young people fail to appreciate what it means to be part of a family or a community. American parents reduce opportunities for unsupervised social activities that might prompt friendship, and instead encourage the acquisition of scholastic honors, athletic achievements, and extracurricular experiences. But these individual gains can come at the cost of recognizing our social responsibilities. And so, more families are raising incredibly accomplished young people who are struggling with basic questions about who they are, what they should do with their lives, and most importantly—what they owe other people.

The Loss of Shared Obligations

On March 13, 2020, the Trump administration declared a national emergency in response to the global Covid-19 pandemic.[21] Two days later, shutdown orders began. On March 15, the New York

City public school system ended in-person instruction, forcing its 1.1 million students back to their homes. Many other school systems would follow suit. For some students, it would be more than a year before they would set foot in a classroom again.

It was not only schools. Bars, restaurants, theaters, and libraries ceased in-person operations—some would never reopen. Many parks and playgrounds were closed as well, much to the consternation of parents. Remote work schedules were implemented for workers who could now only connect with colleagues through instant messaging platforms, email, and video conferencing. In a matter of months, the online video service Zoom became a household name. The Covid-19 pandemic led to the "most dramatic reduction in out-of-home activities and travel in U.S. history."[22]

The pandemic and its subsequent lockdowns not only led to a historic reduction of interpersonal socializing, but it also changed the very nature of the ways in which we interact with one another, and our willingness to trust and accommodate each other. As routine social interactions disappeared, a rash of odd, rude, and alienating behavior emerged in spaces where in-person contact was unavoidable. Our shared responsibility for maintaining standards of social etiquette had completely eroded.

On flights, for example, passengers became more disruptive and even violent in certain instances. In the months and years following lockdown requirements, the Federal Aviation Administration has recorded nearly thirteen thousand incidents of unruly passenger behavior, which included biting flight attendants and stealing liquor bottles off the refreshment cart.[23] Although 2021 was certainly an outlier in terms of this type of behavior, there were still twice as many reported incidents of unruly passenger behavior in 2024 as there were before the pandemic. Many of these infractions were not all that serious—such as watching a movie without headphones—but they are evidence of inconsiderate behavior in public spaces.

And it's not only flying. A Pew Research study conducted in early 2025 found that Americans perceived a rise in discourteous and disrespectful behavior. Nearly half (47 percent) of Americans said that Americans have become ruder after the pandemic.[24] Customers became more hostile with service workers, road rage incidents skyrocketed, and referees faced so much aggression from parents in youth sports that it led to an officiating shortage.[25] It was as if we forgot basic lessons of civility and empathy.

A functioning society requires its members to abide by social norms even when they are personally inconvenient. When I enter a coffee shop, I head to the back of the line and wait until I can give my order. It would be much faster to cut the line, but if everyone engaged in this behavior, it would invite conflict and anarchy. Knowing this, I'm content to wait. But it's not only an understanding and willingness to abide by these conventions that motivates our behavior. If someone violates a norm—cutting in line, for instance—fellow line-waiters must express public condemnation. If no one ever spoke up, line-cutting would become much more common.

Without common standards of public behavior, individuals are obliged to both establish and enforce their own personal boundaries. This is a grossly inefficient and exhausting process. It requires constant vigilance, acute sensitivity to discern whether an action justifies a response, and a willingness to be socially combative to defend your subjective standards. It leaves people to fend for themselves in public places. Few of us are willing to engage in this work on behalf of others, to call out aggressive, demeaning, or threatening behavior. When we witness someone behaving rudely toward someone else, we claim ignorance about the context of the interaction or the relationship between the individuals, giving ourselves permission to abstain. Without robust social norms, we have shifted the burden of correcting antisocial behavior from society to the individual. It's an impossible task.

The task becomes even more daunting when we require children to serve as the enforcers of acceptable public (and private) behavior. For her book *The Second Coming,* journalist Carter Sherman shares a horrific story of a girl named Zoe who sent sexually explicit images of herself to someone she met online. In short order, these intimate images were plastered all over social media, accompanied by comments saying that she was a slut. Nobody stepped in to remove the images or ensure accountability to those who violated this girl's privacy. She was left to face her humiliation alone. Her experience is hardly unique. More than half of teen girls report having sent sexually explicit text messages to someone, and most said they were pressured to do so.[26] Their stories are depressingly similar, and too often the victims are left to fend for themselves.

Although authors like Sherman documenting these cases are clearly sympathetic, they often can't quite bring themselves to condemn the practice of sharing sexually explicit images of oneself. "Like sex itself, sending nudes is not inherently right or wrong," she writes. "It can be just another component of twenty-first century rituals of flirting, dating, and relationships."[27] Despite the agonizing sense of betrayal that so many teen girls have endured after sending intimate images of themselves to someone who violated their trust, as a society we are paralyzed to act because we refuse to even judge it. If teenagers broadly understood that pressuring a girl to send a nude image of herself was wrong, it might not entirely stop boys from asking, but it might make it easier for girls to say no.

And imagine if the consequences for sharing other peoples' nudes was consistent and public? A collective effort by parents and administrators to set clear standards would not ensure violations would never occur, but the social stigma would be carried by transgressors instead of victims. The value of administrative action is not only in providing justice but in what it communicates: the establishment of norms for behavior. It not only responds to behavior; it shapes it.

Expecting teenagers to establish and vigorously police their own moral boundaries, especially for the growing number raised without a strong religious background, is expecting too much. But this is exactly what we have done. So how does this pattern contribute to the division in adult relationships and how men and women relate to each other as a whole? As a wider variety of sexual behavior has become normalized, more is required of individuals to determine what is and is not acceptable. Verbal agreement between two people has become the primary rule of America's sexual ethic. Christine Emba, in *Rethinking Sex,* argues that this is a problem. Consent may reduce some types of violative sexual behavior, but it fails to acknowledge the disparities of status and power that complicate many individual sexual interactions. Certain problematic behavior should engender social judgment and perhaps condemnation. But we struggle to do this. Emba writes, "The bias toward unquestioning acceptance makes it difficult to say no, even when something feels obviously wrong. Because apart from nonconsent, is it possible for anything to be wrong?"[28] There are so many scenarios in which consent is woefully inadequate as a moral system. It makes no accounting of unequal power dynamics, escalatory engagement, or the broader social context, which generally favors one side over the other. Spitting. Slapping. Choking. The most degrading, abusive, and physically violent behavior is potentially permissible, when it should be easy to argue they violate basic standards for how we should treat each other.

Consent typically involves two people coming to a private understanding regarding what is and is not acceptable behavior. It places the entire responsibility on the individual by substituting personal judgment for a collective ethic. What is right or wrong is subjective and dynamic, entirely determined by how an individual feels about it, which may change depending on the particular situation. This can encourage people to test personal boundaries because they are based entirely on how one feels about different behaviors. It challenges our ability to collectively discourage dangerous, disrespectful, or selfish behavior or to hold people accountable for violations. This is about much more than improving the quality of our sexual interactions but speaks to a broader culture that places an increasing amount of responsibility on individuals—including adolescents—to determine for themselves what is required of them and of others. Consent provides maximal autonomy and flexibility when what we need is greater predictability and consistency in our social interactions.

One reason consent fails as a broader ethical framework is that it provides no guidance as to what social obligations we have to each other. In this, it illuminates a much wider problem facing us as we grow more capable of doing things by ourselves and for ourselves: What do I owe you and what do you owe me? There's a growing sense that the answer is: Not much.

In 2013, a new subreddit was launched where users could post questions about moral dilemmas they were facing in their personal lives and ask others to determine whether the behavior violated basic standards of conduct. The subreddit "r/AmITheAsshole" (AITA) has become an enormously popular forum with twenty-four million members (or "potential assholes").

A new study interrogating this forum reviewed 369,161 Reddit posts and eleven million responses and uncovered a disturbing pattern.[29] Daniel Yudkin and his colleagues found that questions pertaining to relational obligations, specifically the refusal to perform an act that another wishes or expects of us, were commonplace. For instance: "AITA for 'ruining' my family vacation because of my period?" Or another: "AITA for locking myself in my office when we have company?" Not only are these types of ethical queries the most common, but they were also the ones most likely to elicit support for the questioner's position. When Redditors asked whether they should feel obligated to do something for someone else—their colleague, aunt, sister-in-law, or whomever—more often than not, they were told they would not be an asshole for refusing.

Without a sense of our obligations to others, how do we know what is required of us in any given situation? What accommodations or sacrifices are we obliged to make on behalf of others, and in turn what might we reasonably ask or expect of them? In my conversation with Yudkin, he said: "We have been forced to develop new ways of understanding and making sense of the difference between right and wrong that is adapted for the modern era."[30] Without traditional sources of moral authority—religion, schools, and the family—more people are seeking guidance elsewhere. In this case, strangers on the internet.

That so many Americans want to understand the moral dimensions of their decisions is a good sign, but crowdsourcing feedback on Reddit is not a sign of a healthy ethical culture. It is tough to know whether the AITA forum reinforces an ethic of noncommitment or simply reflects our broader sensibilities when it comes to duty and obligation. Yudkin believes that our sense of duty to each other has weakened over time. He says, "The role of son or the role of brother or the role of friend was more tightly linked to a set of obligations, of things that are expected of someone in that relationship, in that role, that if you didn't perform those behaviors it was considered a violation of your duties."[31]

Yudkin's research is hardly the only evidence of America's weakening sense of social obligation. Research that tracks personality attributes reveals we are becoming more disagreeable and less considerate of each other. A 2022 study found there had been a significant deterioration of conscientiousness in young people that the authors attributed to the pandemic's isolation.[32] But things have not improved since then. An analysis by *Financial Times* reporter John Burn-Murdoch, who extended the study, found that the level of conscientiousness and agreeableness among younger Americans—defined as those between the ages of sixteen and thirty-nine—continued to fall after the pandemic subsided.[33] Burn-Murdoch attributed this decline to social media. "The advent of ubiquitous and hyper-engaging digital media has led to an explosion in distraction, as well as making it easier than ever to either not make plans in the first place or to abandon them. The sheer convenience of the online world makes real-life commitments feel messy and effortful."

It's not only that Americans are less willing to commit to each other. There also seems to be less appetite for sticking around when problems arise. At least online, people facing relationship difficulties are being counseled to abandon them. This is what George Shao, a computer science student, realized after analyzing posts and comments from "r/relationship_advice," a popular subreddit forum with over two million monthly visitors. Analyzing more than five million posts and fifty million comments over a fifteen-year period, he identified six distinct categories of advice: seek therapy, compromise, give people space or time, set or respect boundaries, improve communication, and end the relationship. No category registered a more significant change than suggestions to leave. He found that nearly half of all the advice users now got on Reddit advocated for ending a relationship or marriage, representing an increase from only about one-third in 2010.[34] When Americans with romantic struggles log on, they are more often advised to take the simplest and most extreme course of action: End it.

Almost anywhere you look, there are warning signs that intimate relationships can be burdensome and risky endeavors that potentially stifle our independent spirits. In making decisions about romantic commitments, we weigh individual costs against individual gains. The societal institutions—families, churches, and schools—once charged with teaching the next generation about the importance of collective commitments increasingly encourage the cultivation of personal ambition, identities, and pursuits. This perspective is regularly affirmed by groups of online strangers, AI chatbots, and social media content creators. Gen Z has learned that the safest path they can take is to find themselves and fend for themselves. And it's had the effect of making simple acts of empathy and selflessness feel radical and even dangerous.

PART II

THE GENDER RIFT

When our formative years are spent growing up in the attention economy, it gets harder to look beyond our own immediate interests. Our worlds become smaller, and making accommodations for others can feel more burdensome. With our access to shared spaces diminished, boys and girls are increasingly growing up in separate worlds, pursuing individual goals. And isolation in the real world leads to greater division online, where young men and women are more often offered stereotypes and caricatures of the opposite sex rather than honest interactions. We understand less and judge more. The gender gap is becoming a chasm, and we've lost sight of why it's worth bridging the divide.

In this section, we're going to examine how the political atmosphere, the erosion of institutional trust, heightened feelings of physical vulnerability, and the rise of accountability culture are making connections between young men and women unavoidably accusatory, more threatening, and less forgiving. A politics of hopeful possibility has been replaced by cynicism as young adults perceive their interests are unimportant to those in positions of power. The country's political leadership—whether Republican or Democrat—has demonstrated less interest in promoting a unifying vision than fostering a culture of aggrievement. We've traded a diligent civic-mindedness in the real world for combative posturing online. The impact on dating has been disastrous. Dating apps encourage singles to become suspicious and defensive when curiosity and openness are needed. Before we are able to find our way out of this mess, we must realize just how divided we have become.

CHAPTER 5

THE DIVIDER IN CHIEF

American politics has grown increasingly polarized over the past few decades, with Democrats and Republicans moving further apart on nearly every conceivable issue. Since the 1990s, Republican Party voters have grown more conservative while the base of the Democratic Party has become more consistently liberal. Gallup polls show that nearly six in ten Democrats identify as politically liberal, nearly doubling their share from decades earlier, while more than three-quarters of Republicans identify as politically conservative.[1] The share of moderates in both political parties underwent a dramatic reduction over the same period. Republicans and Democrats have less in common. Even those who do not follow politics closely generally feel that the country is more divided and our leaders more divisive than they once were. In fact, polls show that Americans believe that it is politics rather than race that most divides the country.[2]

American cynicism over the country's divisive political culture steadily increased, but instead of tuning out, Americans' attention to politics increased. Donald Trump evinced a unique capacity to deeply attract and repel different sets of voters, relishing in both. Through social media and an insatiable thirst for attention, Trump inserted himself into the public's consciousness in ways no previous leader had accomplished. During his first term, Trump broke records in the sheer volume of his public communications, and media companies, who covered every digital utterance, saw their profit margins explode. After Trump's election, politics became less clearly differentiated from entertainment, and with algorithmic advancements, it was increasingly unavoidable.

Political issues became fused to personal identity and as a result, electoral outcomes felt more consequential. Shaped by these forces, young adults developed less of an appetite for political disagreement, and were more willing to dismiss, block, and reject peers who do not share their political affinities. For more young men and women, personal political commitments began to supersede even existing social relationships, and influence the development of new ones. The willingness to self-segregate over politics reveals an abiding sense of insecurity both groups feel about their place in America. As economic opportunities grew more elusive and success less certain, both men and women had come to embrace the idea that their gender was a potential liability, a reason for people to disregard their feelings or deny them advancement. They felt overlooked and undervalued, often by each other.

"We're So Back"

In the 2024 presidential election, Trump accomplished the unthinkable: He won nearly half of young voters, a group whose leftward political trajectory had previously made them largely unreachable to conservative candidates.

In the months leading up to the 2024 election and the year following, my colleagues and I talked with more than fifty college students at eight different schools across the country. We also held eight in-depth listening sessions with groups of young men and women, including those with college degrees and those without, in Philadelphia, Pennsylvania. These conversations revealed a stark gender divide in their views of the candidates and the outcome. A recent graduate of the University of Texas, Jake, explained that, to him and his male friends, the election represented a necessary course change. "Among my peer group, there's a saying, and the saying is, *we're so back* . . . And that's sort of the sentiment among a lot of the people in my peer group with the election results, where it's like, everybody's very satisfied, everybody's very pleased."

Most young women had a very different take on the election. Isabel, a graduate student in San Francisco, felt completely defeated by the result: "I am so, so angry, disappointed, disillusioned, and sad about the state of the country and its people. How could this have happened again? Where is the education system? This is the beginning of the end of America as we know it." This sentiment was shared by many young women, who were in state of disbelief that Trump not only won, but did so with much larger margins than the first time. When I brought up Trump's election in a conversation with a young woman at the University of Virginia, she broke down in tears. It was a stark contrast to her Trump-supporting male classmates, who while not necessarily ecstatic about his reelection, felt generally satisfied and optimistic.

The 2024 election witnessed another sizeable gender gap in the political preferences of young voters. According to AP VoteCast, 58 percent of young women voted for Kamala Harris compared to only 42 percent of young men.[3] The resulting 16-point gender gap reflected the growing political differences between young men and women.[4] In the Trump era, the shared interests of young voters had been overtaken by their diverging political perspectives. It was a political decoupling.

In the rush to interpret post-election polling, many pundits argued the outcome represented incontrovertible evidence that young men were turning right. But Trump's success with young men was not necessarily driven by an ideological drift. A more careful review of their political affinities and issue preferences casts doubt on that explanation. When I first identified the emerging youth politics gender divide in 2022, the polls showed that young men had not become more conservative, at least in how they self-identified.[5] It soon became clear that the gap was entirely driven by the rapid shift in liberal identity among young women. Over the course of only a few years, young women began adopting much more liberal political views. Young men did not appear to be following a similar trajectory—their political views were largely unchanged over the same time period.

If young men did not lurch right in many of their political views, their approach to the two major political parties increasingly became defined by institutional distrust. Rather than basing their choice on detailed policy plans and political agendas, many young men made a much simpler calculation: Which candidate appeared most likely to upend the status quo, to attack the unpopular political establishment? This more populist perspective followed a precipitous decline in their own economic fortunes, and the loss of an abiding faith in the American Dream held by their fathers and grandfathers. Traditional pathways to financial security and stability—namely higher education—were increasingly seen as risky endeavors. As their labor force participation plummeted, so did membership in civic organizations, labor unions, and religious institutions. Cynicism surged.

In the days, weeks, and months following the election, reporters, political analysts, and podcasters dissected young men's dramatic shift toward Trump. They identified many possible causes, such as the #MeToo movement, generalized distrust in the political system, a retaliation against feminism, a backlash to Covid-19 restrictions, the rise in social media, and the growing influence of Joe Rogan–style male podcasters. Many of these explanations were incoherent or incomplete. The changing politics of young men defy a simple explanation. It has become clear, however, that the current trajectory was set more than a decade earlier. Since Obama's first term in office, young men have been steadily drifting away from the Democratic Party. Once a solid Democratic voting group, young men are increasingly expressing an affinity for the GOP. In 2021, aggregated Gallup polling showed that more young men identified as Republican than Democrat for the first time in over twenty years. By 2024, nearly half (49 percent) of young men identified as Republican compared to 40 percent who identified as Democrat. It's a remarkable change. From Obama's first term to Trump's second election, Democratic identity among young men fell thirteen points.

The United States is a closely divided country, but more recent political currents have favored conservatives. Prior to Trump's return to office, the decades-long rise in liberal political identity had stalled, and Republican affiliation was on the rise. In the last five years, public views of the Democratic Party—the popular political choice for most voters for a long time—have turned sharply negative. The most recent polling shows an implosion of Democratic favorability. The party, which once held a commanding lead over the GOP in the hearts and minds of the public, is now deeply unpopular. Gallup polls show that only 34 percent of Americans have a favorable view of the Democrats—the worst showing in roughly thirty years.[6] Even after Trump's public approval rating hit historic lows, there were no signs of a rebound for the Democratic brand.

A single election is generally a poor barometer of the country's political trajectory—incumbents frequently set off thermostatic reactions.* And the current political allegiances of young men are

* The concept of "thermostatic politics" was developed by political scientist Christopher Weizen to describe the tendency of public opinion to move in the opposite direction of government policy. When conservative policies are being passed, the public support for more liberal policies increases.

tenuous because they are not built on strong ideological foundations. Even as young men have become more aligned with Republican politics, their issue positions on climate change, abortion, gay rights, and gun control have not moved in tandem. The same Gallup polls that show a dramatic erosion in Democratic identity do not reveal a corresponding decline in liberal identity. Notably, a plurality of young men are politically moderate.

The 2024 election revealed a mismatch between the issue positions of young men and their voting behavior. Young men and senior men now have similar partisan leanings, but young men are far less conservative than older men. If these political patterns hold—a major assumption—the Republican Party would become increasingly ideologically diverse and less conservative. It's also conceivable that the weak ideological commitments of young men might lead them back into the Democratic fold.

Young Republicans Are Less Conservative

Percentage of Republicans who identify as conservative

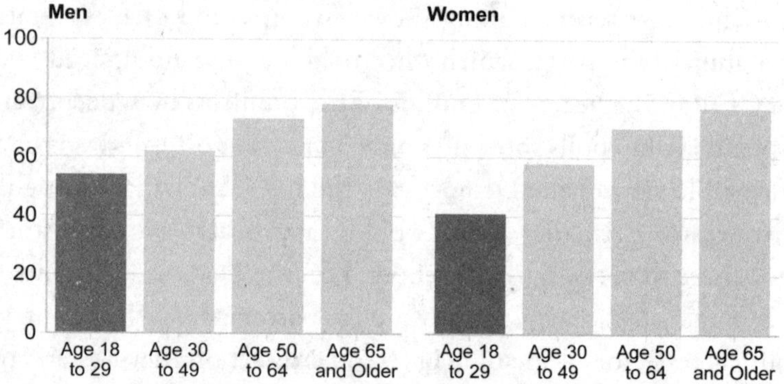

Note: Includes independents who say they lean toward the Republican party.
Source: Gallup Key Indicators, 2024.

The average young male voter is still pro-choice, supports gay rights, believes climate change exists, and thinks greater gun control measures are required to keep people safe. But for the average male voter, none of these issues are a priority. They care more about economic opportunity and inequality and believe that CEOs are untrustworthy and that corporations mistreat their workers in an effort to pad the bottom line. If millennial men's early political experiences were defined by Obama's message of hope and change, the sense of optimism curdled into cynicism for the generation that followed. Young men now believe their political priorities are meaningless, and the issues they care about are unimportant to the people in power. Politics has become performative and pointless. But how does this lead them to Trump? To answer this question, we have to go back to the 2016 election.

Donald Trump was not the preferred candidate for young voters in 2016. Fewer than four in ten young voters cast a ballot for Trump, identical to the level of support Republican Mitt Romney received four years earlier.[7] Hillary Clinton captured a majority of young voters, although her margin was lower than Barack Obama's in his bid for reelection in 2012. Trump was viewed far less favorably when he was a candidate than he was after his election, but during the entirety of Trump's first term in office, Civiqs polling showed him underwater with young men. The 2024 election revealed a startlingly similar pattern. Despite supporting Trump in record numbers, young men's support deteriorated rapidly once he was in office.[8, 9] Trump has always been more effective at campaigning, a role that rewards pugnacity and self-aggrandizement, than he is at governing. Young men have been consistently more receptive to Trump's anti-establishment rhetoric and less repelled by his alienating personal antics. They saw in Trump the actions of a brash outsider who was not afraid to disrupt a broken political and economic system. Young men agreed with Trump that the system was rigged, but saw little evidence that he could or would fix it. Few men believed they were better off for all of Trump's rhetoric.

From the very beginning, young women saw something entirely different in Trump. Unlike Trump's first election, his second victory could not be so easily dismissed as an unfortunate fluke of an imperfect political system. His return to the Oval Office signaled something far more sinister for many young women: It challenged narratives about personal accountability, progress, and power. Many young women took the result as proof that their worth in public life was still conditional and that character and competence could be outweighed by spectacle. The shock gave way to a surge of collective energy, as anger became activism and activism became cultural power. In the years that followed Trump's election in 2024, women would channel that energy into a growing rejection of the country's most central social and political institutions. We are about to see just how far that change reached—and what it set in motion.

Anger, Authenticity, and Aggrievement: Politics Becomes More Perilous

For the last decade, Donald Trump has been an inescapable part of America's public consciousness—dominating the news and captivating the nation's attention. He has been unavoidable, often inexplicable, and omnipresent. A figure inspiring ridicule, adulation, and fascination. For young people now heading off to college, Trump's bombastic, self-aggrandizing statements and his delight in personal attacks have been part of the public discourse since they were eight years old. It's been the only politics they have ever known. Trump's heterodox policy positions make it even more difficult to discern what his voters are truly after. More Americans have come to believe Trump was consistently conservative in 2024 than they did during his first run for president. At the same time, research suggests Trump has redefined the very meaning of *conservative*.[10] Trump's election was not a signal of a broader ideological realignment among young people, or even young men. The gender gap was most pronounced among middle-of-the-road and left-leaning young voters.

Trump handily won conservative young men, as one might expect, but his support among conservative young women was nearly identical. Where the gender gap emerged was among young moderates and liberals. A majority of moderate young men voted for Trump compared to roughly four in ten moderate young women.[11] Perhaps more striking, 25 percent of liberal young men cast their vote for Trump, almost twice the rate of liberal young women.

Moderate Young Men Backed Trump in 2024

Percentage of young men (age 18 to 29) who voted for . . .

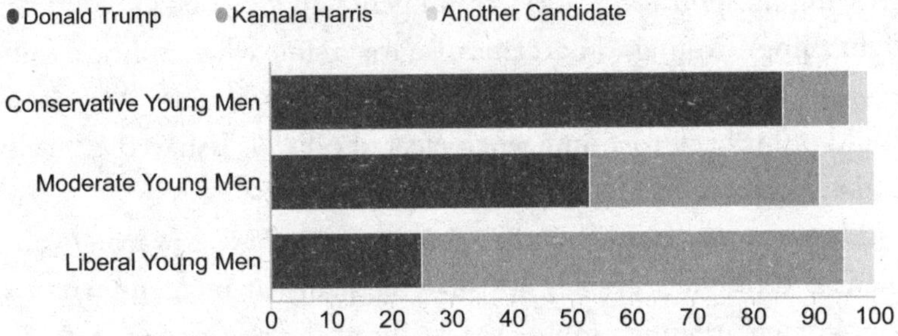

Source: AP VoteCast, 2024.

Trump's penchant for cruelty and personal attacks provoked considerable comment and critique early in his political ascension, but over time the sheer volume of outrageous statements muted the public outcry. It wasn't just exhaustion. In some sense, Trump altered our expectations of political leadership. In 2011, 61 percent of Americans said elected officials should be held to a higher moral standard than people in other professions.[12] A decade and a half later, fewer Americans appear willing to hold elected officials to a high moral standard. It may not be a comforting thought, but it's become clear that we get the politicians that we deserve. Rather than expecting our elected leaders to represent the very best of us, Americans now cynically acknowledge their public representatives reflect our basest instincts and desires. Politics is no longer a vocation meant to inspire.

This is the political legacy inherited by young adults. For Americans under the age of thirty, politics and personal morality are on entirely different planes of existence. By the end of Trump's first term, most Americans said that a politician who commits an immoral act can still behave ethically in carrying out their public duties—a view that was rejected by most Americans less than a decade earlier. Americans over the age of fifty say that when they were growing up, political leaders could generally be trusted to do the right thing.[13] Young adults came of age at a time when political leaders were no longer trusted to do the right thing. If older Americans could point back to a time when elected officials behaved ethically and responsibly, young adults never could.

However, the dim view that young people have toward government and public service is not shared equally by men and women. Young men are much more cynical about the government's ability to deliver on its promises or that there are leaders who recognize their troubles. For many young men, corruption is endemic in the political system and political leaders on both sides of the aisle are untrustworthy. They are more likely than young women to believe special interests have too much influence, that the government is unresponsive to ordinary Americans, and that political leaders are not held accountable for unethical behavior.[14]

Despite how pessimistic young women are about the direction of the country, they do not share the same feelings of cynicism expressed by their male peers. In part, this might be due to feeling they do not have the luxury of political apathy at a time when their rights are threatened. Young women face more intense social pressure to engage in politics as well, especially those in more progressive social circles. The Democratic Party's long-standing support of LGBTQ rights, gender equality, and abortion and reproductive health access—priorities for many young women—made it clear that their concerns were not being ignored even if progress was difficult to discern.

The Podcast President

Most voters recognized that Trump was not honest—polls show this point consistently.[15] But many Americans were unbothered by his dishonesty. It was not simply the low regard with which Americans held politicians either: Trump by most measures was exceptional. By the end of Trump's first term, *The Washington Post* had documented 30,573 false or misleading claims he made while in office.[16] To my knowledge, the *Post* has given up on their counting effort in Trump's second term, and there is little evidence that documenting Trump's serial falsehoods in any way altered public perceptions. The casual and rapid nature of online communication had tempered expectations about its accuracy, and Americans had become more accustomed to the type of self-promotional rhetoric Trump often employed. In the age of influencer culture, Trump's dishonesty was less jarring. Online experiences had socialized many young adults to accept a certain amount of dissembling and performative behavior. On social media, it's generally understood that everyone presents an idealized—and not completely accurate—version of their offline life. Immaculately appointed homes on Pinterest, impressive titles and job descriptions on LinkedIn, and perfectly staged "casual" pics on Instagram have normalized this behavior. Everyone embellishes. In a way, Trump's professions of his own greatness are not that different from what your friend on social media is posting.

This is not the only way Trump was able to leverage the emerging social media culture to his advantage. The social constraints that govern interpersonal interaction in the real world are largely absent online. We post quickly, judge freely, and criticize often without ever bearing witness to the pain or discomfort we cause—maybe we even delight in the response our words can create. Trump's propensity for self-promotion and provocation may have been startling to older voters, but his way of communicating was familiar to many members of Generation Z, who grew up online, where acts of casual cruelty are common. A speaking style that betrays a lack of concern for others is not a sign of corrupted character, but evidence of authenticity. What you say is less important than what you mean.

For Americans less immersed in social media and the online world, Trump's early behavior on the campaign trail, and later as president, was galling. Older Americans, despite their more conservative leanings on many cultural questions, were among the most appalled by Trump's behavior as president. Older Americans had come of age at a time when politics and personal morality were not separate domains.

But some Americans found Trump's unfiltered communication via social media refreshing. Trump, more than any previous president, excelled at communicating directly with voters and his supporters. He was America's first social media president—a leader who relished and reveled in communicating without a filter, and with little regard for the words he used. Before he was ejected from social media platforms for spreading disinformation in violation of user guidelines, Trump posted his own takes on politics, policy, and just about anything else that drifted into his mind. Spelling errors and all. If his habit of posting about policy resulted in confusion and consternation among White House staff, it found a ready audience in young men who appreciated Trump's willingness to say what he felt.

For the young men who supported Trump in 2024, his victory

confirmed that being true to your beliefs mattered more than being endlessly accommodating to prevailing cultural standards. Chase, another University of Texas student, explained what Trump's win meant: "I'll say there's a way in which to be a leader is to be somebody who's unashamedly themselves, . . . being able to stand by something and taking criticism for it unashamedly. . . . That's something that we want to see in leaders, that we need to see in leaders." That Trump not only abided, but embraced criticism was especially appealing to young men who felt they could not always be as forthright in expressing their own political opinions.

What made me believe Kamala Harris was in real trouble was not the polling numbers or Biden's anemic approval rating, but a focus group among young voters conducted by *The New York Times.* Frank Luntz, the moderator, asked the group to share top-of-mind impressions of Kamala Harris.[17] The responses were brutal. Harris was "political PR," "fake," a "politician," "phony and terrifying," a "liar," "rehearsed," a "flip-flopper," "insincere and shallow," "all over the place," an "actress," and "an empty suit." Only one person out of fourteen offered a remotely positive evaluation of the Vice President—that she was confident.

Harris received the lowest level of support among young voters in twenty years. Her inability to explain her political evolution led to skeptical questions from progressives, while moderates never trusted the mainstream persona she adopted. It became impossible for allies to defend Harris because she offered little defense herself. Wavering voters came to believe Harris represented the very worst of the status quo, of political expedience and an attempt to be everything to everyone.

Whatever Trump's evident shortcomings, for many young men these personal defects were far outweighed by his antagonism toward the perceived enforcers of political correctness: feminists, HR departments, and school administrators. Regardless of their politics, commitment to DEI, feminism, or dismantling the patriarchy, the average young man could not avoid being held responsible for the most extreme examples of male behavior. A misstep on their end could be construed as evidence of the systemic abuse that women faced. Even passivity could be problematic—the phrase "silence is violence" communicated that a refusal to actively work against wrongdoing was akin to participation in it. In fact, college-educated young men are much more likely than those without a degree to report facing accusations of sexism and homophobia. Over one-third of college-educated young men said they had been accused of being sexist or homophobic in the past.[18] These experiences coincided with cultural narratives and corporate campaigns, such as "The Future is Female," aimed at empowering girls, while offering critical evaluations of male behavior, such as Gillette's 2019 ad counseling men to hold other men accountable for sexual harassment. On college campuses, the message to men was similar. Duke University launched a course on toxic masculinity, Brown University developed "Pedagogy Against the Patriarchy" aimed at addressing problematic behavior of male student athletes, and George Mason University offered a course titled "What's the Matter with Men: Problems and Possibilities."[19] In most cases, instruction was meant to correct male behavior rather than offering positive models for it. From 2019 to 2025, the percentage of young men who said there was at least some discrimination against men in American society jumped from 32 percent to 51 percent.[20, 21] More than half of young men now believed their gender was a liability. In Trump, they found an avatar for their collective angst, a refreshing model of male behavior. Not only would Trump never require them to acknowledge their privilege, he emboldened them to express themselves unapologetically, regardless of whom it might offend.

Dissatisfaction with the current administration, concerns about inflation, cost of living, and the direction of the economy served as

More Young Men Say There Is Discrimination Against Men in the US

Percentage of young Americans (age 18 to 29) who believe men face some or a lot of discrimination in the United States today

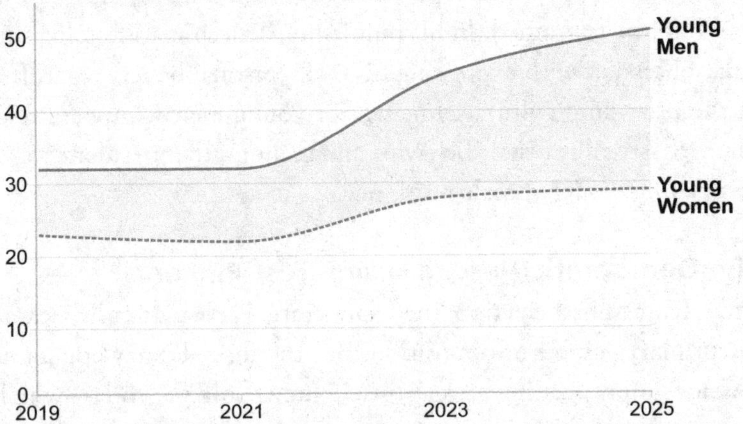

Source: Pew Research Center, American Trends Panel Wave 53, September 2019; Pew Research Center: American Trends Panel Wave 84, March 2021; AEI Survey Center on American Life, American Perspectives Survey, January 2023; Pew Research Center, American Trends Panel Wave 167, April 2025.

crucial advantages for Trump in the 2024 election. Beyond his agenda, what drew young men to Trump was his unapologetic aggressiveness. For most of Trump's adult life, and certainly since he entered politics, he has worked to cultivate an image of masculine toughness. From his career as a New York real estate developer to his authoritative role on *The Apprentice,* Trump's success has hinged on his ability to showcase his brash, bold, and domineering persona. Throughout his presidential campaigns, Trump sought to portray himself as someone who would never compromise or yield to pressure. He would never be on the losing end of a deal, whether in politics or business. In his public appeals, Trump's refusal to give up social media indicated he was not someone who could be handled.

Trump's continual disregard for political conventions resonated with young men who had come to believe that the country's political leaders were only looking out for themselves. Trump could not abide limits to his authority because he saw them as a sign of unacceptable weakness. Many young men who grew up believing that they were either undeserving of help or part of the problem saw in Trump a towering political presence who would not apologize and could not be restrained. In his public life, Trump manifested a singular obsession with expressing his own personal beliefs regardless of the prevailing cultural climate. For young men who were routinely chastised for their behavior and feelings, the president was a compelling model of male resistance.

The Democratic Party's Disinterest in Men

After Trump's first election, the Democratic Party naturally became the primary vehicle of opposition. But the formal party apparatus was not simply pushing back against Trump's policy agenda—which was less identifiably conservative—as much as opposing the cultural project that he appeared to represent. After the *Access Hollywood* tape revealed Trump's dismissive attitude about engaging in sexual assault, his election took on a different meaning for many women. For many young women, Donald Trump's ascension to the highest political office was evidence that American society was unconcerned about the sexual harassment and assault of women. In a single election, they saw progress toward gender equality suddenly imperiled. The energy in the party shifted sharply in response. Over the next two years a record number of women became politically active. EMILYs List, which supports pro-choice women running for political office, reported that twenty-six thousand women reached out in the months following Trump's election—in the previous year the figure was nine hundred.[22] The number of Democratic women who filed to run for the U.S. House more than doubled, and many won. The 2018 midterm election became the "Year of the Woman." The trajectory of the party had changed. Rather than offering a compelling economic vision that could appeal to a broad swath of voters, Democratic efforts became increasingly focused on promoting the rights and interests of women and other marginalized groups.

For at least the last several decades, the Democratic Party rank and file has had a lopsided gender composition. Six in ten self-identified Democrats are women, and about four in ten are men.[23] This ratio has remained relatively stable since at least the late 1990s. Republicans, by contrast, have a more equal gender distribution, slightly more men than women, but the differences are modest.

Underneath this gender gap, a more culturally consequential change was occurring among rank-and-file Democrats. The number of college-educated women in the party ballooned. By 2024, one in three Democrats was a college-educated woman, a demographic whose political priorities differed sharply from other members of the coalition and from the average voter. In contrast, college-educated men make up less than one in five members of the party.[24] The educational realignment of the political parties has been well-documented. *New York Times* columnist Nate Cohn noted, "As they've grown in numbers, college graduates have instilled increasingly liberal cultural norms while gaining the power to nudge the Democratic Party to the left. Partly as a result, large portions of the party's traditional working-class base have defected to the Republicans."[25] This is half right. It's not that *all* college graduates have pressed candidates to adopt more left-leaning positions—it's college-educated women who are largely responsible for some of the party's more aggressive shifts.

The rise in college-educated women coincided with a major shift in Democratic priorities. The issue of gender equality and the treatment of women in society became a central part of the party's DNA. There was growing emphasis on cultural issues, such as LGBTQ rights and abortion, and less attention paid to economic inequality.

For years, the Democratic National Committee's website included a section listing the various constituencies the party represents.[26] Under the tab, "Who We Serve," there was a list of sixteen different groups represented by the party, including: African Americans, Americans with Disabilities, Asian Americans and Pacific Islanders, Democrats Abroad, Ethnic Americans, Latinos, Faith Community, LGBTQ+ Community, Native Americans, Rural Americans, Seniors and Retirees, Small Business Community, Union Members and Families, Veterans and Military Families, Women, Young People and Students. And men? Nowhere to be found.

It seems improbable that the omission was an unfortunate oversight; more likely, it reflects the party's demographic priorities. Representative Jasmine Crockett of Texas argued that the Trump administration's early hiring decisions represented a "coddling" of young men. "The only people that are crying are the mediocre white boys that have been beaten out by people that historically have had to work so, so much harder," she said.[27] This rhetorical approach is not only about signaling who is deserving of help, but who is to blame for the country's problems.

The Democratic Party had abandoned an overarching economic message that resonates with working-class voters and cuts across lines of race, ethnicity, gender, and region. Instead, the party has adopted an identity-group approach that divides deserving from undeserving groups. Columbia Professor Mark Lilla argues that the preoccupation with group membership and individual identity led Democrats and liberals to largely abandon the language of collective responsibility.[28] Policy priorities were determined by filtering through the lens of deservedness, rather than duty. For instance, one of President Biden's first acts on assuming office was the introduction of the Equity Action Plan, which directed federal agencies to address systemic barriers faced by underserved communities, particularly communities of color. It's not even that these types of initiatives were unnecessary or purely performative—although the messaging in certain instances undoubtedly was—but they represented a clear blind spot in the progressive worldview, namely that everyone loses when policymaking is designed to identify a hierarchy of suffering. The belief that the distress of certain groups is more worthy of consideration and empathy undermines the entire project. It squanders the potential for unity necessary to address some of our most enduring social problems—economic inequality, prejudice, poverty—by dividing the world into heroes and villains, perpetrators and victims. Men are on one side, women are on the other.

A Shift in Political Priorities

During the four-day 2024 Democratic Convention, no other issue received more attention, both in side meetings and mainstage addresses, than abortion. There were addresses from women who had received abortions, including Hadley Duvall, an advocate for reproductive rights who was raped by her stepfather as a child, as well as leaders of major reproductive health organizations such as Planned Parenthood and Reproductive Freedom for All. Outside the arena, the emphasis on reproductive health was also on full display. Americans for Contraception brought along an eighteen-foot-tall inflatable intrauterine device named Freeda Womb. After hours, a group of influencers called "Hotties for Harris" hosted a party that included "abortion access Skee-Ball" and a feminist golf course.[29] Whether you attended the convention in person or watched online, it was hard not to come away with the impression that abortion was the defining issue of the 2024 election. It's not a view most voters shared. Although legal access to abortion has solid support among the public, few voters are eager to talk about it and even fewer say it is a top priority.

It was not only how much Democrats focused on the issue of abortion, but the marked change in the way it was discussed. Unfortunate but necessary was the language that Democrats once used to talk about abortion and the conflicted feelings it often aroused. It was replaced by language of empowerment, which less often acknowledged the moral dimensions. This approach resonated among the party's strongest supporters, but it was disconnected from the way many Americans still feel about the issue. The rhetoric failed to recognize the internal tension between the public's views about the legality of abortion and how they felt about its morality.

But it was not simply the party's growing emphasis on abortion and reproductive healthcare that isolated lower- and middle-class voters. The Democratic Party has become increasingly identified with select cultural issues, such as transgender rights, that are as effective at garnering elite interest and agitation as they are unimportant to the lives of most voters. This approach represents a stark departure from the working-class economic agenda that sustained the party's large congressional majorities throughout much of the twentieth century. In 1990, roughly two-thirds of Americans said the Democratic Party, more so than the Republican Party, better represented the interests of poor and working-class Americans. By 2024, only 42 percent of the public believed this to be true.[30]

A *New York Times* poll conducted shortly after the 2024 election found that the American public identified five issues that were a priority for the Democratic Party: abortion, LGBTQ policy, climate change, the state of democracy, and healthcare.[31] Only one of these issues—healthcare—was a priority for most Americans. But the other four issues are far more important for women than men, with college-educated women especially prioritizing all of them.

Beyond policy issues, the Democratic Party, when it's in power, takes very different approaches to the advancement of women compared to the Republican Party. During the 2020 Democratic primary, then-nominee Joe Biden committed to adding a woman to the ticket. He later promised to nominate a Black woman to the Supreme Court. Once elected, the Biden administration was also far more aggressive in trying to ensure gender parity in senior leadership positions. Nearly half of cabinet-level positions went to women—almost twice as many as Trump appointed in his first term.[32] A report from the American Bar Association found that Biden nominated many more women to judicial positions than Trump did during his first term. The report notes: "President Donald Trump, for example, nominated 55 women who were confirmed as federal judges—24% of his total nominations. President Joe Biden has been much more aggressive in naming female judicial candidates. As of Aug. 1, 2024, Biden had nominated 200 judicial candidates who were confirmed as federal judges. Nearly two-thirds—63 percent—were women."[33]

In part, gender disparity in nominations reflects ideological differences between men and women—there are more conservative men than liberal men. But it also reflects priorities. The Democratic Party has institutional interests in advancing women, while the Republican Party does not. The results are stark.

Culture-First Politics

The politics of the millennial generation are often identified with the fight for same-sex marriage, which was legalized by the Supreme Court in 2015 at the tail end of the Obama administration. The debate served as a major cultural touchstone that pitted conservative Christians against left-leaning secular and religious people, a dispute that raged for more than a decade after Massachusetts legalized same-sex marriage in 2004. It became one of the defining issues in the "culture war" of that era. Millennials who were entering adulthood during this period were strongly supportive of the policy. They had gay and lesbian friends in high school and college, watched shows that featured gay characters, and were incredibly open-minded. And yet in poll after poll, the vast majority of millennials repeatedly said that same-sex marriage didn't rank as a top priority for them.

The idea that younger, more liberal generations are defined by these views has warped our understanding of politics for a generation. In the hundreds of polls conducted between 2005 and 2015 that measured the public's political priorities, same-sex marriage was consistently close to the bottom of the list. Millennials were in favor of allowing gay and lesbian people to marry, and they may have signed a petition or put a rainbow flag on their Facebook page, but it was never a critical priority for them when compared with other issues.

Despite this fact, there was a pervasive sense among many Democrats that young voters consistently prioritized cultural concerns above economic ones. Not without reason. Young voters were the earliest supporters of salient cultural issues, such as same-sex marriage. They were less judgmental about various sexual behaviors and practices—such as premarital sex and pornography—and more accepting of alternative family arrangements. And on questions of culture, the Democrats were undefeated. With Bill Clinton and Barack Obama, the Democrats had established themselves as the more forward-looking, modern, and popular political party. The creators and arbiters of American culture—actors, musicians, directors, writers—were mostly Democrats. The Republicans had only B-list celebrities who were awkwardly trotted out during the conventions. The Democrats were not your parents' party—they would never be squeamish about sex or make homophobic comments at Thanksgiving dinner.

For more than two decades, the Democrats were the preferred home for America's young voters. But the advantage that Democrats had with America's youngest generations was not built on cultural affinities or celebrity endorsements. The party had built a reputation as one of the few bulwarks standing between middle- and working-class families and an unforgiving economic system.[34] One attitude that consistently separated young adults from older Americans in 2024 was their support for more aggressive government intervention in the economy and their belief in the overall unfairness of the current economic order. But few believed that the Democrats were willing to or capable of addressing it.

There were signs of young men's growing populist disaffection well before the 2024 election. Young men care deeply about economic unfairness not simply in the abstract, but because of their own struggles. In the 2020 Democratic primary, Senator Bernie Sanders built an incredibly loyal following online—he acquired more than ten million followers on Twitter (now X), more than his leading primary opponents combined.[35] The young men who flocked to Sanders's rallies, and who built online communities to promote his message, were dismissively labeled "Bernie Bros." Sanders supporters were caricatured in media accounts that often focused on their aggressive tactics and mean-spirited engagement—"venomous followers" in the words of one *New York Times* columnist.[36] But their support was driven by growing insecurity that many young men felt about their diminishing opportunities to succeed in an economic system they viewed as rigged. And a politics that had no interest in their fears, only in chastising them for their anger. These feelings were compounded by the fact that young men understood that their value and ability to attract a partner remained indelibly coupled to their economic fortunes. Society valued them not for who they were, but what they could produce.

It's impossible to calculate precisely how many, but research has shown roughly one in eight one-time Bernie Sanders supporters even voted for Donald Trump in 2016.[37] The candidate preferences of these voters swung, but their views about the economy and distrust in traditional political processes have not. Many of the same young men who rejected Harris nonetheless prefer an active role for the federal government in society. Fifty-eight percent of young male voters in the same AP VoteCast survey said the federal government should do more to solve societal problems.

In an interview with *The New York Times* following Trump's 2024 election victory, Tim Chapman, president of the conservative advocacy group Advancing American Freedom, suggested young men were not seeking a specific policy change. "Young men feel the world closing in. They're looking for recognition. And they get recognition from the Joe Rogans of the world, they get recognition from Trump, they get recognition from Bernie Sanders."[38] Trump connected to young men not through a well-defined policy agenda, but through his practice of offensive, irreverent speech. His public persona, and later his political reputation, was built on crusades against "politically correct" expression.[39] For young men coming of age at a moment when language use was being subject to greater scrutiny and criticism, Trump's purposeful violations felt refreshing, and authentic. It was not performative posturing of the type that was popular on social media. The mistake the Democratic Party made was the failure to recognize that offensive speech was not necessarily evidence of malevolent intent. Trump, a recent octogenarian, consistently communicates without grace, or humility; your average teenage boy may engage in irreverent, immature, and transgressive speech, but that sort of speech is not a reliable barometer of his politics or view of the world.

A culture that attempts to silence thoughtlessness will not create a culture of thoughtfulness. How much better would it be if carelessness and inconsiderate comments could serve as an invitation to broaden our worldview, and gain an appreciation for the perspective of others? It's the respectful cultivation of our social responsibility that holds the best promise for success.

A More Fearful Politics

There's not much evidence that young people today are more interested in politics than previous generations, nor are they more informed, but their access to news about government and current events is unique. A study by the Pew Research Center found that young adults are far less likely than older Americans to seek out political news.[40] Rather, seven in ten young adults report that they get political news incidentally, inserted into their social media feeds. Perhaps not surprisingly, the same Pew study found that "young people are more likely to say the news they get makes them feel scared or confused."

These feelings are the inevitable consequence of media outlets that adopt negative emotional framing to compete for public attention, and a social media environment that magnifies and disseminates the most divisive content.[41] Political debates online are far more acrimonious and personal than those that occur offline. For young adults today, their political education comes less often from a trusted teacher, a parent, or a friendly neighbor, and more frequently from strident and objectionable figures representing extreme versions of their ideology. Social media algorithms reward extreme and offensive content, incentivizing trolls and political provocateurs.

The sense of existential angst that young people feel about politics incentivizes them to be risk averse in their exposure to certain ideas or viewpoints. Their political diets become far more curated. A multiplicity of information sources online—even those that share primarily apolitical content such as health recommendations, fashion, or dating advice—facilitate the removal of potentially discordant or uncomfortable ideas. Young people learn to turn off or tune out information that challenges personal narratives because it feels safer to do so. Unseen algorithms generate validating information, and bit by bit they build a worldview designed to be impervious to critical or contradictory information that feels personally threatening.

This dynamic works remarkably well in exacerbating existing tensions between young men and women. When it comes to the gender divide, the same screening mechanisms that allow young people to filter out objectionable political content online can just as easily filter out people. Many online dating platforms now allow users to state their political preferences in a potential partner, weeding out those whose views might not align. Surveys suggest that political affinity has become more important to all singles, especially single women.[42] Our research shows that half of single women, including nearly three-quarters of college-educated single women, say they would be less likely to date someone if they were a Trump supporter.[43]

It is young women more than men who make politics a threshold consideration, and there are many reasons for this position. As I detail in chapter six, recent cultural and political developments—namely, the overturn of *Roe v. Wade,* and the #MeToo movement—have made young women feel more vulnerable and unsafe. But there are also ongoing differences in how women and men are treated, especially online. Young women are far more likely than men to experience abuse when they express their political opinions. Trump's election, which presaged both of these events, communicated to many young women that degrading women was not disqualifying for the nation's highest office. When we asked women in a recent survey why they would not date a Trump supporter, not a single one mentioned Trump's support for tariffs, and very few mentioned his restrictive immigration policies. During our interviews across the country, one twenty-four-year-old woman from Texas explained her reluctance to date a Trump supporter: "It is no longer a political difference; it is a difference in morals. If you are a Trump supporter, I can only assume that you only support the rights of straight white people." This feeling was articulated in a number of different settings, with young women expressing a sense of solidarity with historically marginalized groups. You're either all in, or you're out.

Without a sense of security, it's impossible to develop a sense of curiosity. The walls are built stronger and higher. Because politics has become an unavoidable force in American public life, it can feel necessary to secure greater political alignment in our private lives too. It's not only happening online. Young men and women have become more politically segregated in the real world. More than half (51 percent) of young women claim that they have no close friends who are Trump supporters.[44] Young men practice a different type of avoidance. To preclude potential conflict, some young men embrace a type of strategic disinterest or ambiguous commitments—dating apps are awash in politically "moderate" men. The outcome is the same. Avoidance and apathy limit our ability to engage in honest conversation, to navigate differences and discover shared values. Without regular social contact, political stereotypes rule the day, and more nuanced understandings are lost. We become strangers to each other at best, and threats at worst. The tension builds until we are primed to feel victimized and vulnerable. It leaves us with only one feasible option: to willingly separate ourselves. Unfortunately, it's already happening.

CHAPTER 6

IMPERILED PROGRESS

One of the most difficult parts of writing a data-driven book that deals with so many sensitive subjects is maintaining a sense of balance between my role as an observer and analyst, and my instincts as a human being. There are competing inclinations to keep emotional distance that ensures analytical rigor, and wanting to fully empathize with the struggles young people experience and the pain that they feel. This is more true when I tell deeply personal stories—especially when people see the same situation so differently.

Young women were raised to believe that they could be anything they set out to be, but our research has shown that the rise of abusive behavior online, the collapse of institutional trust, and the coarsening of our political culture have all contributed to a feeling that progress toward equality is unrealized and a sense of personal safety is impossible. Young women have come to believe that they are less safe, more vulnerable, and that men are largely to blame. But men do not need to have daughters, a wife (I have one), nieces (I have two), or other female relationships to care deeply about what young women experience. In theory, it should be easy for men to appreciate women's perspectives. In practice, it's often difficult, especially when we talk about the things that men have done, and do, to women.

You Too? The Rising Specter of Sexual Violence

In all the research I've done for this book, one of the most troubling patterns to emerge is the rising fear of sexual assault. For most of the last twenty years, most younger women (those under the age of fifty) were not overly concerned about the threat of sexual assault. Since 2000, Gallup has asked women how often they worry about being a victim of various crimes, including sexual assault. For most of that time, less than half reported they frequently or occasionally worried about becoming a victim of sexual assault. From 2000 to 2015, fewer than four in ten younger women on average reported that they were concerned. But beginning in 2016, there was a rapid rise in the percentage of younger women who said they were worried about becoming victims. These fears increased steadily such that by 2023, most younger women reported worrying at least occasionally about being a victim of sexual assault.

What accounts for this dramatic rise? For one, there was a massive uptick in the murder rate in 2020 in a number of American cities around the country. Researchers have speculated that the spike in crime was driven by the mass shuttering of schools and workplaces that left teen boys and young men in some of the poorest neighborhoods suddenly removed from structured social environments.[1] Researchers found that teen boys who were not in school and unemployed young men were far more likely to commit violence in their neighborhoods. Public fears about crime generally tracked these national patterns. Gallup recorded a dramatic rise in concern about violent crime, including getting mugged or murdered, but these concerns also reached a high point in 2022.

Younger Women Grow More Worried About Sexual Assault After #MeToo

Percentage of women under age 50 who frequently or occasionally worry about being a victim of sexual assault

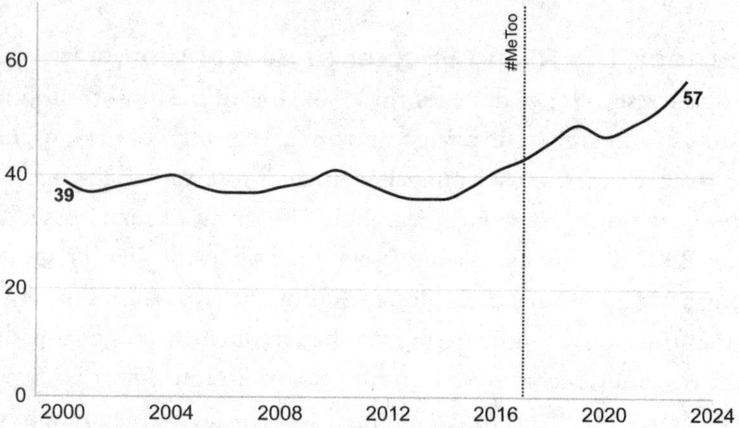

Note: Data represents rolling averages. No data is available for the year 2012.
Source: Gallup Poll Social Series, 2001–2025.

In contrast, the increased concern about sexual assault started earlier and remains at record highs. At first, this might seem puzzling. Why are so many more young women now expressing fear about sexual assault when there is no evidence that their neighborhoods, or workplaces, are any more dangerous?

We can't find the answer in government statistics that track rates of sexual assault and abuse. According to the FBI's Uniform Crime Reports, rates of rape across the United States have remained relatively stable over the past decade.[2] Of course, the reliability of these statistics has frequently been called into question because of the endemic problem of underreporting. Notably, research has long shown that women are at far higher risk of being sexually assaulted by someone they know than a stranger, but polling conducted by Chapman University found that in the case of sexual assault, women are far more concerned about attacks from strangers than from people they know.[3] If you stop a minute to think about it, there's an inescapable and unfortunate logic to it.

We're looking at the wrong metrics. The rise of online sexual harassment, including cyberstalking, has fundamentally altered the risk calculus for many young women. Sexual harassment is ubiquitous, especially on social media. Much of the harassment young women experience comes from strangers. One study found that six in ten women who experienced online harassment did not know who was behind it or said the individual was a stranger to them.[4] One young woman we interviewed, Hannah, had an unfortunate run-in with a man who started stalking her online. "We played one game together because we were randomly matched, and then he tracked me down online, and would not stop messaging me," she said. "It made me really nervous, because my social media profiles were not in any way linked to my game profile. So I was like, 'How did this guy find me?' " After their first interaction, things escalated quickly. He started sending her aggressive voice memos, telling her that she was his "soulmate," and "the love of my life." Eventually Hannah went to the police after feeling unsafe. Her experience is hardly unique. A 2020 study found that more than one in four young women have been victims of cyberstalking.[5] This is all terribly troubling, not only in how common online harassment has become and how easily girls and young women are targeted, but how little accountability perpetrators face. So much of this harassment is completely invisible to those who do not experience it.

Until very recently, women carried the burden of their safety mostly in silence, perhaps discussing their experiences with a few close friends or family members. Unless you were famous, few people would be interested in hearing about your experience, and the repercussions for "going public" with allegations could be substantial. Social media changed all of that. In the wake of #MeToo, stories of predatory behavior once whispered between trusted confidants were broadcast to the world. Suddenly, there was no end to the stories women were sharing and posting online; they were recounting recent incidents as well as traumas suffered decades earlier. An analysis of early Twitter posts using the hashtag #MeToo found that "revelations shared went beyond acknowledgment of having experienced sexual harassment and often included vivid and traumatic descriptions of early life experiences of assault and abuse."[6] It may sound intense or uncomfortable to have these deeply personal and painful stories made public, but for many women, it represented the first opportunity to finally share their experiences openly to an audience that not only cared but understood. It was a moment of honesty and solidarity. But if the #MeToo movement succeeded in heightening awareness of sexual harassment and assault, it may have also changed the way women evaluate potential threats.

A growing openness to sharing deeply personal experiences on social media platforms—including horrific stories of sexual harassment and sexual abuse—created a new way for young women to learn about the world and its threats. Scattered across the internet—from Reddit lists to online women's magazines—there are now endless lists of tactical guidance for women to stay safe. Examples of sexual misconduct have now populated the internet, and young women have become especially adept at identifying it. Strategies to avoid predatory men are often shared widely on social media, as are horror stories of male aggression and violence. Although personal anecdotes of experiences with creepy men are common, many posts also share safety tips. The X account "How Things Work" even recently posted a video to its 2.4 million followers featuring a woman at a bar transforming her hair scrunchie into a drink cover. The caption: "One method to reduce drinks being spiked."[7] It's not that promoting these products or tactics is wrong or even unnecessary—they can make a real difference in helping women avoid a terrible outcome—but an endless stream of content focused on safety will almost inevitably lead to the belief that the world is a dangerous place. In this case, today's social media content reinforces the idea that women need to exercise constant vigilance given the perilous world they inhabit.

A social media–inspired debate demonstrates not only how easily this type of content captures our attention, but how effectively it pits men and women against each other. In 2024, a viral trend on TikTok posed the following question to women: "Would you rather be stuck in the woods with a man or a bear?" It exploded across social media. Thousands of videos were posted in response to the prompt. Late night shows reported on it, celebrities reacted to it, op-eds were written, and it was trending online for weeks. What was the consensus? The overwhelming number of women said they would prefer the bear because that would be the less dangerous situation. One woman shared a personal story that captured the prevailing sentiment: Back in 1996, her friend was tragically attacked by a bear on a hike. Bystanders immediately intervened to help, to distract the bear, and get it to stop. Finally, someone even fired shots at the bear to scare it, and the bear ran off. While the woman recovered in the hospital, the town sent out law enforcement and animal control to track down the bear and kill it. The takeaway for many women is that you have a better chance of being believed and being helped if you are attacked by a bear than a man. Other women responded to her account by posting statistics of bear attacks side by side with statistics of sexual assault, rape, and murder committed by men against women. Another comment, from a woman named Kimbo, cut straight to the heart of the issue. It read: "Women don't want to be attacked by men or bears, but if I was attacked by a bear, people would believe me, and no one would ask me what I was wearing."

If the goal of the viral trend was to expand men's capacity to empathize with women's perspectives, there is little evidence it succeeded. Online, men responded mostly defensively. In an ironic but completely foreseeable moment, a few men became so hostile to the point that they were threatening women who chose the bear, thereby proving their point. There were some responses that accused women of innumeracy—women were far more likely to interact with men than bears, so statistics purporting to show that men were more dangerous than bears were faulty. But many men were dismissive or reluctant to respond, even those—such as the fathers of daughters—who were sympathetic to women for choosing the bear.

If I'm honest, the debate did not leave me wanting to engage in this topic either. It's not that it is not worthy of discussion; we should be talking about it, but it seems too big for the medium. A conversation about sexual assault requires more than 280 characters. But social media rewards pithy posts and provocative comments. And pushes people to pick sides. Actor and comedian Leslie Jones posted: "HEY MEN, you have now become so dangerous to us we would rather take our chances with a wild bear!!"[8] It is not true that men have become more dangerous to women. These types of responses serve to alienate and agitate rather than spur the curiosity necessary for constructive engagement on a topic as sensitive as sexual assault. Instead of a difficult but necessary conversation, we got collective outrage, social media's most reliable product. Women feel unheard, and men come away believing that these moments serve no other purpose than to assign collective guilt and shame. There is no clear course of action or corrective measures to work toward. Everyone is left somewhat further apart, and feeling a little worse about the state of things.

The Resistance Is Female

Trump's 2016 victory reshaped how young women understood safety, power, and progress. Many took the result as proof that their worth in public life was negotiable and their standing in American society was suddenly in doubt. The shock gave way to a surge of collective energy, as anger was channeled into bursts of protests and online activism, and ongoing efforts to reshape or upend cultural institutions. In the years that followed, the optimistic energy gave way to a more pronounced pessimism, and a growing gender divide that profoundly reshaped the nation's political and cultural landscape. Trump's election set off a series of events that not only altered the country's political trajectory but created a deep and enduring cultural rift, leaving more Americans on one side or the other with fewer willing to bridge the distance.

In the space of a few short hours on election night, the country went from being on the cusp of electing the first female president to electing a president who bragged about sexually assaulting women. A president who gave no evidence of being an attentive husband or father, who showed no repentance for his dalliance with a porn star, and who was unfaithful to all three of his wives.

For a generation of young women raised on the ideas of Girl Power and "the future is female," Clinton's loss was a shock. The disappointment many women felt was profound and disorienting. How could Trump's evident character flaws, his inappropriate and lewd behavior, his well-documented infidelity, and his coarse language not disqualify him from office? How could Clinton's political experience, evident competence, and command of the issues not make her the obvious choice for most voters?

In her concession speech, Clinton took the opportunity to speak directly to girls and young women. "To all the little girls watching: Never doubt that you are valuable and powerful and deserving of every chance and opportunity in the world." Clinton framed her candidacy as an opportunity for all women to help "shatter that highest, hardest glass ceiling." For many young women, electing a female president was personally important and represented a meaningful sign of progress and possibility. Few young men registered it as such. Rather, it was a choice between two flawed candidates. But the loss took on a different meaning for many young women, who asked themselves what Trump's election meant for women in America. In the years following Clinton's loss, fewer women believed they would see a woman in the White House during their lifetime.

If Clinton represented a step forward for women, Donald Trump, who once bragged to a radio show host that he had never changed a diaper, was assuredly many steps back. "I'll supply funds, and she'll take care of the kids," Trump said in a 2005 interview with Howard Stern.[9] The MAGA movement was not articulating a political or economic argument but a cultural one. One of the young men we interviewed at the University of Texas in Austin, Ethan, articulated this phenomenon, particularly as it related to guys his age. When asked about Trump's appeal to this demographic, he said:

"I guess Trump's our guy, right? He's our guy. . . . It's like, I guess he's our guy, which is to say, yeah, advocating or standing up for not just policies and a vision politically that I agree with, but also advocating maybe more deeply for something like . . . conveying a vision of, you know, masculine strength and courage that is respectable and good that we don't see really anywhere else, right?"

It was the simplistic nature of Trump's masculine persona that made it accessible, and attractive to many young men who found themselves navigating uncertain cultural terrain.

Although Clinton lost the electoral college, and the presidency, by an incredibly slim margin, the surprising outcome signaled to many women that the country was in a very different place than they had thought. In an important way, Trump's election suggested to many women that the country's inevitable climb toward gender equality may have stalled out. It was, for many, a bitter realization that both credible accusations of sexual abuse and grotesque boasts of sexual assault against women were not dealbreakers for the nation's highest office.

After Trump's Election, Women Grow Less Satisfied with America's Treatment of Women

Percentage of Americans who are satisfied with the treatment of women in American society

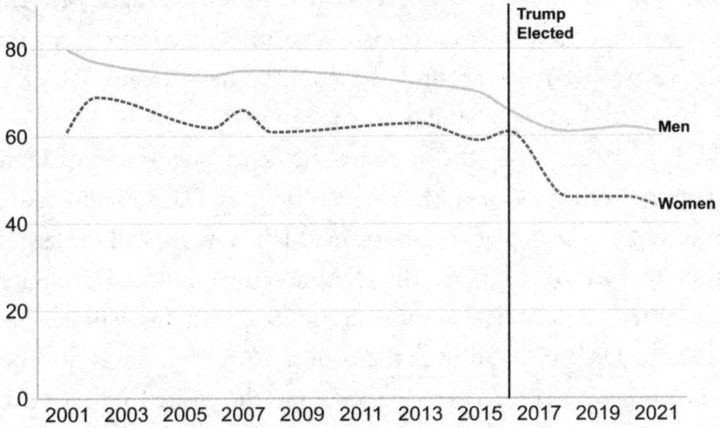

Source: Gallup Poll Social Series, 2001–2021.

For more than two decades, Gallup has been asking Americans how satisfied they are with the treatment of women in American society. From 2001 to 2016, most Americans reported being relatively satisfied with the way women are treated (although men report somewhat higher satisfaction). Things changed rapidly after Trump's election, especially for women. In 2016, more than six in ten (61 percent) women said they were at least somewhat satisfied with how women were treated in the United States. Two years later, only 46 percent of women, and even fewer young women, said they were satisfied.[10] Men were largely unfazed—the majority of men continue to report feeling content with women's treatment.

A few weeks after the shock of Trump's first election victory started to wear off, many women who opposed him looked for a way to respond. Ideas circulated online about what could be done that would send a message that would communicate the resolve and dismay so many women felt. The answer came from a grandmother and retired lawyer in Hawaii, Teresa Shook. After Trump's victory was confirmed, Shook posted on the popular Facebook group "Pantsuit Nation" suggesting that someone should organize a pro-women's march in Washington, D.C. The message caught fire. The next morning, Shook was astonished to find that more than ten thousand people from around the country had already RSVP'd, with hundreds more pouring in by the hour.

On January 21, 2017, the day after the first inauguration of Donald Trump on the National Mall in Washington, D.C., the inaugural Women's March took place on that same Mall. It was one of the largest protests that ever took place there. Almost five hundred thousand people marched that day. Some were local, but many women had flown in to D.C. from all over the country. And hundreds of other "sister marches" were held in solidarity across the United States and all around the world. An estimated three to five million people participated globally. It was a physical manifestation of female solidarity and empowerment, both with the sheer size of the crowds as well as their adornments: Many of the women wore pink "pussy hats" and carried signs with slogans such as "Ovaries before Brovaries" and "This Pussy Grabs Back." The rally signaled female resistance to Trump, with many women repulsed by his personal background, character, and brand of performative politics. In the months that followed, the energy and agitation evident at the rally fueled support for political organizations and politicians willing to forcefully challenge the president.

It was not simply a grassroots movement. In Congress, the 2018 midterm elections saw the Democrats sweep back into power. Notably, four outspoken progressive women were elected in the Democratic wave: Alexandria Ocasio-Cortez of New York, Ilhan Omar of Minnesota, Ayanna Pressley of Massachusetts, and Rashida Tlaib of Michigan. Collectively, the media dubbed them "the Squad," a group that quickly earned a reputation for combative engagement with their GOP colleagues and Donald Trump. The sparring between the two sides was both political and personal, and it received considerable media attention.

But Trump's chief political adversary during his first term in office was Democratic Speaker Nancy Pelosi, a veteran liberal lawmaker from San Francisco. The two tangled regularly, and she was perhaps his most visible foil. In one provocative act, Pelosi ripped up a copy of Trump's State of the Union speech as she stood behind him. The clip immediately went viral online, inspiring hashtags such as #NancyTheRipper.

If Trump's election served to energize opposition from women, his checkered history with women—including numerous accusations of sexual abuse—also helped set the stage for a momentous shift in public conversation about sexual harassment and assault.

The #MeToo Moment

The night of the 2016 election, Kathy Spillar, executive director of the Feminist Majority Foundation, offered a prescient observation about what Trump's election might mean for American society. In an interview with PBS, Spillar said the election represented an inflection point on the issue of gender violence.[11] "A sleeping giant has been awakened on this issue of sexual assault," she said. "Women have made it very clear that they're not going to be treated this way by men."

A few decades ago, the casual harassment of women in the workplace, often carried out under the guise of playful banter, compliments about physical appearance, or expressions of sexual interest, was an unremarkable and unfortunate part of their daily lives. Nearly every woman had an experience she could share. In fact, these stories emerged during casual conversations. One memory that comes to mind was when one of my colleagues told us about something that happened to her middle-aged mother. When she was at home visiting her family, her mother mentioned offhandedly that while she was working at a pizza joint in the late 1980s as a teenager, her boss wrote "cute butt!" on her paycheck. Her daughter was shocked not only at the retelling, but at how unremarkable her mom viewed the entire experience to be—it was something that young women were once forced to deal with. "It didn't really seem like a big deal, just a weird joke," she said. Today, such behavior would be grounds for an HR intervention or a sexual harassment lawsuit, but at the time, many women did not believe these episodes were worth a response, perhaps no more than an annoyed eyeroll or a private complaint to friends. Perhaps the most amazing aspect of this story was how nonchalant this mother of five daughters was in her recounting of it.

The #MeToo movement was the culmination of a decades-long shift in American attitudes about gender roles, power dynamics, and women's place in American society. It was a volcanic release of energy and anger long submerged under coercion, control, and cultural norms. The conversation about sexual harassment, assault, and consent erupted suddenly online after many women who felt pressured to keep silent about their experiences were encouraged to share them.

Within the first twelve months, the MeToo hashtag had been tweeted roughly nineteen million times. It rapidly took on a life of its own. News stories featuring the words "sexual harassment" skyrocketed, peaking at more than nine thousand a day.[12]

On the left, the mantra of "Believe Women" became the operating response to every story that was shared. This phrase captured an emerging cultural imperative of addressing widespread sexual harassment and abuse. It was a powerful slogan, reflecting the dismissiveness with which sexual allegations often had been treated, but it suffered from a lack of nuance on an issue that demanded it. The implications of the statement were less easily addressed. In fact, on many college campuses "believe women" had been the operative approach to handling issues of sexual misconduct. It led, perhaps inevitably, to accusations of unfairness and a lack of impartiality.

In 2011, the Department of Education's Office for Civil Rights issued new guidance that substantially lowered the evidentiary standard of proof for colleges and universities to take administrative action on sexual misconduct allegations. The directive not only required administrators to end sexual harassment, but to "eliminate [the] hostile environment" in which it occurred.[13] It was an attempt to change campus culture. To this end, the definition of sexual misconduct was expanded to include "verbal conduct," a category that meant off-color comments, dirty jokes, and offensive gestures could lead students to face administrative consequences. It didn't come out of nowhere. The aggressive posture was a response to growing concerns about the prevalence of rape on college campuses. A few years earlier, a blockbuster finding from the 2007 Campus Sexual Assault Study concluded that one in five female college students could expect to be sexually assaulted at some point during their college career. Deeply concerning, this statistic appeared in hundreds of news stories and opinion pieces as evidence of "rape culture" on college campuses. But not everyone was convinced. In an eleven thousand-word article for the left-leaning *Slate* magazine, Emily Yoffe noted that the one in five figure was not actually based on a nationally representative sample of female college students, but surveys of students at two public universities.[14] What's more, the definition of sexual assault used in the study—an incredibly thorny question for researchers—was fairly broad, including "rubbing up against you in a sexual way, even if it is over your clothes."

Because a single incident of sexual assault is one too many, schools should aggressively investigate allegations of abuse, but portraying the problem as an epidemic can lead to the adoption of policies that effectively abridge due process rights for those accused. In certain schools, the lack of due process was so egregious that it provoked strong criticism from those generally sympathetic to the problem. At Harvard University, more than two dozen law faculty wrote an op-ed for *The Boston Globe* accusing the school of adopting "procedures for deciding cases of alleged sexual misconduct which lack the most basic elements of fairness and due process."[15] However well-intentioned the original effort to root out sexual harassment and abuse, it had predictable results. Everything became more adversarial. If women on campus still felt unsafe, an increasing number of their male peers now felt that they could be unfairly targeted.

I heard from several young men about what they felt was an unfair or inconsistent application of Title IX, a law prohibiting sex-based discrimination in schools that receive federal funding, to cover a broad range of behavior. One student I talked to at Claremont McKenna College, a small liberal arts school in California, said: "I've heard so many stories about guys doing the smallest things and getting Title IX cases against them, like calling their ex-girlfriend a slut or another guy jumped out in front of a girl and tried to scare her as a joke," he said. Both of these interactions were undeniably immature, disrespectful, thoughtless—but did they warrant an administrative response? Our research shows that even the existence of these types of accusations had social repercussions—another male student said that at his school there was pressure not to associate with people who had pending Title IX cases. Maintaining a friendship with someone accused could have negative social consequences, whatever the merits of the case or the behavior involved. In most of my interviews with students, few young men worried about facing Title IX complaints themselves, but stories like these circulated among their friend groups widely and led to heightened anxiety.

Relatively quickly, young men and women adopted differing attitudes—not about the principle of gender equality—but about the ultimate purpose of the #MeToo movement and the process of enforcing standards of accountability. A 2022 report by the Pew Research Center documented how large a gap had emerged between the views of young men and women. The report found: "Women younger than 30 particularly stand out: 72% say they support the movement, compared with 52% of men of the same age. No other age group comes close to matching the level of support of women under 30."[16] For young women, #MeToo offered a clear and positive vision for change, but young men were far less convinced.

I never got the sense that young men were not sympathetic to women's experiences with sexual harassment or feelings of threat. Their ambivalence about the goals and purpose of the #MeToo movement emerged from the general rising criticism of male behavior—from mansplaining to manspreading—along with endless conversations online about toxic masculinity. They felt bombarded by criticism, and there was little interest in hearing their side of the story—their opinions did not matter. The goal was not reform but retribution. None of it felt fair. In our interviews about #MeToo, young men talked a lot about their anxieties around fairness and equal treatment. They especially were concerned with the issue of due process. One twenty-six-year-old man said something that captured the sentiment of this defense: "I do not support the idea of 'believe all women.' This country was built on innocent until proven guilty."

Another young man expressed the potential risks of unsubstantiated allegations, claiming that plenty of women had nefarious motives. He said, "I believe there are people falsely claiming 'me too' for their own financial gain and potentially destroying the lives and reputations of the people they are accusing. Too many people are taking advantage of a serious situation because it's trendy or they are greedy or just want attention." There is no credible evidence to support the claim that false reporting of sexual assault is widespread. Nonetheless, we found that nearly one in four young men believe that it is very common or extremely common for women to report experiencing sexual harassment or assault when it did not happen.[17]

Instead of coalescing around a shared vision, many young men sought to distance themselves from the movement. In our interviews with young men who acknowledged the issue of sexual violence and harassment, many were leery of engaging too much with it. Uncertainty about what type of behavior might land them in trouble had a marked chilling effect, but even more, there were some men who seemed to write it off as an inconsequential pop culture phenomenon. One young man simply sidestepped the issue: "You know, I don't revolve my life around celebrities. I don't have anything to do with rape culture. And I barely paid any attention to it."

It's hard not to feel frustrated by how the #MeToo discourse ultimately played out. That women felt empowered to share their past sexual abuse on social media was a significant societal achievement, and in many cases it represented a profoundly courageous act. Unfortunately, for half the population, the public airing of these experiences changed little on the ground. Again, the medium was part of the problem. Even as posts featuring MeToo hashtags quickly populated the social media feeds of women, few men were exposed to much of this content. And the posts that did find their way into men's feeds more often featured the most divisive and incendiary language, stripped of its initial context.

This feels like a missed opportunity. It's impossible to change a culture through administrative action alone. Men do need to listen, but they are finding it harder to know who they can trust. Social media provided women a meaningful outlet to share painful experiences, but it was less effective in getting men and women to engage with each other. In my work, I've seen that progress rarely occurs as the result of grand gestures. It happens through incremental adjustments in individual behavior and beliefs, which are brought about through regular interactions with trusted friends and family members. Of the young men I talked to, the ones who were typically most understanding of the challenges that women faced had one monumental thing in common: they heard these "unbelievable" stories from their female friends and classmates. Those genuine, personal connections made a difference. They broke through the noise, providing the necessary time and space for men and women to see each other and gain an appreciation of their unique experiences. That's the way forward.

Shout Your Abortion

If more girls are being raised to prioritize financial independence, career success, and educational goals, there is one experience that could derail all of it—unintended pregnancy. Campaigns to prevent teenage pregnancy had been a staple of government policy for decades, but a cultural event may have had an even more profound impact in shaping the way young women thought about parenthood. In 2009, MTV released the TV shows *16 and Pregnant* and *Teen Mom,* which followed teen moms during the early days of motherhood, depicting the struggles of early parenthood, from strained relationships to financial stress and absentee fathers. Nearly every episode traced a similar narrative arc: A girl who had been participating in conventional high school activities—playing sports, hanging out with friends, attending parties—was suddenly separated from all of it. For anyone watching the struggles of teenage girls with newborns, it was difficult not to come to the conclusion that parenthood was an alienating and isolating experience. And girls did watch. *16 and Pregnant* was a massive ratings success for MTV: It was consistently one of the most popular programs among teen girls and young women.[18] It was a cultural force, not only shaping the way teenagers thought about pregnancy, but altering their behavior as well. A report from the Brookings Institution found that the show was responsible for a nearly 6 percent decline in teen pregnancy during the eighteen months after it first aired.[19]

With parents and educators more aggressively encouraging girls to invest in their education, the risks of unintended pregnancy became much clearer. Yet this renewed focus on encouraging teen girls to avoid unintended pregnancy coincided with a concerted effort by Republican state lawmakers to restrict access to abortion. With new majorities in many statehouses following their successful 2010 midterm election, Republicans pushed aggressively to reduce access. In just two years, from 2011 to 2013, more than two hundred laws restricting access to abortion were introduced in state legislatures across the United States.[20] These restrictive laws caused considerable alarm among left-leaning women. Abortion, once a difficult conversation even among supporters, was increasingly embraced as a key part of young women's capacity to pursue the life they wanted.

A couple of years before a five-letter hashtag forced a public reckoning over sexual harassment, a thirty-year-old graduate student, frustrated and upset about Republican plans to defund Planned Parenthood, posted about an abortion she had had a year earlier. Amelia Bonow wanted to normalize abortion by getting women to talk openly and publicly about their experiences. She posted on Facebook: "Having an abortion made me happy in a totally unqualified way. Why shouldn't I be happy that I wasn't forced to become a mother?"[21] Her friend reposted it on Twitter, adding the hashtag #ShoutYourAbortion. The post took off, garnering thousands of replies and reposts. The Shout Your Abortion (SYA) movement had begun. Bonow has since written a book and turned SYA into a nonprofit organization dedicated to furthering abortion access. SYA has been covered widely in the media, has garnered a large online presence, staged multiple demonstrations at the Supreme Court in support of maintaining access to abortion pills, sponsored billboards along rural Interstate 55 that runs from the Great Lakes to the Gulf of Mexico, and more.[22]

In the United States, abortion attitudes are difficult to summarize. For decades, Americans have maintained consistent support for legal abortion in at least certain circumstances. But the robust support belies considerable reservations about its morality, and polls also show that Americans are generally comfortable with some degree of restriction on its availability. In a word, attitudes are complex. In fact, when we asked Americans whether they believed abortion was simple and straightforward or complicated, most said it was the latter. The views of men and women were once quite similar, but something happened that pushed them apart. On every metric, women became more supportive while men did not.[23] Gallup polling showed double-digit gaps open up between men and women about abortion access, pro-choice identity, and attitudes about morality. To understand what happened, we have to go back to 2016.

Donald Trump was not an obvious contender for pro-life champion. If Trump was a late arrival to national politics, his commitment to pro-life policies came even later and less definitively. In a 1999 interview with NBC's *Meet the Press,* Trump stated: "I am pro-choice in every respect in as far as it goes."[24] Two decades on, Trump reversed course, identifying as "pro-life" in an address to the Conservative Political Action Conference (CPAC). It was not an inspired conversion, and few conservative Christians were won over—at least at first. Trump's flamboyant lifestyle was hardly an example of personal fidelity and virtue, nor was it evidence of a commitment to the traditional family values that many pro-life Christians sought in their political leaders. His personal piety and religious faith were notably absent. Trump's 2016 vice-presidential pick of Mike Pence, a stalwart conservative Christian, was an explicit acknowledgment of this political liability.

Even after Trump became the architect of Roe's unraveling, his commitment to pro-life principles was never obvious. Where Trump did find common cause with many conservative Christians was in championing traditional gender roles and supporting the social and cultural structures that enforced them. A growing number of young women who supported reproductive autonomy came to believe the conflict over abortion access was not about the rights of the fetus or an ethic of life but was instead a matter of control. The goal of abortion restrictions proposed by powerful men and the institutions they presided over was to roll back progress on gender equality. To them, abortion restrictions would limit the educational and professional opportunities of women and require them to return to roles as wives, mothers, and homemakers.

Pro-life leaders had often expressed concern about how abortion negatively impacted women, but with Trump as the cause's most visible ally—with his long history of belittling women—this argument became less convincing. Trump's record, which included allegations of sexual abuse against multiple women, made a multifaceted, morally complex issue seem simpler, or at least much more straightforward than it once was.

The overturn of *Roe* in 2022 confirmed the worst fears that many young women had about their place in American society. It galvanized them to think collectively about their experiences and challenges. That same year, in fall 2022, we found that young women were uniquely likely to see their lives as being connected to those of other women. Two-thirds of women under thirty said that what happens to other women in the United States has a direct bearing on their own lives, compared to less than half of women age thirty or older.[25] This feeling of connectedness, known as "linked fate," is often born out of a sense of collective threat and vulnerability. It was especially strong among young single women.

Young Women Feel More Connected to Other Women

Percentage of women who, when asked how much of what happens to women in the US affects what happens in their own life, said . . .

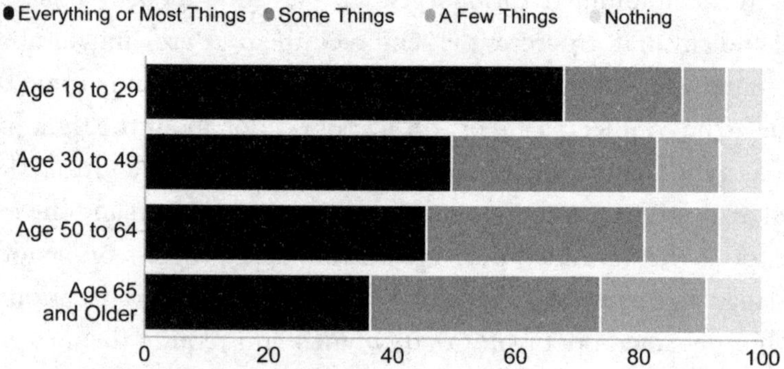

Source: AEI Survey Center on American Life, Abortion and Religion Survey, August 2022.

If the politics of the abortion debate at one time required a minimal degree of performative ambivalence, after *Roe,* young women were less inclined to see the issue as morally complex, and fewer supported any restrictions on access. Gallup polling revealed a 10-point jump in the percentage of women who said abortion was "morally acceptable" between 2020 and 2022.[26] Men were more circumspect in their views about abortion, showing no signs of change. In a survey we conducted in late 2022, more than seven in ten single young women said abortion was morally acceptable or not a moral issue to them. Only about half of single young men shared this view about abortion. On one of the most enduring moral questions in American politics, young single women and young men see things quite differently.*

Young Single Men and Women Differ in Their Views on the Morality of Abortion

Percentage of young singles (age 18 to 29) who believe abortion is . . .

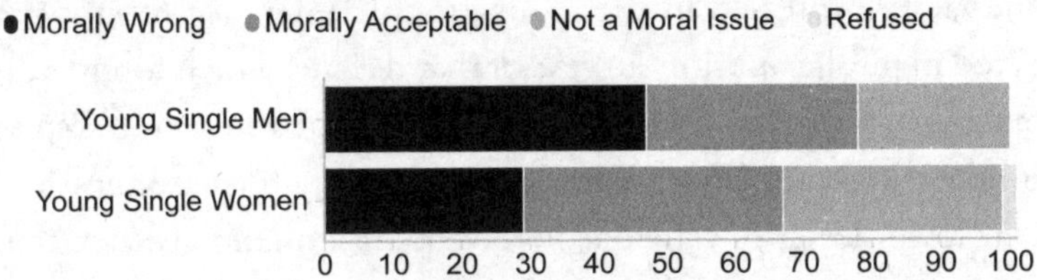

Note: "Singles" refers to those who have never been married.
Source: AEI Survey Center on American Life, Abortion and Religion Survey, August 2022.

As young women's attitudes about the morality of abortion evolved, they grew less willing to abide any type of restriction on abortion access. In 2004, the General Social Survey found that only

* Even after the news coverage of the Dobbs decision receded, the gender gap on abortion endured. A 2025 survey by the Pew Research Center found that seven in ten young single women said abortion is morally acceptable or not a moral issue, far more than men.[27]

26 percent of young adults—a historic low—believed that a pregnant woman should be able to obtain a legal abortion for any reason. Twenty years later, that number rose to 64 percent, marking a stark change from the previous generation of young adults.

In the early aughts, I participated in a set of focus groups among millennials on the topic of abortion, sexuality, and gay rights. As part of the discussion, we had participants write down their immediate reaction to seeing the word *abortion* written on a notecard. The participants undertook the same exercise again, this time with *same-sex marriage* on the card. The responses could not have been more different. When it came to same-sex marriage, participants were almost overwhelmingly supportive, especially millennial women. Participants wrote "Awesome" and "Go for it!" When it came to abortion, the tone was entirely different. Abortion was not celebrated but viewed as an unfortunate experience, even among those who believed it should be legal. The most positive response to the abortion prompt we heard was: "Fine by me."[28]

The views expressed in the focus group conference room were reflected in public opinion surveys of that decade, which found millennials surprisingly conservative on the issue of abortion. Despite their liberal attitudes on sexuality, higher levels of formal education, and far lower levels of religious involvement, millennials' views on abortion mirrored those of the broader public.

Until recently, even ardent supporters of abortion rights readily acknowledged the moral and ethical dimensions that went into the decision. Outside liberal enclaves and friendly media echo chambers, few Democrats wanted to talk about the issue. When they did address it, they often spoke in hushed apologetic tones, expressing the belief that abortion should be "safe, legal, and rare."[29] There was a tacit acknowledgment that abortion—whichever side you were on—was a complex moral issue. It was a deeply personal decision that required significant deliberation and care.

Much has changed. Young women who feel their rights are being taken away and their freedom is under threat are responding by more emphatically and vocally supporting unqualified access to abortion. To them, it is not simply a necessary medical intervention that should remain available, but also a tool of female empowerment. Increasingly, they express no interest in finding common ground with those who do not share these goals.[30] Nearly half of young women now say compromise on the issue of abortion is not possible. For single young women, no issue is a bigger romantic deal-breaker than disagreement over abortion.

A climate of fear makes it impossible to render complex moral judgments. When women believe their most fundamental rights are imperiled, there are no appropriate half-measures to take or compromises to broker. Social media and online media content expediently affirm their worst fears. It has taken society far too long to acknowledge the harms, indignities, and risks that women endure. And yet, encouraging young women to maintain a state of constant vigilance against potential harms is not relieving these burdens, but adding to them. Without the ability to discriminate between various types of behavior—that which we can learn to abide and ignore, and that which we must address—young women find the cost of social interactions and public engagement crushing, every encounter a potential minefield of microaggressions. And they largely endure it alone.

CHAPTER 7

ACCOUNTABILITY CULTURE

If there is one unavoidable fact of modern life it is that we feel a pervasive sense of exhaustion. We feel burned out, anxious, and agitated. Whether we're fatigued workers, exhausted parents, or stressed-out students, it feels like each one of us is shouldering excess weight. We are tired because we are doing more than we should. Individuals have taken on roles and responsibilities that were once primarily reserved for collective enterprises—the burden has shifted. Our social lives were once primarily, if not exclusively, structured by neighborhoods, schools, sports leagues, civic associations, workplaces, and churches. Many of these institutions still serve critical social functions, but more of our social interactions now occur outside them. We communicate using instant messaging apps and email, comment on group text chains, and post on social media platforms. Less socializing occurs in the church parking lot, the office breakroom, or in the school cafeteria.

Today, as more of our social interactions are unmediated, they occur unconstrained from social conventions established by particular organizations or spaces. This type of unfettered independence comes with a steep cost. Institutions not only provide physical spaces for people to come together; most are governed by reasonably well-articulated values and norms. Sociologist Emile Durkheim had a name for it: "collective conscience," a morally binding and socially enforced set of rules and understandings that govern behavior. These social conventions and norms defined not only what is expected of us, but what we could reasonably expect of others. In the absence of these shared norms, individuals are left on their own to "police their boundaries." In the age of social media, we have deputized ourselves to serve as vigilantes of interpersonal behavior, maintaining a watchful eye for potential problematic acts. But when we identify negative or threatening behavior, enforcement is not individual, it is often tribal.

Institutional Failure

The push for personal accountability online has emerged as a reaction to the diminishing role of our social, political, and civic institutions to establish social norms and aggressively enforce their violations. The rise in fear of sexual violence is unfolding against the backdrop of collapsing mistrust in institutions and authorities to identify abuse, protect victims, and hold perpetrators accountable. When these systems fail to keep us safe and hold offenders responsible for their actions, people feel a need to create their own rules.

In the early 2000s, the global sex abuse scandal in the Catholic Church rapidly eroded confidence in religious leaders and the institutions they ran. As the horrific abuse came to light, and the extent of the efforts of religious leaders to protect abusers became clear, confidence in religious institutions plummeted. In 2001, 59 percent of Americans expressed a great deal or quite a lot of confidence in churches; that number fell to 46 percent the following year.[1] Although confidence rebounded slightly in 2003, trust continued to erode over the next two decades. In 2020, Gallup found that only 42 percent of Americans expressed a great deal or quite a lot of confidence in religious organizations.

The abuse in the Catholic Church captured considerable public attention, but it was hardly the only religious denomination wrestling with the problem of sexual abuse. There was a huge exposé about how the Southern Baptist Convention (SBC), the largest Protestant denomination in the United States, had protected perpetrators of sexual abuse for years. In 2019, a joint investigation by the *Houston Chronicle* and the *San Antonio Express-News* identified seven hundred women and children who had been victims of sexual abuse since the late 1990s.[2] Facing mounting pressure from inside and outside the denomination, the SBC released an internal report documenting how "top church leaders suppressed and mishandled abuse claims, resisted reforms, and belittled victims and their families."[3] As often happens, protecting their own reputations and the welfare of the church had been the overriding priority for church leaders.

The criminal justice system has a long history of failing victims of sexual assault as well. In one infamous example, Brock Turner, who was convicted of raping an unconscious woman outside a fraternity party at Stanford University, received only a fraction of the maximum sentence. Instead of being imprisoned for fourteen years, he got six months in jail and three years of probation for the offense. Lenient sentencing of sexual offenders is not the only issue within the justice system; the lack of aggressive prosecution and vigorous investigation of sexual abuse allegations by police remains a problem as well. A few years ago, the City of Memphis was the subject of a class-action lawsuit for its police department's failure to process roughly twelve thousand rape kits over a twenty-nine-year period.[4] One study that interviewed sexual assault victims about their interactions with investigating officers found that many victims faced insensitive treatment, aggressive questioning, and victim blaming.[5]

The mounting examples of corruption and systemic abuse not only violate the trust women have in these organizations but risk collapsing the entire collective effort to address social problems that these institutions are uniquely equipped to take on. When organizations designed to serve the public are more responsive to institutional interests, it communicates a clear message: You're on your own.

The failure of America's religious and legal authorities to protect vulnerable people from abuse undermines their integrity and capacity to function effectively. Only about half of young women say they have a great deal or a fair amount of confidence in law enforcement to respond fairly and responsibly to reports of sexual harassment or abuse.[6] An even smaller number of young women—four in ten—express confidence in church and religious leaders to handle these issues responsibly. In contrast, older women express far more confidence in these institutions despite their well-documented failures and shortcomings. Their formative information environment had a lot to do with shaping their opinions—the internet and social media-based criticism could undermine trust more effectively than leadership could build it. The most critical information—highlighting abuses and scandals—could go viral in a matter of hours, leaving a church's reputation in tatters. The internet, by reducing the control organizations had over their own reputations, fundamentally altered the relationship that members had with them. Where older women saw flaws in a system that required correction, their daughters and granddaughters believed the entire system was essentially corrupt, deserving nothing less than dismantling. And when we don't believe in the possibility of reform, the burden of carrying out essential functions—ensuring safety and providing accountability—shifts from institutions to individuals.

The collapse of institutional trust more broadly has led more young women to believe they cannot rely on formal authorities to ensure their safety or processes to mete out justice. The world has not become more dangerous, but we're becoming increasingly comfortable with the personalization of public safety. Young women are taught that they must take the necessary precautions of protecting themselves. And that is precisely what has happened. Between 2007 and 2021, the percentage of women who carried pepper spray or mace doubled.[7] Nearly four in ten women travel with these personal safety devices. A growing number of women have turned to websites and apps to help ensure their safety as well. There are apps designed to share location information to connect immediately with first responders, and for occasions when women may be in more vulnerable situations, such as running.[8]

The existence of these resources further reinforces the notion that individual safety is a personal responsibility as opposed to a collective one. Women come to expect that they must provide for their own security simply because there are tools designed for them to do just that.

Young Women Have Less Confidence in Authorities to Handle Sexual Abuse and Harassment

Percentage of women who have a great deal or fair amount of confidence in the following to responsibly address reports of sexual harassment or abuse . . .

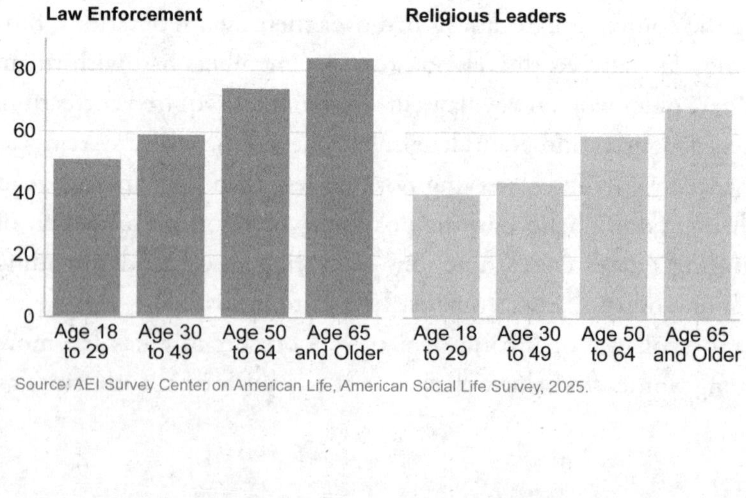

Source: AEI Survey Center on American Life, American Social Life Survey, 2025.

Highly involved parents and their heightened anxieties about danger have also prompted more conversations on these topics. Abby, a senior at Claremont McKenna College in California, said that her parents taught her and her two sisters to be constantly vigilant about potential threats. "I remember the Brock Turner case really vividly, also because I'm the oldest of three girls, and so my family's very conscious of the fact that all of us are never going to be 100 percent safe, which is scary. And I feel like I was very much socialized to be kind of, not on guard, but aware. My dad was always like, be situationally aware." This is further proof that young women are socialized to believe two things: that the world is not safe, and they cannot trust others to help them.

Social media was not the only change in the way information about sexual assault was made public. One study found a marked shift in how journalists covered allegations of sexual assault.[9] The authors showed that between 1980 and 2013, news coverage of sexual assault was typically episodic. Reporters would cover a specific instance or allegation, especially if it involved an element of scandal or it featured a celebrity. Rarely did these stories delve into the structural nature of the issue. But beginning around 2014, more news stories framed the issue in thematic terms, addressing the prevalence of sexual assault and exploring the dynamics behind it. "Thematic coverage focuses on the sheer prevalence of campus assault, which no one supports, while giving less attention to individual institutions or to accusations that the victim was somehow responsible for the assault." Sexual assault is now often contextualized in news accounts to encourage a broader understanding of the contributing factors involved, and is less likely to be framed as a discrete incident.

A focus on the cultural forces involved in the perpetuation of sexual harm against women is the first step toward ensuring accountability—but it may leave women feeling more vulnerable as well. They may feel less disposed to trust institutional policies and processes, and more inclined to engage in a more aggressive style of vigilance.

Spilling Tea: Crowdsourcing Accountability

When institutions prove that they're untrustworthy, the demand for accountability doesn't simply evaporate—it moves elsewhere. In our digital era, that looks like people going online and managing this accountability from person to person. However, the lack of guardrails combined with the affirmation culture online creates a space where safety is crowdsourced without crowd control.

The ability to identify sexual abusers could be a potentially life-saving advantage, especially when institutional protection is lacking. And since the rise of online dating upended the social dynamics of courtship, young people are being offered more romantic options and thus more intimate interactions with strangers. Today, fewer young adults are dating people they met in real life—friends of friends, people they met at the gym, or even their co-workers. Dating strangers removes a built-in accountability mechanism for individual behavior. The knowledge that colleagues, friends, or family members will learn about your behavior is a powerful social incentive.

As the popularity of dating apps grew, single women became increasingly frustrated with the quality of their romantic experiences and their inability to hold strangers accountable for rude, creepy, or threatening behavior. Sometimes, the actions of one's date are off-putting yet harmless, amounting to no more than a wasted evening. Other times, behavior can make women feel truly unsafe. The question became: How could women identify and avoid dangerous or deceitful men who were otherwise able to operate with impunity?

The answer, it turned out, was easy: online crowdsourcing.

Historically, women have relied on "whisper networks," to keep themselves safe in potentially dangerous circumstances. These networks were traditionally based on preexisting relationships that served as informal word-of-mouth information-sharing systems, which helped women avoid problematic men who could pose a threat to their safety. They were especially important as women moved into male-dominated spaces, where they were more vulnerable. In the 1990s, a group of women who worked at Bear Stearns, an investment bank, formed the "Glass Ceiling Club," to share information about problematic male colleagues. The group advised new female hires to avoid certain men and stay in public places, such as the trading floor. "Survival hints like that were shared pretty freely," said Maureen Sherry, a former Bear Stearns employee, in an interview with *The New York Times*.[10] These kinds of networks in the workplace have historically helped women avoid men with a history of harassment or inappropriate behavior, especially in times when reporting men to HR was largely seen as ineffective, or subjected women to office discrimination, unfair punishment, or even the loss of their jobs.

The internet changed how these mostly informal groups worked, especially in the case of crowdsourcing specifically for romantic situations. With social media, women could create private groups and share information widely with far less effort. There was less vetting of allegations as well, as these groups became full of women who were mostly strangers to each other, rather than colleagues or friends. This made the information more difficult to corroborate because the women providing it were not always impartial and their motives for sharing were not always clear. If these sites solely served the purpose of warning women about dangerous or violent men, this would not be an issue, but when they are used as a forum to discuss a much wider range of behavior, these issues loom large.

One of the most influential online crowdsourcing forums was started in 2022 by a woman named Paola Sanchez. Paola started a Facebook group called "Are We Dating the Same Guy?"

(AWDTSG) with the purpose of identifying abusive and unsafe men that women have dated in specific cities. It also served as a space where women could go to confirm the faithfulness of their partners by posting screenshots of men they were dating. In some cases, the intuition that first drove women to check the site was proved right, revealing that their partner was involved with another woman, sometimes multiple women. Even if the answer revealed the worst about their partner, many women felt grateful for the site's existence. The women-only groups grew rapidly, spreading to more than two hundred cities, and now boast more than six million members.

But what began as self-defense quickly evolved into digital offense.

The purpose of the private, women-only group is to inform each other about and then avoid potentially dangerous and dishonest men. If you don't want to end up on the page, don't engage in predatory behavior or rampant infidelity. Easy as that, right? Not exactly. If we've learned anything about social media, it's that it readily encourages users to see signs of mendacity or malevolence in good intentions and earnest awkwardness.

If the original intent of the groups was to keep women safe, many women are now using them to post about any type of behavior or qualities they find objectionable. Women are not only posting about sketchy or creepy guys, but making shallow comments that nobody should be judged by publicly. There are hundreds of posts that focus on subjective qualities, such as guys who are too "clingy," comments about physical appearance, sexual performance, and even sharing medical information, such as whether men may have a sexually transmitted infection.[11] One post from an anonymous member read: "This guy is a Tinder fixture. No good intentions. He also talks like an Italian duck. Spit everywhere. In his defense, I think it's a lisp. Anyway . . . he was super rude after I declined his cigarette breath kiss. I went to the bathroom and came back, and he drank the rest of my drink." Off-putting and unfortunate perhaps, but this is hardly behavior deserving of being immortalized online. It should be easy for us to agree that publicly insulting someone in deeply personal terms without their knowledge is simply wrong. It is vindictive and serves no purpose other than to normalize the practice of ritual humiliation.

Although the groups have moderators, enforcement is often lax. Members are encouraged not to screenshot posts and share outside the group, but sometimes posts travel across social media platforms. A single post with the hashtag #AreWeDatingTheSameGuy or #AWDTSG has garnered 3.6 million views on TikTok.

Although crowdsourcing efforts to review women have not taken off in the same way, men are no less interested in enforcing their own standards of accountability, and it stems from similar feelings. A growing number of young men see America as a place that does not offer a level playing field but one tilted against them. There are spaces where young men do feel free to express themselves, where they are heard and their experiences are validated. Plenty has been written about the manosphere, but fundamental to its appeal is that it acknowledges what many young men feel: They inhabit a world that is uncaring or hostile to their experiences. Plenty of young men feel that while they are being criticized for manspreading, mansplaining, or embodying toxic traits, women do not receive the same level of scrutiny for their harmful behavior.

Some of the most misogynistic material emerging out of the manosphere is based on the premise that women do not face accountability for their actions. It is a regular theme on Atlas's *Whatever* podcast that I discussed in chapter one. Although the guest lineups change, the entire setup is adversarial, mostly pitting men against women who are criticized for being hypocritical, vapid, or immoral. It's also quite popular. An episode that featured a debate between a

Whatever host and an "Ivy-league feminist," garnered more than one million views and more than twenty thousand comments, nearly all of which were critical of her argument.[12] Although not particularly unique in terms of its tone or emphasis, one comment offers a representative sample of the way men in the comments typically respond. "This is clearly the first time she's ever had her indoctrination challenged." It received more than six thousand likes.

The conversations are degrading, and frankly, very difficult to watch. The hosts routinely demean their guests, pressing them to reveal deeply personal information about their sex lives, and then rebuking them for their answers. Listeners can pay to have their questions asked to the women. For a price (typically somewhere around $100), you can ask these women anything or have anything read out loud. It's almost always something objectifying. Listening to just a few minutes of these conversations was enough to make my stomach turn, and perhaps that's the point.

Other examples of men crowdsourcing women online are found on a number of social media accounts, such as "Why Women get Ls," and "Women Being Awful," that traffic in content featuring women engaged in excessive promiscuity or acts of infidelity. I tracked down "Jon," who runs the Women Being Awful account, and asked him why he spends his time promoting the most controversial, degrading content he can find to his millions of followers. He said it was because no one holds women accountable for their behavior. Our conversation took some unexpected turns. It was not all masculine bravado. He acknowledged that many men suck, but his motivation in highlighting women's behavior was his belief that society gives them a pass. "I believe we are gynocentric in many ways, especially with the court systems. And like, you see women having sex with students all the time, and they're getting slaps on their wrists," he says. "White cis men are kind of at the bottom rung, and they're free to make fun of, criticize, and dehumanize in the ways that have been used to dehumanize others in the past." But Jon also revealed that he lived a fairly lonely existence, and that he had been mistreated in past relationships—not only in romantic relationships, but by friends who treated him poorly.

Does he have a point? Given that 94 percent of sexual abuse offenders are men, this is a less than compelling argument.[13] There are known sentencing disparities between men and women, but there's little evidence to suggest that women are not held accountable for engaging in child sex abuse. Therefore, the core purpose of accounts like these is to highlight unfairness and double standards that trigger feelings of grievance. What matters to these users is that the claims feel true, and it is offered as another example of the injustices that many young men relate to.

Our failure to apply the same standards of behavior to everyone has been an enduring societal problem. Without universal standards of behavior, enforcement becomes tribal. We accept violations from our allies but punish them severely in our enemies.

Accountability requires a collective response. No one can claim immunity from social norms because of their race, ethnicity, gender, sexual orientation, or political allegiances. A society that refuses to discourage antisocial behavior—shoplifting, littering, line cutting, fare dodging—will only see examples of it multiply. We all need to exist within the same moral system, subject to the same social norms and with the expectation that we will face the same repercussions if we transgress them. If the authority structures are seen as preferencing certain people at the expense of others—even if there are benevolent intentions behind it—we will have undermined the fragile sense of fairness that societal comity is built upon.

Existing gender norms can make this process difficult in practice. Men and women face different societal expectations for their behavior. Weakness in men is more often viewed as a moral failing. Men can face social stigma for avoiding confrontation, while women can be punished for engaging in it. Acknowledging these distinctive cultural constraints should not preclude us from expecting decency, respect, and honesty to serve as the basis of our social interactions and communal life. This goal can't be accomplished through provocative or performative online behavior. We need to start modeling the behavior we want to see in others.

Confidence, Creepiness, and Reputational Risks

The problem with women sharing personal details about men in chat rooms and private forums is not that the information is unhelpful, but that these sites became indiscriminate clearinghouses for any and all types of behavior. In the absence of more formal structures to ensure accountability, wasn't social media better than nothing? Providing an early warning system to help women avoid abusive men is inarguably good. But it also reduces a complicated social interaction or relationship into a one-sided complaint. There's no expiration date on an accusation, and no way to respond. Broadcasting someone's misbehavior is a fairly poor way to change it. It was effective in making men more guarded and less trusting of women. In our research, we're seeing that for every online tool that makes women feel safer, there's a parallel fear that men are experiencing: What if one awkward moment or vulnerable text could turn into a blemish that lasts forever?

One of the fascinating things about modern dating is how unequal it is. Even as it has become more common for men and women to split the bill on a first date, there are strong norms for men to cover it. So much of courtship is reliant on male initiative. Ellen Lamont, author of *The Mating Game: How Gender Still Shapes How We Date,* observes that despite the goal of equality in many modern romantic relationships, men are still expected "to ask for, plan, and pay for dates; initiate sex; confirm the exclusivity of a relationship;

and propose marriage."[14] Polls bear this out. Female-friendly dating app Bumble was designed to only allow women to make the first move, but many female users grew exhausted and dissatisfied with their experience. It's not just traditionally minded women either. In talking with a young woman attending Barnard College, being feminist for her did not mean a less conventional approach to dating. "I want to be asked out. I don't want to have to be asking, I don't want to pay for my dinner, and I want them to open the door for me."

Men still do largely take on the role of initiating romantic interactions. And when it comes to rejection, the experiences of men and women are not remotely comparable. In a poll we conducted, among Americans who had experienced regular romantic rejection, men accounted for 70 percent of this group.[15] At the other end of the spectrum, those who reported they had never been turned down, two-thirds were women. Making an embarrassing misstep is more likely if you have to make the first step. When private mistakes can result in public ridicule, ambivalence and insecurity are often the consequence.

When I started talking with young men about their concerns, any time the topic veered into dating, a surprising number talked about how risky they felt the process had become. Many young men worried about reputational damage. When a bad date, mistake, or misdeed is shared online, it becomes part of your permanent record, an unerasable personal history. Saying or doing the wrong thing would result in disparaging comments on social media that would be seen by thousands, or perhaps millions, of people.

For women who have had dates go awry, sharing these uncomfortable, off-putting experiences can feel validating and even empowering. It's a bid for social solidarity. "It can feel freeing to share your story with others, lightening the weight of the dating mishaps that could otherwise continue to bother you," said Miranda Nadeau, a licensed psychologist.[16] I once heard a story from a young woman whose date, instead of the dinner that was promised, took her grocery shopping and asked for advice about developing a menu he was planning for another social event. (Advice he then dismissed.) I've heard a surprising number of women and men say they have gone out on a date only to be accompanied by their date's sibling or friend. Exes appear in plenty of these stories as well. One young man reported that his date announced that she had come directly from her ex-boyfriend's house, but she assured him that they had not hooked up in a while. How do I know this? It's all public. You can find it on TikTok, Facebook, and Instagram. Many of these stories spread rapidly across social media platforms or wind up in compilation articles on mainstream outlets, such as *Cosmopolitan, BuzzFeed,* or *Bored Panda.*

As I've noted, in the days before social media, women typically relied on other precautionary measures to warn others about potentially malicious men. Typically, the worst offenders were called out or identified—men who likely engaged in repeated problematic behavior with women. But the definition of what constitutes "problematic" seems to have expanded, along with the ease with which it can be publicly shared.

For many single men, Facebook groups and apps like these are not simply about ensuring women's safety, but about embarrassing and punishing men for a subjectively negative dating interaction. It's clear that some men who have been posted have engaged in abusive or menacing behavior. I doubt very much that most men would object to using social media to help women avoid serial abusers, but the standard for everything less than "clearly wrong" is somewhat subjective. If the judgment is how a certain interaction made you feel, posting about the intimate or personal details of an interaction with someone else without their consent is not so clear-cut. Our research shows that fewer young men are entering adulthood with dating and relationship experience, so their immaturity and inexperience invariably contributes to awkward romantic encounters.

In addition to punishing both harmless and harmful behavior with the same consequence, the prevalence of groups like these also makes it harder for men who have made mistakes to move on and find loving relationships. One man we met in a 2024 focus group in Philadelphia, Jayden, said he had been posted on the AWDTSG Philadelphia page. While he is not the most sympathetic character, his experience sheds light on a key problem with online-only accountability mechanisms. He described his experience to us: "They made [a post about] me, and it had so much bad stuff on there . . ." After finding himself on the page, he kept scrolling and reading the posts about all the other men on there. "What if he had three bad dates and twenty good dates? Those good dates aren't going to comment on there and say, 'we had great dates,' because they already see that some other people had bad dates. And any woman that's dating him is going to see that and be like, okay, red flag. Stop talking to him. Didn't even give him a chance. That could have been your future husband, right?"

Jayden himself explained his own dating past with what seemed like sincere remorse: "I used to be a serial cheater once upon a time, and I've perfected the art of hiding things. . . . yeah, I was horrible at one point. It's not good. It's not good."

I, of course, do not have the ability to confirm or deny if this man is truly reformed from his "serial cheating" days, but if he is and now seeks a new start, any woman he goes out with can find the posts from when he cheated in the past and make a decision about him before he has had the chance to prove his penitence. There's another problem with having a permanent record cataloging mistakes and misbehavior: It robs us of our capacity to grow, to mature, and to develop authentic feelings of remorse for past wrongs. Without the possibility of redemption, we become forever defined by our failings.

Crowdsourcing safety makes a lot of sense in a dating environment that throws strangers together, but it is rife with abuse as well. There is an element of subjectivity in all social interactions—particularly those that fall within the spectrum of socially inept yet harmless interactions. What we perceive to be problematic behavior might not bother someone else. Maintaining impartiality was never going to be possible, and it's even less so given the personal stakes involved.

For some of the young men I talked to, there was a sense that women might exaggerate a negative sexual experience to gain sympathy from friends or people online. The more outrageous the story, the greater potential for virality. In some ways, it matters little if their concerns are valid; what matters is that they exist and that they are shaping the attitudes and behavior of young men when they interact with women.

When "Believe Women" became a rallying cry of the #MeToo movement, it was meant to challenge a culture that serially diminished and discounted the experiences of women. It was a potent corrective, but it grew to mean something different for young men. It created a sense of imbalance on an issue that men still believed encompassed two legitimate perspectives, and that to fully affirm the statement meant the discounting of their own experiences. For many of those who have experienced sexual abuse or serial harassment, they develop deep reservoirs of shame and self-doubt that create lasting inhibitions to talk about it. Yet, on social media, many young men see women sharing their traumatic stories easily and often, gaining clout and validation along the way. Many men would feel uncomfortable sharing deeply personal and vulnerable experiences, especially if they were victims, but young women face a very different set of social incentives that can influence how they interpret and respond to various personal experiences.

Trauma Bonding and Gender Solidarity

Writing a book about dating, relationships, and social connection can often generate curiosity and interest, especially from young people who are living it. One young woman I met named Ella had a story she was eager to share with me. In her sophomore year of high school, Ella joined Global Visionaries, a Seattle-based nonprofit group that works with high school students to foster "socially and environmentally conscious" leadership. Her cohort would be sent to Guatemala to participate in reforestation efforts in the country. Before she and her fellow students embarked on the trip, Global Visionaries leaders gathered the students together and separated the girls and boys. The girls sat in a circle and, according to Ella, were instructed to share a difficult moment from their lives that happened to them because they were girls.

Many of the girls talked about negative interactions they had with boys or men. When it was time for Ella's best friend to share, Ella was startled by what she heard.

"My friend shared this experience about how she, herself, had been sexually molested when she was a child by her doctor, and then later on by a teacher, and that her brother had also been sexually molested by this same teacher." It was not a story that her best friend had ever shared with Ella, but she told it to a group of strangers. "She went into a lot of detail about it," Ella said. "It broke my heart to hear that this had happened."

Except, it turned out the story may have been completely fabricated. After the staff of Global Visionaries followed up with her friend in preparation to share the accusations with law enforcement, the girl said the story she told in the circle was not true. "She had lied about all of it," Ella said about her friend. It may not be possible to sort out the entire truth. Victims of sexual abuse, especially children, sometimes recant their stories for any number of reasons. Ella was sympathetic and understood why she told the story she did. "In that circumstance, she felt so much pressure to share something," Ella said.

She wasn't the only one. Ella remembers another girl who broke down in tears that day because she did not have a traumatic experience to share. She said: "I don't have anything to say, like nothing bad has ever happened to me, but I'm just so terrified of being raped."

What's striking about the entire episode is that Global Visionaries' work is not focused on addressing gender discrimination, sexual harassment, or assault. It's an environmental group. Their goal is to plant trees.

At the time, Ella remembers the experience made her feel more anxious that the risk of sexual assault was far greater than she imagined. "I was like, wow, maybe I need to start feeling so scared of being raped too."

After some reflection, Ella, who is now a junior at Brigham Young University, is more troubled by the experience. "When you're in an environment where individuals are sharing very vulnerable stories, it's very easy to want to be a part of the camaraderie," she said. "There's almost this weird environment that forms where you feel left out if you haven't had an experience like that."

This experience shows us something startling: Trauma and fear can be used as relational currency. When young girls are in a setting where they feel like vulnerability can help them belong, the story of suffering can be the price of admission. It's most obvious in online spaces, where tearful testimonials and emotional breakdowns serve this very purpose. Whether it is dealing with a breakup, getting a speeding ticket, or having a tough day at work, these posts are meant to elicit sympathetic responses. In showcasing their vulnerability, social media creators are trying to establish an emotional bond with their followers. These videos provide the illusion of closeness without the reciprocal work typically involved in fostering deep and meaningful connections with another person. The bond is built entirely on a shared sense of vulnerability.

Traumatic experiences can create powerful bonds that work to provide a sense of solidarity and support among victims. Past research has noted that shared experiences of hardship, like among combat veterans, can create deep social bonds even across generations.[17] Victims of sexual abuse who share their stories can form meaningful connections that serve as sources of support. However, research has also shown that broadcasting these experiences can result in heightened feelings of anxiety and stress.

One study showed that, "given that social groups function, in part, to promote identification among members . . . those who share social identities with victims of traumatic experiences that are broadcast widely may share their feelings of threat, anxiety, and distress."[18] The authors of the study described this as "a double-edged sword"; it can create community but amplify feelings of distress as well. It can also reduce their sense of agency.

At a time when so many young people feel uncertain about where the country is headed and unsettled in their personal lives and relationships, the impulse to seek affirmation is strong. That solidarity strengthens collective purpose but sustains collective fear. The more women identify with the struggles of other women, the harder it becomes to imagine the experiences of people with an entirely different set of problems.

For young men observing from the outside, it can feel disorienting. They sense the fear but fail to fully appreciate its weight. "I just left feeling really guilty for being a boy," one male student told Ella after the Global Visionaries session. That guilt mirrors the fatigue many young women feel. If one side feels overexposed and vulnerable, the other feels defensive and disregarded. In many of the conversations I had with young men, they expressed feeling that they were less deserving of help. If they faltered or failed, no one would come to lend them a hand. Johnny, a thirty-year-old from Philadelphia, put it this way: "As a man you get no sympathy from the world. Nobody is coming to save you." It's difficult to hear, not least because of how often this feeling is shared. We have become preoccupied by our own pain. It's kept us paralyzed.

We cannot solve any of this by retreating to the safety of our own side. In fact, it requires that we nurture the opposite instinct—a sense of curiosity. If men feel a sense of aggrievement over being called out or criticized in group chats and private Facebook groups, they should consider women's experiences on dating apps. Nearly half of women who have ever dated online report that a man continued to contact them after they were rejected. The same study found that nearly half of women report that a man—presumably someone they did not know all that well—sent them an unsolicited message containing a sexually graphic image or explicit content. This type of sexually aggressive behavior is jarring, uncomfortable, and in some cases scary. On the other side, women would find it difficult to comprehend the amount of rejection many ordinary men face on these same platforms. It's never been easy for men to express vulnerability because their value is in some part based on the security they are supposed to provide. Instead of acknowledging the unique constraints men and women face, it's easier to ignore or exploit them.

Our goal shouldn't be for women to stop sharing painful experiences, but to reestablish the guardrails that make unfortunate incidents less common. What's missing is a framework of understanding that allows people to learn from past mistakes, and more fully appreciate the consequences for other people. Social learning is best when it occurs in an institutional context—when rules are clear, consequences are consistent and proportionate, and models are readily available. We exist in one place at one time, and a certain amount of tension and friction is inevitable, and necessary. We don't have to like it, but it doesn't have to define us either.

The internet has greatly expanded our social world. The online world feels nearly infinite, populated by so many different people and personalities, making a single action feel inconsequential. In fact, it's the opposite. The consequences of our actions are significant, and we are more closely connected than it seems. We were never meant to navigate through this life without help, but at every juncture, our culture seems intent on communicating this message to young people. We were meant to depend on each other. The recognition that our lives are collectively constructed should not simply encourage young people to ask for help; it should create the imperative to provide it.

CHAPTER 8

HOW DATING GOT WORSE

If the preceding chapters have given you the sneaking suspicion that dating has become more complicated, your hunch is correct. Generation Z is entering adulthood with a less clear sense of their relational priorities, a greater preoccupation with their own interests and needs, and far less early romantic experience than previous generations. Rising fear about sexual violence and concerns about surveillance culture have contributed to a greater sense of distrust. This has encouraged singles to adopt a more defensive posture in their romantic interactions. Online dating platforms have also torn down geographic barriers and social boundaries, erasing shared norms in the dating process. Monitoring and vigilance become more important and the simple act of sharing a meal with someone is a far less rewarding experience. And so young adults do it less often. An entire generation has been taught that opting out of romantic commitment can be the better course of action, and in doing so they deprive themselves of the most consistent provider of personal growth, meaning, and support.

Dating Troubles

"In one word, how would you describe modern dating?" Our focus group moderator posed this question to a group of ten women sitting around a table on a hot summer evening in Raleigh, North Carolina. She did not have to wait long for their responses. The mostly twenty-something single women responded in rapid succession: "Frustrating," "Disappointing," "Disheartening," "Garbage," "Repetitive," "Difficult," "Traumatizing." Even the more neutral descriptions were tinged with pessimism: "Fast," "Fleeting," "Minimal." When our team talked to their male peers, they were not any more optimistic. It's not only in Raleigh—nationally there is a growing pessimism about dating. More than six in ten Americans say that dating is more difficult today than it was ten years ago. The sense of gloom has become more pervasive as well. In 2019, less than half of all Americans said that dating had become more difficult than it had been in the recent past.

Americans Believe Dating Is More Difficult Today

Percentage of Americans who say that, compared to 10 years ago, dating today is . . .

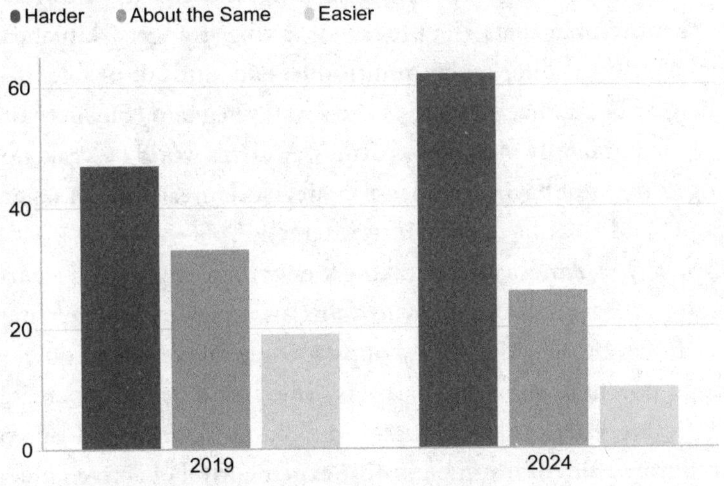

Source: Pew Research Center, American Trends Panel Wave 56, October 2019; AEI Survey Center on American Life, American Perspectives Survey, December 2024.

But if the adjectives single men and women use to describe dating sound similar, the substance of their complaints is quite different. One of the most frequent complaints single women voiced in our research was how difficult it was to find someone they were interested in dating. In fact, in a survey we conducted on the topic of dating, we found that this was one of the most often-mentioned reasons women gave for being single.[1] For many single women, attracting attention was not the problem. Perhaps predictably, single men's chief complaint was being ignored or disregarded.

Conversations about modern dating practices have always featured a fair amount of handwringing over the meandering, imperfect ways young men and women get together. But there is something truly unique about the courtship process today. Online dating platforms have reordered the dating landscape by pushing strangers together and displacing traditional ways of meeting romantic partners. Many young people find it, for lack of a better term, undeniably strange. The regular rhythm of romantic exchanges can feel rushed, moving too quickly toward commitment or sex. Or they lack direction, with half-hearted conversations over text that go nowhere. But it's more than that. The process of letting strangers skip ahead straight into the inner sanctum introduces all kinds of problems—the biggest being that it removes the social safeguards our network of friends and family members provides. And in a world of weakened dating norms, not having these social safeguards greatly increases uncertainty and volatility in romantic interactions.

On average, Americans are taking longer than ever to find a partner, and a growing number who want a permanent partner may never find one. Facilitated by apps, people move more quickly through potential romantic partners. The dating landscape creates considerable relationship churn as people move into and out of various romantic commitments more expediently. For active singles, this can mean more dates, but it also means more negative dating experiences. Online dating can also leave people in a state of perpetual romantic ambiguity. The anxiety and exhaustion are palpable. No one believes it's fun, and some are so tired of it that they've thrown in the towel completely. Demographic forecasts are daunting. One demographer estimates that one in three Americans today will never get married.[2] Morgan Stanley estimated that 45 percent of prime working-age women (age twenty-five to forty-four) will be single and childless by 2030.[3]

The decline of marriage is often characterized as a troubling societal development—one that will lead to population decline and economic malaise. But the implications may be even broader. Marriage encourages men and women to merge interests and resolve their differences for the sake of partnership. To maintain intimacy and longevity in a romantic relationship necessitates a posture of compromise, patience, and empathy. Our understanding of the opposite sex does not emerge suddenly, the result of a single enlightening event, but is built through small conversations and intimate interactions with our partners. When we lose this connection, we close a window of understanding on a world very different from our own. A society with large numbers of dissatisfied and permanently single men and women is not a healthy one. It increases the possibility that women and men will perceive each other as adversaries operating in a zero-sum environment. It undermines the development of mutual understanding regarding the distinct challenges that men and women face in everyday life. Without close and consistent engagement, we become more rigid in our thinking; we become less able to acknowledge, let alone respond to, the distinct needs and concerns of others. Every accommodation we are asked to make may start to feel like a concession—a loss for "our side."

The way young singles meet is part of the problem. Despite fatigue with online dating, it has grown to be one of the most common ways for young people to meet. And it's not just that singles are wary of meeting up with complete strangers, but that online dating excels at making introductions that go nowhere. A Stanford University study found that roughly half of those on Tinder were not actually using the platform to find a partner.[4] For many users, the dating app was simply a source of entertainment, a distraction, or a way to boost their self-esteem.

To make matters worse, young singles are entering adulthood with less dating experience than ever. Close to half of Gen Z men report not having had a romantic partner during their teenage years, a sharp break from the past when teen relationships were common.[5] The lack of romantic experience is a considerable liability for young men who are having to adapt to new cultural norms, and whose behavior is now subject to greater scrutiny. And they're having to figure out these road maps alone. Positive models for men when it comes to modern dating are largely absent in popular culture. Meanwhile, modern expectations for young men are higher when it comes to their level of emotional intelligence and communication skills. Additionally, many young men still feel tethered to certain norms of traditional masculine behavior, not necessarily out of a sense of insecurity, but because women still expect it. That's a lot to manage all at once, especially on your own.

Today, there is far less agreement about basic dating conventions. We should celebrate that women have attained greater economic parity with men, but it makes the question of who finances dating activities less clear. Our culture now encourages young women to self-advocate, strive, and achieve, but it has not defined how these imperatives transfer to dating. In a world where the ambitions of young women are given equal weight to those of young men, who leads and who follows? Dating traditions of the past are being challenged and discarded, but new models have not emerged to replace them. There is no agreement or consensus.

All of this has made dating more difficult and unpleasant. Worryingly, there are signs it is also becoming more contentious. Rising levels of mistrust and the belief that the interests of men and women are inherently misaligned exacerbate the tensions between men and women. These tensions then spill out in dramatic fashion online. Everyone is in it for themselves, there are few rules to follow, and the very worst of male and female dating behavior is displayed on social media with depressing regularity. Even as most young singles report wanting to get married, young men and women appear less able to accomplish this goal. It feels a bit like watching a slow-moving train moving inexorably down the tracks, unable to stop when the bridge is out. Even recognizing what's wrong is not sufficient to stop it.

Sadly, relationship failures are common. Some relationships just aren't meant to be, whether that's because of timing, different priorities, or misaligned values. A failure rarely leaves people feeling good, even when they believe it is necessary. Relationship failures can serve as critical opportunities for personal reflection and resilience. They can also leave people feeling hurt, confused, and bitter. And wanting answers or affirmation of their experience. Social media content can provide both. Young men and women are invited to see each other as the problem. The online tools that are meant to streamline the process of romantic connection have compromised the trust and reciprocity that relationships are built on. They set expectations for curation without compromise, and possibility without patience.

Dating Online: The Perils of Endless Possibility

Dating apps have turned courtship into a numbers game, but men and women play it differently. Typically, young men receive far fewer likes and messages than women, so they are incentivized to try to match with as many women as possible to increase their odds of getting a date. On the other hand, young women can become inundated with attention and message requests from people they are not all that interested in. Because a single rejection is relatively costless on dating apps—the risk of public embarrassment is almost nil—both men and women tend to "shoot their shot" with individuals more attractive than themselves. In both cases, the volume of romantic prospects creates perverse incentives that make the dating experience worse.

Carey, a young woman we interviewed last year, said the impact of dating apps is obvious. "People think that they just have a million options. It's like when you want to watch a show, and you put on Netflix, and you literally find yourself not being able to decide for like an hour, and then you wind up not watching anything."

This results in a high failure rate for users. Nearly one-third (31 percent) of young Americans who have used dating apps report that it has never led to an actual date.[6] Many dating app users spend hours scrolling or engaging in cursory communication with prospective matches without ever making it out into the real world. Even when they do move offline, many dates turn into disasters. Online dating creates a problem of volume and optionality—there is a risk in making an early investment because something better may come along. Sarah, a single woman in our Raleigh focus group, said: "Even if they are interested in you, there's the thought of 'Well, what if there's somebody else?' "

Having too many options can sap motivation. A common critique that many young singles make is the lack of effort that people put into any one date or person. Why would you go all out to impress someone you do not know and may never see again? The ease of access to potential romantic partners decreases the value of a single match or date. There is always another option waiting in the wings. The possibility that a "better match" exists and only requires a bit more swiping undermines the satisfaction people have with their relationship choices.

Studies have shown that having abundant romantic options can leave people feeling less confident about the decisions they eventually make. In one research experiment, Jonathan D'Angelo and Catalina Toma offered one group of online daters six possible matches to choose from, while another group was presented with twenty-four possible matches.[7] They found that the users who had fewer options to choose from were ultimately more satisfied with their choices.

A quantitative approach to dating, one that maximizes exposure and the accumulation of inbound likes and messages, tends to devalue individuals. At a certain point, it's just a game of numbers. It encourages daters to prioritize expediency, which can leave people feeling disposable. Ghosting—the term used to describe abruptly cutting off communication with someone without explanation—has become commonplace in dating. A Pew survey found that 42 percent of young adults reported having been ghosted before, but that figure is far higher among those with online dating experience.[8] More than six in ten (62 percent) Americans who are currently dating online report having been ghosted; for those who never dated using the apps it's less than one in five (19 percent).* Let that sink in: Your odds of being ghosted are three times higher when you date online.

The reasons for cutting off contact can be incredibly superficial, reflecting the ease with which alternatives can be found. On one viral social media post, women shared their reasons for ghosting men, which included: using "your" instead of "you're," not waiting until she was inside her house before driving off, not holding the door open, laughing like her dad, ordering calamari, and getting a new haircut. The comments section was flooded with additional examples and affirmations of the original post. It's dispiriting but

* This analysis includes anyone who has used an online dating app or dating site within the last 12 months.

not surprising how many people believe this is a perfectly valid approach to dating. Or even to treating people. Both men and women live in a world that encourages the practice of making snap judgments and shallow evaluations based on limited information. The more plentiful we perceive our options to be, the more mercenary we become.

Perhaps the most problematic aspect of online dating is that it artificially accelerates the courtship process. In her book *The New Laws of Love: Online Dating and the Privatization of Intimacy,* sociologist Marie Bergström argues that, for active users, "dating platforms yield many dates, many of which become sexual, but only a minority of the resulting relationships are long-lasting."[9] Like so many other recent technologies, online dating introduces expediency into a process where purpose and patience result in better outcomes. A system that produces more failed relationships and false starts is one that will breed resentment and recrimination. Bergström argues that this is a central feature of online dating rather than an unfortunate side effect. She writes: "The specific tempo of online dating makes short-term relationships a constitutive part of the user sexual experience even when users do not necessarily want this feature."[10] For many young singles, the entire thing seems like a bad deal.

By offering a great quantity of romantic prospects, online dating also reduces the quality of romantic interactions. In an interview with *The Atlantic,* Manhattan-based therapist Matt Lundquist shared how he counseled many of his single patients on managing expectations with online dating. "So the assumption is, the odds are pretty good that [any given date] will suck, but, you know. Whatever. You've gotta do it," he says.[11] For a while, many young singles did. They dated a lot. In fact, young singles today have access to more potential romantic connections than any previous generation, despite their lack of formative dating experience. But social media and dating apps provide more false starts and rapid flameouts. Singles spend more time in a strange liminal state, sometimes referred to as "the talking phase," that often includes awkward introductions, matches who never respond, texting conversations that fizzle out, and unpredictable delays between replies. Over time, these types of interactions have left people feeling confused, resentful, and burned-out. So more young singles are deciding that they do not, in fact, *have* to do it. Instead, they are choosing to walk away from the dating market.

It's Complicated: Romantic Relationships in Digital Space

Despite all the frustration they engender, dating apps continue to draw users for two reasons: Most singles want a partner, and dating apps are the easiest, most obvious way to do it. And yet, even for those who have successfully navigated the pitfalls of online romantic interactions, it doesn't end when a relationship begins. There is an entirely new set of potential problems that arise when it comes to merging digital lives. For a generation that has assiduously maintained a constant digital presence, the process of sharing this highly personalized space can create complications. Even for millennials, who came of age with Facebook, toggling relationship status was an important moment, formally announcing the status of the relationship. The most popular social media platforms for Gen Zers don't include any formal indicators of relationship status. There's no "committed" button on Instagram or any way to identify as "single" on TikTok. Some young women talk about "soft launching" their new relationships, like they're introducing a new product. But there is no standard way to handle these transitions.

Romantic relationships work differently in the digital world than in the physical one. Before social media, being in a committed relationship meant regularly sharing physical space, especially when a couple lived together. One would often be aware of what their partner was doing, who they were with, or how they were spending their time. But our lives online operate independently from our partners'. The vast majority of young people maintain an active digital presence on social media platforms whatever their relationship status. And these digital lives offer abundant opportunities for people to browse potential romantic alternatives without committing obvious violations.

For those in committed relationships, there are few social norms governing acceptable online behavior. Is it acceptable to post a provocative image of yourself that garners lots of male attention when you are in a relationship? What are the rules about liking or commenting on other women's posts when you have a girlfriend? These behaviors may seem harmless, but they can cause friction in a relationship. Online forums like Quora and Reddit are littered with comments from young people who are frustrated by their partner's online activity. Take for example a young woman named Kayla DeChant, who posted about being upset with the amount of time her boyfriend spends following and watching other women online:

"I always feel like I'm not good enough for him because he's always watching some sort of TikTok half-dressed girl. He says it just shows up too but like, he's got to be looking them up or watching TikTok nude porn for it to show up. Honestly, it almost disgusts me, and it tears down my self-esteem."[12]

The specter of infidelity has always been a source of relationship angst, but as our social and romantic lives have adapted to online spaces, couples are wrestling with an entirely new variety—attention infidelity. The competition for our attention, one of our most valuable possessions, has become extraordinarily intense. Roughly one in three young women report feeling "jealous or unsure of their relationship because of the way their current partner interacts with other people on social media."[13] In many instances, attention infidelity is not exactly cheating by traditional standards, but it can be just as pernicious.

Even if this behavior does not amount to a relationship-ending offense, it can increase anxiety and feelings of insecurity. It can engender resentment and make people feel the need to constantly monitor the online behavior of their partner. The perception of unlimited romantic options changes how people behave. It may reduce how much we value our current partner and undercut the stability of the relationship.

Digital dating also makes it easier to conceal these activities. In response, more young women have developed a keen intuition for suspicious behavior and a talent for online sleuthing. In a recent *Saturday Night Live* sketch, Sydney Sweeney played an intern recruited by the police department to assist in solving cold cases. She solved the cases within minutes by jumping around various social media sites. Her lines were illuminating: "We're twenty-two-year-old girls in situationships . . . we can find out literally anything about anyone with no information."[14]

It's an entertaining sketch, but the message is bleak. The phenomenon of young women feeling compelled to engage in this type of monitoring does not suggest anything healthy about the state of romantic relationships in the United States.

Unfortunately, keeping tabs on their partner's digital lives has become a common relationship practice for many young women. One study found that a majority (63 percent) of young women in romantic relationships reported having looked through their current partner's cellphone without their knowledge.[15] Few Americans condone this type of behavior, despite its prevalence. The same report noted that most Americans say it is rarely or never acceptable to look through your partner's phone without their knowledge. Young men tend to object to this behavior more emphatically than young women, but few people who have had the experience feel good about it. "It feels a little bit violating. But I mean, it's like the day and age where that's like, normal," said a thirty-one-year-old man we talked to in Philadelphia. Mariah, a young woman from Philadelphia, said that when she caught her current partner going through her phone, it left her feeling confused and unsettled. "I don't know what his past traumas are or whatever, but I'm just like, 'What do I do with this?' "

Attention infidelity is not limited to engaging with attractive strangers on social media. Our devices have embedded themselves into our daily lives, influencing our most routine interactions, altering the regular rhythms of relational life. An essay in *GQ* magazine documented the rise of "laptop boyfriends," which are young men who consume hours of YouTube podcasts, often lugging their laptops into bed with them to the consternation of their partners.[16] Women are no less susceptible to these algorithmic enticements. In fact, it is probably more often a mutual activity. Many couples—my wife and I included—find themselves bowed over their phones, immersed in entirely different worlds, while sitting only a few feet apart. Instead of reaching for each other, we snatch up our digital devices that flood us with an endless stream of hyper-curated content.

A Problem of Extremes: Online Relationship Content

It was inevitable that the volume of information we consume online would eventually shape our behavior offline. The moment you demonstrate even a passing interest in personal stories about dating or romantic relationships on social media, the algorithms take over. For the growing number of young adults with little dating experience of their own, these social media stories offer a distorted curriculum for intimacy. The lessons offered through the repeated consumption of social media relationship content is that complex human interactions can be used to create overly simplified maxims.

We're made to believe that the most emotionally charged and outrageous behavior, the type that is rarely witnessed in the real world, is not the exception, but the rule.

Online relationship content is varied, but much of it falls into two extremes. On one side, you have posts showing spouses or partners engaged in acts of exceptional thoughtfulness like planning elaborate trips, spending a whole day setting up a surprise, morning coffee in bed, and so forth. Some of these posts are accompanied by the popular tagline: "If he wanted to, he would," a catchphrase that tells women they shouldn't settle for less than absolute devotion. On the other side of the internet, you have viral stories about the most appalling behavior that people experience with their partners. These posts cover everything from intense neglect to screenshots of rude conversations to messy breakup stories—and they tend to garner a disproportionate amount of attention. The most shocking of these, like the eight-hour-long TikTok saga "Who TF Did I Marry" that received nearly 200 million views, attract significant interest and reinforce the idea that relationships today are either fairy tales or nightmares—with little room for nuance in between.[17]

Social media posts documenting unhinged behavior are routinely shared on social media, and relationship content is no different in that way. But what makes them so engaging is also what makes them so harmful as templates for relationship dynamics. They make extreme or dangerous situations appear worryingly normal. Consuming this content has a real impact on how people feel about their dating lives, especially for those exposed to a lot of it. Young women who regularly watch social media content that features negative dating experiences are far more pessimistic about single men than those who see this content less often.[18] But it can also leave them unprepared to walk into a dating experience where they're compared to the best and the worst examples of male behavior. This often means that there's little room for error or patience as a relationship develops. Since women are being fed extreme portrayals of relationship dynamics, many feel fatigued before they even start dating, and the internet is ready to take advantage of that too.

These online patterns have generated opportunities for exploitative creators to step in and promise a path forward that ends up being both personally lucrative and socially destructive. There's been a boom in self-styled "relationship experts," such as YouTuber SheraSeven, who encourages women to start viewing relationships in purely transactional terms. On her account, Shera offers advice for single women on "How to Get Him to Spend His Money on You," warning that "no young men are trustworthy."[19] This type of polarizing negativity has become very profitable for some creators. As of spring 2026, Ms. Seven has amassed 850,000 subscribers on her YouTube channel and roughly one million followers on Instagram. But this "advice" isn't actually helping anyone. It's reinforcing the transactional logic that elevates a sense of collective mistrust. It encourages singles to shift from following their curiosity to engaging in threat detection.

Even when the relationship and dating commentariat have mostly benign intentions in sharing their personal stories, their experiences are typically not all that representative of your average single seeking a partner. The people who are most passionate about a particular topic—whether its politics or love—tend to have more extreme views or experiences. There are multiple writers who have written about going on forty, fifty, and sixty dates over a twelve-month period, and these accounts are chock full of embarrassing, weird, and highly entertaining anecdotes, but ultimately the information shared is not particularly instructive or useful to other singles. Worse, these types of stories can give us a warped perception of how the dating world works and shape our expectations of dating behavior.

The things we devote our attention to ultimately shape what we think and how we act. The greatest thinkers across time and culture have recognized this: Buddha said, "We are what we think. All that we are arises with our thoughts. With our thoughts we make the world." Confucius and Marcus Aurelius offered similar insights about how attention shapes behavior. Today, we live in a day and age where these patterns operate on a global and instantaneous scale. When hundreds of thousands of people watch the same videos and internalize the same harmful messages about dating, we are not simply recipients of this cynical culture—we cocreate it. And this unforgiving loop doesn't just hurt us; it keeps putting money in the hands of people and companies that have no stake in our welfare.

Dating Without a Shared Purpose

Why do people date? It's a question with an obvious answer: to find a partner or spouse. But behind that answer lies a plethora of varying reasons: To avoid feelings of loneliness. To expand their social circle. To share meaningful experiences and adventures. To help pay the bills or afford the rent. To get married and raise a family. Sex. Validation. Or even perhaps as entertainment. The list is potentially endless. These days, modern dating can feel like traveling on a road to anywhere with no road signs. But it didn't always feel so open-ended.

It was not so long ago that Americans generally agreed about the pace, direction, and progression of courtship. You meet someone through mutual friends, family, or at work, you spend time together, begin formally dating, and then enter into a relationship on the way to a more permanent commitment, which was most often marriage. Not too long after came kids. The purpose of dating was to find a single person with whom to build a family. However imperfectly a couple might come together, the relational goals of marriage and family formation helped establish clear parameters. Increasingly, these goals are being called into question.

If the purpose of dating is less clear than it once was, it's because marriage and parenthood are less desirable goals for many young people today. In the last thirty years, government-funded surveys revealed that the percentage of teenage girls interested in marriage plummeted, dropping from 83 percent in 1993 to 61 percent in 2023.[20] Boys have remained relatively stable over the same time period—about three-quarters say they want to get married someday. When it comes to parenthood, both teenage boys and girls express greater doubts. The same study found the percentage of teenagers who believed that they were at least "fairly likely" to have kids at some point in their lives is now less than half. In the early 1990s, nearly two-thirds of American teenagers said it was at least "fairly likely" they would become parents someday.

Societal norms have evolved rapidly toward greater acceptance of a wider variety of romantic arrangements. Sexual practices and relationship types that were once less accepted—polyamory, ethical non-monogamy—now appear in the pages of *The New York Times,* or turn up in relationship advice columns. In one recent column, the *New York Times* ethicist answered the question "I Let My Wife Have an Affair. Do I Have to Console Her Now That It's Over?"[21] That kind of arrangement would have been unheard of a decade ago. Not to mention completely mystifying. But the more we write about, share, and participate in these types of romantic experiences, the less unusual it becomes. On Facebook, users who for years could say their relationship status was "complicated" can now identify as being "in an open relationship."

If relationships are evolving to primarily function to serve our personal interests, it makes sense that any configuration might be a plausible option. Flexibility is prioritized over permanence, mutual betterment, or stability. Not surprisingly, this orientation invites considerable confusion about longer-term relationship goals. More young singles are left in a kind of relationship purgatory with partners who take full advantage of the ambiguity with little social pressure to clarify their interests or intent.

Young adults have become more circumspect about marriage, but even those who are excited about the proposition are less certain about when it should happen. There is no consensus on the ideal age when this lifetime commitment should be made. Nearly half of Americans say there is no ideal age to get married.[22] The remaining responses range from early twenties to early thirties, or later. I can appreciate that singles looking for partners do not need any additional pressure, but the alternative is that we accede that every choice is equally valid without considering the costs. The longer we spend on our own, the more our personal routines and habits become entrenched—accommodating the needs of someone else begins to feel like an imposition on our lifestyle.

Researchers Scott Stanley and Galena Rhoades argue that central to the rise of dating anxieties is the growing ambiguity about relationship status—singles have fewer cues about where they stand or where the relationship is headed.[23] The labels may vary—"hanging out," "just talking," "hooking up," "situationship"—but the experience is the same, and far more common today than it once was. We found that close to four in ten young adults reported having ever been in a romantic or sexual relationship that was undefined, which means they were uncertain how to describe the relationship.[24] Although older Americans have far more total relationship experience than those under thirty, far fewer report ever having this type of relationship ambiguity. It's no wonder so many young people feel lost.

The indeterminate nature of these types of relationships maximizes personal agency while providing some elements of emotional intimacy and commitment, but it all comes at a cost. Marriage, whatever flaws it possesses, engenders greater trust and stability than its competitors. The Pew Research Center found sizable advantages among married people in reported feelings of trust over those in cohabitating relationships.[25] Seventy-four percent of married people said they would trust their spouse to act in their best interest, compared to 58 percent of cohabitating relationships. More than two-thirds of married Americans said they would always trust their spouse to tell them the truth; only about half of cohabitating couples said the same.* These are not minor differences; they reflect the greater sense of security that married people feel about their partner. An ambiguous relationship status can sometimes feel safer than fully committing, but it undermines the confidence we have in our partner and ourselves. It keeps us locked in the present. Marriage is a uniquely future-oriented institution; it compels us to think about what lies ahead.

Partnership has all sorts of benefits, but without agreement on the parameters and purpose, relationships can become a source of anxiety and insecurity. Romantic relationships in which both people are moving toward a shared goal, such as marriage and family formation, create a sense of stability. A shared goal does not ensure against relationship problems, but it allows for greater emotional, social, and financial investment. Our sense of security is critical because it allows us to sacrifice more freely. Without a shared understanding about the purpose of romantic partnerships, they can devolve into utilitarian exercises, serving only specific functions. Then the entire project begins to feel mercenary. When the individual cost of meeting a particular need outweighs the benefit, there is one obvious choice to make.

Admitting what we actually want is not easy. One of the barriers to asking for real commitment is that it can invite judgment and criticism. Courtship requires clear and consistent communication

* There's not a way to control for the duration of the relationship, but these gaps are evident in every age category. Young married adults who have probably only been married a relatively short time are still far more trusting of their spouses than those who are cohabitating trust their own partners.

about expectations and goals, but engaging openly and honestly with another person in this way can make us feel exposed. And so, many young singles use social media and dating apps to help safely shroud their romantic interest. They use memes, emojis, and tersely worded texts to soften the emotional impact of rejection. Given the dismal state of interpersonal trust among young adults, it's understandable, but it is a poor substitute for in-person communication. Psychologists have found that verbal expression is uniquely effective in conveying information about someone's emotional state.[26] You have probably had the experience of being able to discern what someone is feeling simply by listening to the tone of their voice. When swiping and texting become the primary forms of romantic communication, we deprive ourselves of critical information about who people are—and what they want.

It can be easy to lose sight of what's at stake. When relationships don't work out, it often feels devastating. Heartbreak is a near universal human experience, but our current approach to dating and relationships seems to be producing so much more of it. The answer lies not in more flexibility but less, not in leaving options open but closing them down. For a generation that grew up amid digital abundance, this is not so easy.

CHAPTER 9

THE SOCIAL DEFICIT

Take a moment to imagine your typical teenager. How is she spending her time? What types of activities is he participating in? Who are they spending time with? These were the questions that prompted me to conduct a survey that would allow us to explore the way teenage experiences changed across generations. It was clear that today's teenagers were having qualitatively different childhoods, but we wanted to document exactly what was happening. The results were startling. A previous generation of teenagers could be found listening to music, hanging out at the arcade or the mall, or riding bikes around their neighborhood. Whatever the activity, they mostly did it together. Today's teenagers are less likely to do all these things, and even when they do, they are more likely to do them alone. Even activities that once incorporated a substantial social component, like playing video games, have evolved into a more solitary pastime. In my late teen years, two of the most popular games were Mario Kart 64 and GoldenEye 007; I logged many hours on these two games, but only ever with friends in the same room, playing together. When we asked young men whether they typically played video games alone or with someone else—either in person or online—a majority (55 percent) said they usually played alone.[1] Gen Z has spent less time participating in critically formative social activities. Compared to previous generations, today's teenagers are found less often at church, hanging out at corner stores, parking lots and parks, drinking at house parties, attending a scout meeting, working a part-time job, or out on a date. So, if they're not roaming around their neighborhoods and generally causing mischief, where are they?

They're at home. Today's young people spend a great deal more time at home than they once did. Americans age fifteen to twenty-four are spending roughly two more hours each day at home than the previous generation of young people.[2] Much of this time is spent alone. The American Time Use Survey, a diary of how Americans allocate their most precious resource, revealed that time spent socializing has declined over the last decade.[3] Journalist Derek Thompson has gone so far as to suggest that mass social separation is the defining social trend of the twenty-first century. I'm inclined to agree.

My own research on the state of American friendship shows a similarly disconcerting trajectory. Since 1990, the number of "close friends" that Americans have has plummeted, especially among young adults. Nearly one in four young men and nearly one in five young women report having no close friends, an astonishing fact given that almost no respondents reported this when surveys questioned Americans about their social networks three decades earlier.[4] When we originally published research on declining friendships in 2021, it set off a torrent of coverage and concern about the causes of what I coined as America's "friendship recession."[5]

Follow-up research that explored the various ways social connections develop and influence our lives revealed something fascinating: that our connection crisis has contributed to siloed experiences of boys and girls. It's not just that Americans are lonely. When young people retreat from standard socialization—friendships and interactions with their community as a whole—they are encouraged to seek out frictionless relationships, which are often transactional. We're seeing that without regular socialization and friendship, romantic relationships deteriorate. The lack of support and feedback from an inner circle further exacerbates relationship problems and even hampers our ability to form a relationship. We need to be living in community; America's relationship problems are made worse by the disappearance of regular and routine social interactions.

Pandemic: Antisocial Accelerant

There is no representative Covid-19 pandemic experience. Your age, gender, where you lived in the country, the type of job you had, and the school you attended all affected your degree of isolation and how destructive the experience was. Living in a community with more restrictive policies might have meant more extended school closures and longer time away from other public places such as restaurants, coffee shops, playgrounds, and parks. Certain groups were more vulnerable to the prolonged social isolation required by public health officials. Teenagers had an especially tough time being cut off from their friends and classmates.

Even among teenage boys and girls who attended the same school, the pandemic had a notably different impact on their behavior. With more leisure time, boys were far more likely than girls to spend their time playing video games. Researchers found a 55 percent increase in the time boys spent gaming, with an average of more than two hours per day.*[6,7] The same study found that while

* This category includes various types of games, including board games, but evidence suggests most of the increase in the time that teen boys spent playing games is attributable to video games.

boys were more likely than girls to spend time alone, the increased social isolation may have taken a greater toll on girls. The authors concluded that technology may not have effectively served to mitigate the damage caused by the impacts of social distancing. No kidding. At an especially critical time for social development, when friends and peers take on a far more important role in identity formation, emotional support, and social learning, social distancing policies effectively denied access to them.

Whether due to the sudden increase in social media use or social deprivation, or some combination of the two, negative health outcomes for girls increased significantly during the pandemic years. In the months and years that followed, hospitals reported a dramatic uptick in admissions of adolescent girls related to anxiety, depression, obsessive-compulsive disorders, eating disorders, and tic disorders.[8] Emergency department visits doubled for eating disorders and tripled for tic disorders.

In one way, the public health recommendations introduced by various governmental bodies revealed a crucial societal blind spot. Quarantine policies rarely acknowledged the long-term social costs that prolonged isolation inflicts on both individuals and communities. There was little mention of the possible far-reaching effects of policies requiring mass social separation. For the most part, public health officials and local government leaders were so focused on reducing transmission of the Covid virus that they made little effort to mitigate the profound damage prolonged isolation caused.

The pandemic was a powerful lesson in the consequences of mass social deprivation. Social cohesion and community trust are sustained through repeated interactions. Social competence and confidence are acquired through the same process, through regular engagement with others. Young adults lost critical opportunities to develop and refine their social skills, while the rest of us experienced a steady erosion not only in our abilities but in our appetite for social engagement. Without regular social interactions, we became less gracious, more guarded, and overly sensitive to friction; our willingness to accommodate personal inconvenience deteriorated rapidly. The pandemic also amplified our worst antisocial tendencies.

For America's teenagers, the pandemic was life-shattering. Overnight, their friends and classmates simply disappeared from their daily lives. They felt trapped not only in their homes but in a permanent state of uncertainty. One young person we talked to, Sophia, was fourteen years old when the pandemic closed her school in Boston. Even now, she remembers the feeling of fear she had as she contemplated all the unanswerable questions swirling around her. "Am I ever gonna be able to see people again? When is this going to end and when am I going to have a normal life after this?" She told us, "We didn't know, we couldn't see the end and we didn't know how bad it was. We didn't know what to believe."

Like so many teenagers, Sophia turned to the internet for entertainment, escape, and connection. She found communication over social media could be unpredictable: coming in rapid bursts and then not at all. Not all teenagers felt lonely; many reported feeling closer to their parents, but they still craved opportunities to feel a sense of belonging.[9] To be seen and accepted. Without their classmates and friends to provide a sense of camaraderie and connection, where did they go? How did they reallocate their time that was once spent hanging out with friends? You probably already know the answer.

The Rise of Parasocial Relationships

In its earliest days, the internet functioned largely as a way to facilitate rapid information sharing. ARPAnet was designed to facilitate the rapid transfer of scientific and technical knowledge between scientists and their respective institutions. But the most lasting social impact of this revolution of global connectivity was not instantaneous information sharing across vast distances. The internet fundamentally altered the way humans communicated with one another because it dramatically lowered the cost of doing so. Whether email, text messages, or DMs on social media platforms, electronic communication could be accomplished with very little personal effort. It also introduced substantial ambiguity into personal exchanges—when does a text-based conversation end? Yet, perhaps one of the lasting ways that online communication altered the social and romantic landscape was by giving individuals access to many more people to communicate with. On social media platforms, a single user can engage with hundreds or even thousands of followers in mostly one-sided interactions. Social media reoriented courtship and social strategies to prioritize attention-seeking, audience-building activities rather than establishing mutual understanding between individuals.

When the pandemic forced young adults into extended social isolation, their relationships deteriorated, including their dating and sex lives. Of course, men and women relate to one another in countless ways in different contexts, but their approaches to sexual relationships are uniquely revealing—they expose our personal priorities, intimate longings, and vulnerabilities. The sale of condoms dropped 40 percent during the pandemic, according to the world's largest manufacturer of contraceptives.[10] But the demand for companionship, physical affection, and sex all increased as people were simultaneously largely shut off from these experiences. And so, if the pandemic was bad for Americans' sex and romantic lives, it was great for social media platforms offering an approximation of those things.

When OnlyFans launched in 2016, it was a niche website. That changed dramatically after 2020. From 2019 to 2023, the number of registered users on the platform increased from 13.5 million to 305 million.[11] Now, OnlyFans has 4.6 million content creators and, at least among young adults, has become as well-known as other popular social media platforms.

The OnlyFans user base is predictably male. There are no official statistics of OnlyFans users, but in a nationally representative survey we conducted in 2025, men accounted for roughly three-quarters of the subscriber base.* They also tend to be young. Younger men report higher rates of use than older men—roughly one in eight young men report that they've subscribed to OnlyFans at some point in their lives.[12]

The economics of paying for content produced by a single creator make little sense. Even the most prolific podcaster or writer can only offer a single perspective, based on limited personal experience and knowledge. *The New York Times,* with its army of more than two thousand writers and editors, delivers hundreds of well-researched news stories from around the world to readers each day, and it costs about the same as a Substack subscription to a single author. Because of authoritative content and access, a *New York Times* subscription provides so much more bang for your buck both in terms of the topical variety and amount of original analysis and reporting. But the size of the *Times'* readership has always made it challenging to cultivate personal connections with individual readers. Americans are not seeking more reliable information, but opportunities to be seen and heard, and new platforms emerged to fill this need.

The tremendous growth of Substack and OnlyFans is not due to the fact that this type of content is not accessible anywhere else; rather, it's because these platforms connect creators and writers di-

* This figure includes respondents who indicated they have ever used OnlyFans, as well as those who have used the site in the past year.

rectly to their subscribers. Gen Z's growing trust in social media for news, most of which is sourced to traditional outlets, is largely based on the personal connection influencers develop with their followers. Asynchronous communication is a critical ingredient in the rise of parasocial relationships. It's not possible for creators to have an individual relationship with each of their thousands of followers, but they can host Ask Me Anything–style chats, respond to follower questions in real time, share individual messages (DMs), cultivate inside jokes, and broadcast unguarded feelings. And this is precisely what they do. Social media platforms offer a range of features to facilitate creator-subscriber relationships, including private group chats, live and prerecorded videos, and virtual events. All these features were designed to create a sense of connection and community.

Similarly, paying a single creator to produce sexually explicit content when the internet is awash with pornography makes no sense. But what if that creator knew your name and responded to your personal requests? What is that worth? Mary Harrington of *The Wall Street Journal* writes that the success of platforms like OnlyFans is not about the product but the experience. "What it offers isn't just sexual release, but something that feels a bit like a relationship—a subscription girlfriend, if you will, without any of the inconveniences that come with a real one."[13] The success of OnlyFans is built on twin pillars of male loneliness and sexual objectification. One of the chief ways OnlyFans attracts a male audience is by making the creators feel real and accessible. They aren't professional performers, but relatable amateurs.

If men—who are the vast majority of OnlyFans subscribers—prefer this type of relationship, who are we to judge?[14] But it's not clear if they actually do. Many men who became subscribers to OnlyFans did not seek out companionship from creators on the site. They were first enticed after encountering the creators' profiles on other social media platforms. For single men ignored on dating platforms, with few friends and limited social outlets, the immediate availability and instant gratification provided by an OnlyFans creator is potent medicine. But it's not real. There is a level of deception involved in OnlyFans transactions that is inherently manipulative. The goal for OnlyFans creators is to provide subscribers with a manufactured intimacy that will entice them to keep spending their money and time. This, it turns out, is a key competitive advantage. Private chat fees—what users pay to interact with creators—account for 70 percent of OnlyFans's total revenue.[15]

A subscription to an OnlyFans account is only the beginning of the transactional relationship. Creators use a variety of tools to upsell their already paying subscribers. They will offer premium content, in the form of images or videos, that all cost extra. The goal for OnlyFans creators is essentially extractive—it is to use whatever means necessary to squeeze a bit more out of their often desperate or deluded subscriber base. The primary method of hawking additional content is through online chats or DMs that connect subscribers directly to creators. But this too is often an illusion. Even modestly popular OnlyFans creators have management agencies taking on the work of communicating with their many adoring subscribers. They hire out low-wage workers (both men and women) to engage in intimate and erotic conversations with subscribers on behalf of creators who will never speak to them. In a revealing exposé, *Wired* reporter Brendan Koerner set out to work as an OnlyFans "chatter," as they are commonly referred to in the industry.[16] The agency Koerner signed up with offered various learning sessions to teach him various skills: The titles included "Scripts and Storytelling" and "High Spender Retention." The goals were always to get subscribers to spend more money, even if it meant engaging in various forms of dishonesty. For instance, it is not uncommon for creators to claim images and videos taken a year earlier were created solely for the subscriber.

Certainly, the men who subscribe to OnlyFans content are guilty of some amount of self-deception. On some level, subscribers must realize what Koerner reveals in his exposé: "The mathematical realities of the platform"—there are 4.6 million creators and 377.5 million subscribers—would make it impossible for individual creators to hold conversations with each of their subscribers.[17] I still think it's difficult to argue the entire enterprise is not in some way predatory. OnlyFans promises a way for creators to "monetize content and develop authentic connections with their fans," but there is nothing "authentic" about any of this.

The problem with parasocial relationships is that they are fundamentally transactional—the relationship ceases when the subscription ends. Even in the least manipulative instances, these relationships only provide an illusion of closeness and connection. Ultimately, they fail to provide what all people need: genuine human connection. Social media platforms like OnlyFans are designed to create this illusion. Worse, they prey on people, mostly men, who are seeking some form of intimacy.

It may feel uncomfortable to sympathize with an OnlyFans creator who uses the platform to earn a few extra dollars. Sex work is still consistently condemned in the United States even as the consumption of pornographic material has become more widely accepted. Before we rush to judgment, we might reflect on how we got here. A society that routinely sexualizes girls and young women, that fails to adequately protect them from exploitation, and introduces them to technology that rewards their exposure, cannot possibly be surprised when some number are willing to take the next logical step. I won't deny the importance of personal agency, but the responsibility is collective. Pornography consumption has become a nearly universal experience for young adults. That's not a sign of a broken person but a broken culture.

Not everyone will agree. What seems abundantly clear at this point is that whatever the financial benefit to OnlyFans creators, the widespread use of the platform creates relational problems between men and women. The type of transactional intimacy offered by OnlyFans comes at a significant emotional cost. Men who focus their romantic attention on OnlyFans creators deprive themselves of the opportunity to practice empathy, communicate respectfully, and learn to put the needs of others before their own. They learn that what women value about them is their finances and, in turn, that women exist primarily to serve their immediate sexual and emotional needs.

It's probably inevitable that many, if not most, men who use the platform will come away feeling disappointed or rejected. Their need for intimacy and connection will remain unmet, and they may start to blame women for their feelings of inadequacy. For risk-averse young men, OnlyFans offers a much safer way to engage with women—if you have money, there is no fear of rejection. The longer they inhabit the twisted fun house of online parasocial pornography, the more difficult it will be to return to the real world. It's not difficult to see how these types of transactional interactions with women might lead to an incel chat forum.

Single men are hardly the only ones affected. Despite a reputation for attracting socially awkward singles, many men who engage with OnlyFans creators are in romantic relationships. In fact, more than half of men who visited the OnlyFans website in the last twelve months are in a committed relationship, cohabitating, or married.[18] Not everyone will care and certainly many women will not be surprised, but this feels tragic. The more our emotional energy and attention is diverted into maintaining these artificial connections, the less we have for the people in our lives who truly need it.

America's Dating Problem Is a Social Problem

America's romantic recession won't be solved with more sophisticated dating algorithms or creative mating strategies. Hinge, for example, recently launched an AI dating coach to teach users to flirt more effectively, while others are experimenting with AI concierge services that can make the first move for you. But technology that reduces incentives for social interaction is ultimately self-defeating. This is fundamentally a problem of social connection. Over the past thirty years, the number of close friends that Americans have has declined dramatically. Americans are less likely to have a best friend, too. We also have fewer siblings on average and, consequently, fewer cousins. Our social worlds are also populated less with weak social ties—the type of people we run into occasionally but do not know well. The fact that we also have fewer romantic partners, spouses, girlfriends, and boyfriends is simply an extension of this larger societal trend. Every type of relationship we've lost has made our lives smaller in both measurable and immeasurable ways.

When it comes to our social networks, size matters. In one recent survey, we found that the number of close friends people have was closely tied to feelings of belonging, inclusion, and isolation. Previous research has found equally strong correlations with feelings of depression, anxiety, and even self-reported physical health.[19] The largest differences are found not between those with no friends and those with only a few, but rather between those with only a few friends and those with many friends. A vast body of research has shown that the robustness of our social networks is linked to greater interpersonal trust and more active civic participation. Without strong social connections, establishing trust with others is nearly impossible, and the wounds we inevitably experience run deeper and heal more slowly. A variety of social connections provides us with opportunities to participate in a wider array of activities and experiences. This was the central conclusion of the Harvard Study of Adult Development, an eighty-six-year-long longitudinal study focused on human flourishing: It is nearly impossible to live a good and meaningful life without a lot of people in it.

Americans With Fewer Friends Feel More Isolated, Left Out, and Ignored

Percentage of Americans who say that, in the past 4 weeks, they sometimes or often felt . . .

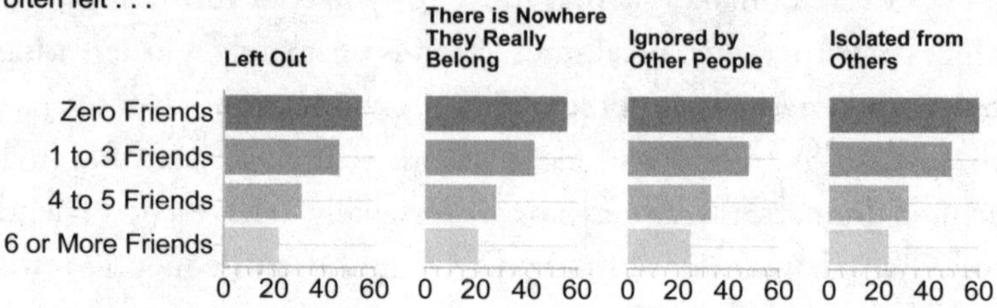

Note: "Friends" refers to close friends, excluding relatives.
Source: AEI Survey Center on American Life, American Social Life Survey, 2025.

Technologists are unlikely to be saviors of American social life. In an interview with podcast host Dwarkesh Patel, Mark Zuckerberg said he trusts that people using AI chatbots are the best judges of how they spend their time—and if they want to devote hours talking to an artificial companion, who is Meta to stop them? Zuckerberg is, however, right when he says, "The average person wants more connection than they have." Our 2021 study on friendship found that less than half of young adults reported they were satisfied with the number of friends they had. They are even less satisfied when you ask them about their broader social lives. However, Zuckerberg's prescription is wrong. So is that of every person working on AI products that are designed to help people with "social tasks." There is a growing body of research focused on the social impact of AI chatbot use, although little on the long-term implications of extended use. The early evidence is alarming. AI companions are not helping young people establish firmer connections with their peers, but instead offering an attractive, low-risk substitute to real social interactions. In one month, Character.AI found that users spent an average of ninety-three minutes a day talking to their personalized chatbot.[20] Teaching adolescents and young adults to use AI companions for advice, to navigate challenging social situations, and for emotional support is teaching them not to rely on one another.

Interestingly enough, though dating apps have become an increasingly common way people find a romantic partner, more Americans are still meeting offline than on. Even for Americans under age forty, most met their spouse or partner at work, at school, or through shared social ties.[21] Churches and places of worship are still effective ways to find a romantic partner for those who attend regularly—one in five report having met their spouse or partner there. But even though many of us still meet out in the real world, and prefer it to the alternative, the attraction of apps is undeniable. No matter how unpleasant the overall experience, the single act of asking someone out requires so little effort of them.

Social media and dating apps are marketed as a complement to real-world experiences by making the act of connecting with people easier and more efficient. What they accomplished instead was to cannibalize our valuable time and attention. They have diminished our shared social experiences by separating us from one another, even when we inhabit the same space. The rise of social media exacerbated America's growing social and civic vacuum. We continue to live in the shadow of civic decline that Robert Putnam first noticed more than a quarter-century ago. The solution to this decline is not novel; we must set about the work of reinvigorating our social, civic, and religious institutions. Individual relationships—that can require so much time and attention—are more easily sustained and fortified through shared institutional or community membership.

For this rebuilding to happen, we need to find places in the real world to spend time with and around each other. Our most lasting relationships are formed in places we spend the most time: neighborhoods, schools, workplaces, and churches. Close to half of college graduates report having made a close friend at their office or workplace.[22] The reason is not difficult to understand. At least in the recent past, Americans spent a considerable amount of time with their colleagues, which helped foster trust and a sense of companionship. There are a number of reasons why religious communities have been such powerful drivers of social connection and civic participation, but the routinization of in-person contact is undeniably a critical component. Attending worship services requires no scheduling or coordination, and in many communities, the strong social expectation for attendance reduces the burden of individual planning. Even living in a community with a high density of local commercial and public places—bars, restaurants, coffeehouses, parks, and libraries—is associated with a stronger feeling of belonging. Most Americans used to have a regular place they could go where they'd engage in planned or impromptu social exchanges with members of their local community. After the pandemic, fewer do.

Our romantic lives are downstream from our social experiences. To me, this is a central insight Christine Emba offers in her book *Rethinking Sex*. "Our sex lives are still socially constructed: how we talk about sex, what we expect from our interactions with each other and how we behave."[23] If our social experiences are limited, our romantic lives are more likely to be constrained through fear, doubt, and insecurity.

Frictionless

The modern world is designed to reduce friction. Good design is meant to make our interactions with the world seamless, requiring less physical or cognitive effort. Relying on DoorDash eases the burden of feeding ourselves, but we lose the opportunity to sharpen our cooking skills in the process. Having GPS has allowed us to easily navigate without consulting maps, road atlases, or help from strangers. But I feel less confident driving around the city without it. There's no doubt that these conveniences make our lives easier, but they diminish our sense of capability. We're increasingly applying this same principle to the social world. A frictionless society is one that becomes less patient, less tolerant of ambiguity, and less willing to deal with uncertainty. It's been a disaster.

The problem with trying to make social interactions seamless is that they lose their value in the process. The modern dating marketplace has become so much more seamless that social interactions are less memorable and less meaningful because they require little risk and even less effort. Because dating apps present us a sea of strangers, singles are often less invested in romantic connections in their early stages. Prioritizing frictionless interactions makes us more productive—we can swipe through more profiles, message more people, and go out on more dates. But the experience teaches us to value each interaction less. Nobody owes you anything, not even basic courtesy or respect. That's why so many early online interactions never materialize into real-life exchanges. Instead, singles filter through endless profiles, decipher curt messages, and endure periods of silence, last-minute cancellations, and dismissive affectations. It makes the entire process feel exhausting.

The more first dates singles go on, the less inclined they are to give any one person the benefit of the doubt. This is even more true when the people they are dating have no connection to their social network. Only 11 percent of single women (and 16 percent of single men) say they would go on a second date with someone they met online if the first date was subpar.[24] That number jumps up by over thirty points when it comes to someone who was introduced by a mutual acquaintance or a close friend. In this scenario, close to half of singles report that they would be willing to give their date another shot. There are plenty of reasons people have mediocre dates: nervousness, lack of chemistry or interest, even simple miscommunication. Yet whatever the reason, your odds of having a second shot are far better if your date has some small connection to your social world.

The steady accumulation of mediocre dating experiences further undermines confidence and trust in the process. One YouGov poll found that 57 percent of women reported having gone on a "terrible" date, compared to 44 percent of men.[25] I've heard plenty of these stories. There was the guy who talked about airplanes and their various features for much of the three-hour date, the gentleman who kept taunting other drivers to street race on the drive home, the woman who was constantly texting her friends during dinner, and so on. These stories monopolize our attention on social media, altering our expectations in the process. It can leave singles feeling unnecessarily anxious. More often, first dates are uneventful experiences in which one or both parties walk away simply feeling "meh" about the other party. They make for boring stories and so we don't tell them.

Heightened sensitivity to social miscues can lead to a broader range of behavior being flagged as potentially disqualifying. It explains why so many singles, especially women, end up dating the people already embedded in their social network—their colleagues, classmates, and friends. Half of young women who are in a committed relationship reported that the person they are currently dating was a friend first. This statistic may surprise some people. There is a vigorous online discourse on whether women "friendzone" young men who would otherwise make good romantic partners. In more misogynistic spaces, women are accused of trying to date above their status and leaving quality men as backups or placeholders. The truth is that when young women can fully evaluate young men on a broad range of qualities—and young men have the opportunity to demonstrate value beyond their earning potential or attractiveness—it results in better outcomes. These relationships emerge out of repeated positive social interactions.

The cultivation of a robust group of friends provides considerable benefits in dating. Having a larger number of close friends increases opportunities to meet new people. Whether it's a music festival, happy hour, house party, or volunteering in the community, having more friends means getting invited to participate in more social activities. Men with a deep roster of close friends are also more likely to count a few women among them. It also signals to women that they are trustworthy, reliable, or, at the very least, interesting.

Research backs this up. Younger men with more close friends are less likely to be single, and the disparity in relationship status is large. More than half (51 percent) of younger men who have no close friends report they are currently single.[26] In contrast, only one in three younger men with at least six close friends are single. Even among singles, having more close friends is associated with having a more active dating life. Single men with at least four close friends are three times more likely to have gone on a date in the last month than those with three or fewer (27 percent versus 9 percent).

Young Men With Fewer Close Friends Are More Likely to Be Single

Percentage of single younger adults (age 18 to 34) with the following number of friends

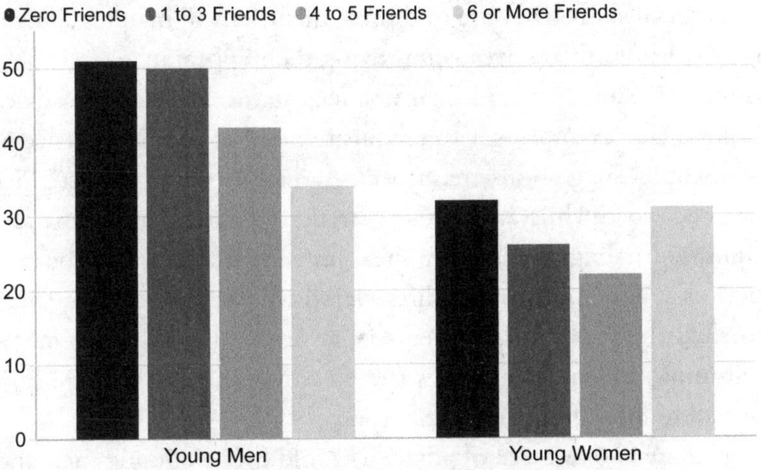

Note: "Friends" refers to close friends, excluding relatives.
Source: AEI Survey Center on American Life, American Social Life Survey, 2025.

In our surveys, young women do not seem to benefit as much from larger friend groups, but other research shows that for both men and women, vibrant social connections are associated with romantic success. A longitudinal study that followed 165 teenagers and young adults found that strong friendships in adolescence were a stronger predictor of romantic life satisfaction in adulthood than dating experience.[27] Even if you're not dating someone, the benefits of having a friend group are enormous. One study found that "doubling the number of friends in real life has an equivalent effect on well-being as a 50% increase in income." The same research found that having a larger network of online connections had no measurable impact on subjective well-being.[28] Fortunately, the very best thing you can do to improve your overall life satisfaction is the same thing that will make you a more attractive partner: Build out your social network.

Instead of cultivating deeper social connections, the advice so many young men get from various internet personalities is to engage in various forms of ascetic self-improvement. Single men are told their romantic success hinges on superficial qualities rather than social skills. They are told these qualities will manifest only if they work on themselves—improving their appearance, their physique, their intellect, and their financial status. Some of the advice is good (for example, get the requisite number of hours of sleep), while other suggestions are suspect. Actually, most of the activities deemed worthwhile are solitary: strength training and sauna sessions, journaling, meditation, meal prep, or listening to educative podcasts. The "monk mode" lifestyle, which encourages young men to shed their social attachments in favor of adopting a regime of self-improvement, exemplifies the idea that relationships are burdensome and solitude is productive.

If there is one piece of advice I would give to young men and women aspiring to find romantic connections, it is simply this:

Hang out more often with your friends offline in ways that maximize the potential for unpredictable outcomes. Not every awkward interaction or perplexing behavior is a dealbreaker or deserving of your derision. Relationships are extended conversations. Hopefully, the early moments are suffused with the heady excitement of possibility, while we fumble around to find a rhythm. Only in novels does the dialogue sing between newly acquainted characters. In the real world, social interactions of all varieties come with a certain amount of risk—usually it's fairly low. What makes them valuable is their capacity to surprise and change us. When an experience becomes too curated, when it becomes predictable and safe, it loses value. The only way to improve our ability to navigate social friction is to experience it, and that means more embodied experience in the physical world.

We're stuck in a vicious cycle where more of us are willing to sacrifice interpersonal interactions because we believe it will spare us from potentially uncomfortable consequences. Ironically, our in-person interactions tend to engender less friction than conversations that occur online. Christine Rosen, in her book *The Extinction of Experience,* cites research that proves our online behavior varies significantly from the real world, even when we're engaged in the same type of activity—for example, trying to impress someone we like. Those findings showed that the quality of conversation was far better in person: "Men and women in online conversations asked fewer questions about the other person and referred to themselves more frequently than the couples meeting face-to-face. Face-to-face conversations—exchanges where we can read bodily cues, facial expressions, and tone of voice—offered a 'deeper and smoother form of social engagement.' "[29] This finding is intuitive. We are better able to recall our experiences with others in the real world than those that happen online. We feel more strongly connected to someone after meeting them in person for a coffee than we do after a Zoom call. We feel this way because real social interaction requires more investment from us. When we are more invested in the interaction, we subsequently care more about the experience and the outcome.

A pair of psychologists, Nick Epley and Amit Kumar, tasked participants in a study to contact an old friend via phone or email.[30] Although most study participants expressed a strong preference for sending an email, Epley and Kumar randomly assigned only half the group to draft a written message. Compared to the group that sent an email, the group that talked to their friend on the phone felt "a significantly stronger bond" and left the conversation feeling that they had "really connected." When we fully commit to a social interaction (for example, being present and attentive), it does require more energy, but it provides a much greater social return as well.

Young adults are not oblivious to what has been lost. There are more conversations happening online about the erosion of the "small favors economy"—or the notion that communities are relying less and less on one another for favors like borrowing a friend's dress for a special event, mowing a neighbor's lawn, or the all-too-dreaded helping a friend move. These are tasks that could—and likely will—inconvenience us to some extent. Why offer to drive your neighbor to the airport during rush hour when they could just order an Uber? Do you really need to help your friend build their new bed frame when they could just hire someone on Taskrabbit?

Our current social standards tell us that inconveniencing a friend, neighbor, or colleague can jeopardize the relationship. In fact, the opposite is true. Research has found that when we help someone out, we actually feel closer to them. Asking for help is additive, not subtractive. One young woman on TikTok explains that we all need to get "a little more comfortable with the idea of inconvenience." She says: "If you ask your friend for a favor, they'll ask you for a favor, and it's a great cycle and great way to deepen that friendship and stop our loneliness epidemic." The video received over a million views and has thousands of comments, many of which voice a similar desire to be "inconvenienced" by their friends.[31] We aren't alone in wanting change. But we need to relearn what it means to ask for and receive help—it's not about solving discrete tasks or individual problems; it's about the work of weaving our lives together.

CHAPTER 10

THE THRESHOLD QUESTION

In all the ways that dating has evolved to reflect modern sensibilities, gender roles, and new mediums of communication, there is one way that heterosexual coupling remains inflexibly traditional. Money. More specifically, the role that financial standing plays in the evaluation of romantic partners.

For men, financial success is a critical component of their dating outcomes. A couple years ago, as part of a major national study on the state of dating, we developed an extensive set of personal qualities that Americans deemed important for a romantic partner to possess. In a list of nearly twenty attributes, there was one that stood out for single women looking for a long-term partner or spouse: employment status.[1] This was judged as more important than height, politics, religion, or education, and was true regardless of a woman's politics, religious background, race or ethnicity, or educational background. Economic potential was the most consistent and key consideration in partner selection. For most single women looking for a committed relationship, this is the threshold question.

Despite the immense educational and economic progress that women have made, there remains a basic asymmetry in how men and women evaluate potential romantic partners. A Pew survey found that for singles dating online, occupational information carries far more weight for women than for men. Less than one in three noncollege men said it mattered whether a dating profile included someone's occupation. In contrast, more than six in ten noncollege women—and eight in ten college-educated women—said occupational information was an important factor in evaluating a potential match.[2] In the eyes of both men and women, a man's capacity to provide is still inextricably tied to his financial prospects. Women are not subject to the same standards. More than seven in ten Americans believe that "what makes a man a good partner" is his ability to support a family.[3] Only 32 percent of the public say the same of women. Importantly, men and women have nearly identical views when it comes to evaluating men. Men recognize that their value as partners is in large part based on their material contributions.

This feels profoundly dissonant given the kind of conversations we have about dating and relationships. That men are still expected to be providers is not a quirky holdover from traditional courtship; it is still a central feature that governs much of modern dating dynamics, yet it is so rarely addressed. At the same time that boys are taught to celebrate the achievements and success of women, they are coming to realize that their value as men is still based on their capacity for provision. These lessons are often not subtle. In social media posts that garner millions of views, women discuss their dating standards that frequently include financial requirements that can include a six-figure income, that a man "pays for everything," or even a 750+ credit score. There are certainly less ridiculous examples, but the overall message communicated to young men is that their own financial status is a critical part of their appeal.

To be sure, there are a lot of ways societal standards for men and women are unfair or harmful. For centuries, women have had to negotiate unrealistic demands regarding their physical appearance. They are still excessively judged and casually maligned for what they wear, their weight, and how they carry themselves. They are also socialized to care about their physical presentation and bear the attendant financial burden that entails. Entire industries are dedicated to altering women's physical appearance, from cosmetic surgery, nail salons, makeup, and skincare, to fashion—and these products and services are not cheap. Beauty routines and regimens are not costless either. They take up time and energy as well. Women in their twenties spend on average about twenty minutes more per day on personal grooming than men the same age.[4] But while women are pushing back against pernicious beauty standards, men seem more resigned to the societal pressure placed on them to be providers. For men already floundering in unforgiving economic conditions, these societal expectations feel like throwing them an anvil.

The Class Divide in Dating

Both single men and women can make strong arguments about whether dating is worse for their sex. In the world of online dating, single men can feel invisible or that their value as a partner comes more from what they are rather than who they are. Women can feel overwhelmed having to manage a barrage of incoming messages that can quickly turn aggressive or hostile.[5] Overall, there are abundant examples of romantic disasters—acquired from firsthand experience or secondhand through social media—that support the claims of both single men and women who believe their side has it worse. It's not a competition, and in many cases the challenges are not comparable or even relatable. While single women tend to report a higher number of negative dating experiences, they are also going out on more dates, on average, than men. Many men could not afford to go out on multiple dates a week even if they had the opportunity. If the purpose of dating is the formation of an exclusive relationship or even marriage, which seems like a reasonable assumption, there is one group that has far worse outcomes than almost everyone else. By this metric, young single men without college degrees are struggling the most in the modern dating market. Fifty percent of young men (between ages twenty-four and thirty-five) who do not have a four-year degree are single, compared to only 31 percent of young men with college degrees. The education divide in dating experiences is a chasm for young men. Twenty-eight percent of younger women without a college degree are single, a rate roughly similar to college-educated women (24 percent). Obviously, these statistics tell us nothing about the quality of romantic experiences or the stability of these relationships, but for men without degrees the struggle is more fundamental: It is about being chosen at all.

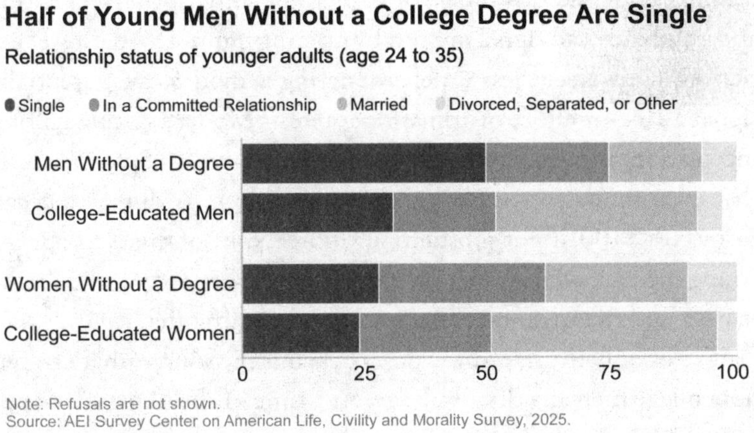

So why are so many men without degrees single? It's not necessarily due to a lack of effort or interest. More than anything, studies consistently show that what seems to be damaging the romantic prospects of these men is their comparative lack of financial resources. The reason is obvious. For men, dating can be an expensive proposition. In one study of singles, roughly nine in ten men paid for the first date, and a majority paid for subsequent outings as well.[6] Despite dramatic changes in the economic fortunes of men without college degrees, in this way, dating culture remains locked in another era. The same study found that nearly 80 percent of men, and most women, still expect that men will pay for the first date.

Wealthy men have always had an advantage on the dating market, but dating apps have, if anything, increased it. Men are more likely than women to pay for dating apps, and those who struggle to get matches are offered additional ways to boost the visibility of their profile—for an added cost.[7] Hinge offers users a "Superboost" feature that will elevate your profile for twenty-four hours for a one-time fee of $29.99. Higher-income men tend to spend more on dating apps, in all likelihood because they can afford to. Men with resources can take advantage of higher-tier subscriptions on dating apps, and they can signal interest by offering impressive dating experiences. Conversely, less expensive dating activities can potentially signal a lack of effort or romantic interest. Modern dating culture incentivizes meeting and dating a larger pool of people, meaning that even modest expenses can quickly add up. A dinner out can easily cost $100, if not substantially more. None of this is a secret—young men are well aware of the asymmetry they face in the dating market and the advantage that status and wealth offer.

It's not only the size of the paycheck, but the source, that can put noncollege men at a disadvantage. At a time of shrinking social opportunities, the workplace frequently serves as a critical social hub, especially for younger workers who have less established networks. But white-collar work environments tend to more effectively promote social connection. Our research shows that college graduates establish closer and more enduring connections with their co-workers than those without degrees.[8] While the same social dynamics that help colleagues form friendships can foster romantic connections, these opportunities vary considerably across workplace environments. Noncollege men tend to work in more gender-segregated professions, such as construction or building trades, and thus have fewer opportunities to meet and socialize with women in the workplace. They are also far more likely to work in solitary occupations, whether that's long-haul trucking or gig work, such as driving for Uber or DoorDash. Even when noncollege men work in service-oriented industries that include more even gender ratios, turnover tends to be common, making it difficult to foster social or romantic connections.

It's not only a deficit of workplace connections that limits potential romantic opportunities for these men. Compared to college graduates, men without degrees are less socially active by almost every conceivable measure—they report lower levels of membership in gyms, churches, book clubs, and intramural sports leagues. They are far less active in their communities as well, spending less time out at restaurants, bars, and coffee shops than college graduates. This is not entirely a question of financial resources either. These men are also found less often in places that have no financial barrier to entry, such as community centers, public parks, and libraries. Whether due to economic constraints or individual initiative, they demonstrate lower rates of social and civic activity by nearly every conceivable metric. It reinforces social separation and reduces opportunity. Everything becomes harder.

Dating platforms are an obvious solution for less socially active men, but digital dating has its own challenges. Single men without degrees are far less successful dating online. Only about six in ten of these men say they have ever gone on a date with someone they met on a dating app; it's north of eight in ten for college-educated men.[9] Research has shown that while male evaluations of female attractiveness tend to be fairly stable, there is greater variability in what women find attractive in men.[10] Being able to signal resources in profile photos—such as a finely decorated apartment, expensive clothes, or an exotic travel destination—offers a competitive advantage in a dating environment that requires rapid and superficial evaluations. Single women value honesty and generosity in romantic partners, often more so than many single men realize, but it is far easier to advertise wealth and status on dating apps than kindness, consideration, or loyalty. Thus, dating apps provide more of an advantage for well-resourced users who can more effectively attract strangers using superficial cues. As a result, there is a massive experience gap in dating platforms. Only 47 percent of men without a college degree compared to 64 percent of college-educated men reported a positive experience dating online.[11]

To make matters worse, the acute economic anxiety many young people feel about the future alters their risk calculation. Marriage is increasingly viewed as a potential liability—what it might cost if it fails—rather than the stability and security a lifetime partnership provides. At one time, marriage offered a sense of financial security for two people trying to make it in the world. Marrying early meant having a partner to contribute socially, emotionally, and financially during the earliest part of adulthood. Marriage was a cornerstone institution on which a good life was built. Today, more young singles have adopted a capstone view of marriage—it is an achievement that is unlocked only after having secured at least a modicum of financial stability. Damian, a young man we talked to in Raleigh, said that a good life required investing in yourself before taking on additional responsibilities. "[It's about] taking care of yourself first, then worry about building the family and all that . . . everything else will fall in line." Too many young men I have talked to over the past year believe that they are not going to be an attractive option if they cannot demonstrate some degree of professional or financial success.

I don't believe that young single men without college degrees are less interested in finding a partner, although many are more cynical about the endeavor. Their pessimism is not the result of failures to find someone who meets their criteria. Compared to other singles, men without degrees demonstrate greater flexibility in their dating preferences. They place less emphasis on political or religious alignment, a potential partner's employment status, or lifestyle factors such as smoking. Physical appearance—a critical dating criteria for most of us—is arguably less important to them as well. One study found that these men were much less likely than women with or without degrees to require online dating profiles to include a photo.[12] This research challenges the stereotype that these men are seeking bombshell "tradwives" who are equally servile and supportive. The reality is that men struggling economically are aware that their social and romantic fortunes are indelibly tethered to their financial outcomes. American culture has sold young people on the idea that they can be anyone and do anything, but experiences on the dating market quickly shatter this illusion. It's a lot to ask anyone to work themselves to the bone all for the sake of the chance of meeting someone on a dating app. Making personal sacrifices for the ghost of a romantic possibility is a good deal harder than it is to do for someone real.

Invisible Men and Disappointed Women

Before the internet, social life and romantic opportunities were geographically limited, determined by where you lived, the type of work you did, and the organizations you belonged to. It was a smaller and more socially controlled world, with clearer boundaries. A young man could meet a potential girlfriend at church, at school, at the animal shelter where he volunteered, or at the restaurant where he bused tables. Today, the same young man faces competition from a greater number of peers. The girl next door might have been his neighbor for his whole life, but her world now includes a vast pool of strangers vying for her attention.

The rise of dating apps has coincided with a remarkable increase in the number of dating partners reported by the most romantically successful men. One study found that the top 5 percent of sexually successful men increased their number of sexual partners by a whopping 32 percent from 2003 to 2013, while men who had fewer sexual partners to begin with reported dramatically fewer partners.[13] In our own research, we find the number of romantic or sexual partners that men have is stratified by educational attainment. Younger men (age twenty-four to thirty-nine) with a high school education or less are far more likely than those with a college degree to report that they have not had a sexual or romantic partner (39 percent versus 21 percent).[14]

It's not only that less financially successful men are ignored on dating apps, but when they turn to social media, they see what they're missing. It's an experience that feels deeply personal and profoundly discouraging. For Joseph, a single man who participated in one of our studies, dating has been a trial. He currently lives at home with his parents in Jacksonville, Florida, and has tried to connect with women online, without much success. He wonders if that's because of the things he's doing. After all, there are plenty of men who are successfully attracting attention from women online. On Instagram, Joseph says he regularly sees attractive male content creators receive objectifying comments from women who post eggplant emojis and make sexually explicit requests. For young men like Joseph, there seem to be different rules for different types of men. He's not alone. Social media is awash in posts arguing that judgments about toxic and creepy behavior operate on a sliding scale. Physically and financially desirable men seem to be able to engage in sexually suggestive back-and-forth with women, while other men cannot. It's not as if women are not subjected to social constraints on their behavior themselves—they face plenty—but they generally have greater latitude in how they interact with men online. The lesson many single men take away from these virtual experiences is that being kind and considerate is less important than maximizing their attractiveness and wealth. This attitude manifested in the "looksmaxxing" movement, which holds that advancing one's aesthetic appeal should be the highest priority.

The shallowness of online dating culture doesn't just impact male self-esteem; it's also changing the way romantic relationships play out as well. Today's dating landscape has made it easy for attractive and affluent men to find short-term dating prospects, but our research has shown that an abundance of options can reduce interest in long-term partnership. It is easier for sexually successful men to pursue multiple women concurrently with little social constraint. This has led some men to adopt dating strategies that maximize opportunities for casual sex and delay long-term commitment. Dating apps just heighten this approach by allowing a smaller group of romantically successful men to monopolize attention from an even larger group of women. It creates an asymmetry of dating interest as wealthy and attractive men engage with different goals—prioritizing short-term sexual relationships—than many of the women they interact with. It is a recipe for disappointment and disillusionment.

This is happening not just on dating apps. On the college campuses we visited, it was not uncommon to hear female students, with a note of weariness, mention how easy it was for their male peers to get girlfriends. Many of these universities have gender ratios that favor men (women outnumber men on college campuses overall, with three female students for every two male students). Studies have shown that these women go on fewer traditional dates yet are more sexually active, and rate the overall dating experiences worse when the gender ratios on campus become too imbalanced.[15] The authors concluded that when men exercised greater control over dating dynamics, without social controls to moderate their behavior, traditional dating and coupling was less common. With more women competing for fewer single men, there is less incentive for men to commit because of the widespread availability of romantic alternatives. For women, dating and relationship preferences remained the same, but their bargaining power was greatly diminished.

Too many interactions with disinterested men leads to predictable results. When dating becomes too grueling, more ambitious young women may decide to opt out altogether, choosing instead to focus their energies on their education or career. William Costello, a psychology professor at the University of Texas whom I spoke with, believes that the rising levels of financial autonomy may lead more women to simply give up on dating entirely. "What we might find is that for the first time, women are free to choose singlehood rather than settle for a man that they need out of economic necessity or a really strict social norm," he said.[16] In our own research, we found that, for college-educated women, one of the most frequently cited reasons they reported for being single is the inability to find a partner who meets their expectations.[17] This finding was used as "evidence" that women have ridiculous or unrealistic standards, but the answer is hardly so clear-cut. Women face less pressure to find a partner and enjoy greater financial security than they once did, but they are often less certain about whether the person they want to date shares the same relationship goals. Uncertainty can rapidly sink into indecision when the stakes feel so high. In individualistic societies, partner selection is crucial because so much of our affection, support, and companionship rests in a single person.

The pressure to get it right, and the fear of making a poor choice, weighs heavily on those who want to find a partner. But not everyone pays the same price when dating culture breaks down. When any system malfunctions, it almost always punishes those with the least while leaving an escape hatch for those better off. For non-college men, the social and civic structures that once provided them a way to move forward have largely disappeared, leaving them romantically adrift. Disadvantages compound. Those with the least social support struggle the most to build it.

There is a risk in focusing too much on current relationship challenges between these social classes and not enough on what's at stake long-term. Most college-educated men and women will get married at some point, even if they have to endure a fair number of mediocre dates to get there. At age forty, one in three Americans without degrees is currently unmarried—it's about half that number for college graduates.[18] Because men without college degrees have fewer close friends, they will go through their lives receiving less support, love, and companionship. At one time, social class indicated the things you could afford to buy, or the places you could afford to live. Now, it strongly predicts the type of social life you have, the number of people who will care what happens to you, and your odds of finding a meaningful long-term relationship. Worse, many young working-class men blame their social and romantic failures on themselves. This self-blaming erodes their confidence long-term. Perhaps this is due to masculine norms that encourage stoicism and self-reliance, or a resistance to acknowledging structural influences. Or perhaps it is simply their lived experience. One large-scale study found that there was less public support for programs designed to help disadvantaged men, and Americans more readily attributed poor outcomes for men to their own lack of effort.[19] Regardless of the reason, many young men feel expendable, that society cares less about their welfare, and that they are less deserving of help.

When sociologist William Julius Wilson first introduced the

term "marriageable men" in 1987 to describe a man's relational value, it was based on a single economic metric—their employment status. What made a man a worthy partner was his ability to hold down a full-time job. Since then, scholars have developed more sophisticated definitions that incorporate criminal record, dependencies, and mental health status. I can't say I much care for the term, and not because it is offensive or reductive, although it clearly is the latter. At least in popular usage, the term overly focuses on current circumstances without regard to an individual's trajectory. We are more than a snapshot of our lives at a single point.

Even after we've reached adulthood, we are still capable of unimaginable growth. We can acquire wisdom, learn patience, and develop perspective. After fourteen years of marriage, and nearly a decade as a parent, I would argue that I am more marriageable today than I was when I first proposed. Relational value should be determined by the strength of someone's commitment, the burdens he carries, the attention he gives, and the compassion he shows. I don't think being able to financially support a family is irrelevant dating criteria, but we've lost sight of what makes someone truly valuable as a partner and a person.

CHAPTER 11

COUPLING IN A ME-FIRST CULTURE

In countless conversations with young adults on the topic of dating and romantic relationships, one recurring theme that regularly emerges is how risky commitment seems to be. Men argue that women will take advantage of them financially, or that once committed their partners will become sexually disinterested in them. Women believe that domestic responsibilities will not be equally shared, or that their partners will become social and emotional burdens on them. Both sides appear to be motivated by a strong sense of loss aversion. More young people are motivated to avoid negative outcomes rather than the pursuit of positive ones.

Today's dating culture has a preoccupation with identifying potential relationship pitfalls and problems. Lifetime commitments—such as marriage and parenthood—entail proportionally greater risks, and young adults are proceeding cautiously. Surveys show that of the varying critical life goals, marriage tends to rank toward the bottom. For me, one of the more remarkable developments—and certainly one of the most tragic—is how impermanent young singles believe marriage to be. Only about half of teenagers believe that it is "very likely" that they would stay married to the same person for their entire life, down from roughly six in ten a few decades earlier.[1]

Why is this happening? Why do romantic relationships feel so risky?

Much of it has to do with a warped understanding of our purpose in life. As I've noted throughout the book, American society is increasingly governed by the principles of expressive individualism, which emphasizes authenticity, personal fulfillment, and the pursuit of self-interest over adherence to shared social norms.* Our actions are affirmed not based on the impact they have on others but on the degree to which they are aligned with our true selves. Sociologist Robert Bellah argued that, were it to become the dominant ethic, expressive individualism could lead people to forgo the development of a shared moral framework in pursuit of their own "authentic" truth. It's an appealing ethic at least superficially, but as we've seen, it creates all sorts of relational problems. Commitment feels conditional when relationships are instrumental, serving only individual interests. Compromise can feel like a betrayal because it's no longer about negotiating between competing values or interests, but the suppression of identity.

Things haven't always been this way. But as the practice of regular self-expression on social media became more fully integrated into adolescent experience, young people have taken these early lessons and dutifully applied them through every stage of life. Young adults are trained to see individualism as the highest societal value. They have been taught to mistrust public institutions, taught that they have to compete in a sink-or-swim economic system, and taught to

* Robert Bellah, in *Habits of the Heart,* argued that the rise of "expressive individualism"—the belief that we come to know ourselves through intuition and self-reflection—erodes social solidarity and community.

participate in an all-or-nothing political process. It leaves them without the proper tools or even a serviceable vocabulary to express a commitment to something larger than themselves. America's embrace of hyper-individualism has had disastrous consequences for communal life, but the impact is most evident in how it changed our understanding of one of our foundational social and civic institutions: marriage.

Individualized Marriage

Young adults have not given up on marriage, but their expectations about the institution reflect a culture that understands romantic relationships as transactional rather than formative. Its purpose is to satisfy individual personal needs—social, emotional, and physical—and promote personal growth. The combination of rising economic insecurity and investment in their education has led many young people to express concern about the potential consequences of making a lifetime commitment. Marriage is something that can threaten both their carefully cultivated identity and their well-exercised sense of autonomy. We see this insistence on individuality play out both in the lead-up to marriage and during the actual relationship, and how these small shifts ultimately cost us more than we realize.

Personalized wedding culture is exploding across America. A survey of nearly ten thousand couples by The Knot, a wedding planning website, found that 63 percent of couples felt that personalization of their celebration was critical.[2] More people want their wedding ceremonies to reflect their personal values, their aesthetic, or their "brand" by choosing unique themes, locations, and even merchandise. Some couples design and create their own wedding logos; others incorporate games into their celebrations, such as scavenger hunts, bingo, or trivia.[3] Whatever the aesthetic or the entertainment choices, the goal is to stand out. It's not uncommon for couples to hire brand consultants. In an interview with *The New*

York Times, Becca Atchison, the founding partner of an event-planning company in North Carolina, said that at least one-quarter of their company's wedding budgets are allocated to the development of distinctive branding. "Couples are looking for a level of customization that is so far beyond what was out there even as recently as five or six years ago," she said. For young people, especially women, who have come up documenting major life events, marriage is the ultimate milestone to share online. Where marriages were once primarily community-led celebrations, they are now public performances meant to reflect a couple's unique style and personality.

National surveys bear this out. Few couples are choosing traditional wedding venues, such as a church or place of worship, as they provide less opportunities for customization. Only 30 percent of Americans who were married after 2012 report having their ceremony in a place of worship.[4] Assuredly, this reflects the waning importance of religion in American life, but it also marks a shift in the purpose of these ceremonies. A ceremony that once served to usher a couple into a community has instead become a promotional opportunity to highlight their distinctive aesthetic tastes, values, and lifestyle. Commitment has become content.

It's not only on the day of the wedding that our preoccupation with individuality is apparent: The lives of married couples are less integrated than they were in previous generations for the same reason. By marrying later, more couples have developed their own spending habits and established their own credit profile. They have spent more time managing their finances. For those who have done this successfully, there may be a desire to keep independent control over their financial life even as they merge other parts of their life. Relatedly, there has been a sharp rise in the percentage of couples entering prenuptial agreements. In 2022, The Harris Poll found that 15 percent of engaged or married couples had prenuptial agreements, an increase from 3 percent in 2010.[5]

The rising age of marriage has also altered incentives for some women to keep their maiden names. By their late twenties and early thirties, many women have achieved significant career success or established a professional identity under their given name, making them less enthused to change it. Three in ten married women under the age of forty did not take their husband's last name when they got married.[6] Young women who are currently single express a greater deal of uncertainty about the decision—only 41 percent say affirmatively they would take their future husband's last name.

It's not only worries about work: The expansion of possible lifestyles—what to eat, where to live, what entertainment to enjoy, activities to pursue, people to meet—means there are more ways an individual might have to compromise to make a marriage work. If someone has spent most of their adult life on their own, making their own decisions regarding what to eat, where to live, and generally managing their own affairs, giving up that sense of autonomy can feel disquieting. Making room for another person can limit how fully you can optimize everything for yourself. Even if many of these personal decisions are not all that important, giving them up can feel constraining, especially as singles become more comfortable in the solo lives they have built. If getting married is like stepping off a cliff together, more couples appear to be wanting to keep one foot firmly on the ledge.

Practically speaking, these concerns are understandable, but the instinct to retain personal autonomy can come at a cost. For instance, a study published in *The Journal of Consumer Research* found that couples with joint bank accounts tended to have higher relationship satisfaction than those without.[7] Merging finances can encourage people to have open and honest conversations about their financial goals and plot out their future together. The same is true for maintaining independent social lives. One of the less understood impacts of online dating is that it often means that couples share no common social connections in the real world—people who might be invested in both members of a couple. When couples develop or maintain a shared network of friends, these social connections can reinforce commitment. Research by sociologist Claude Fischer found that relationships in which people have overlapping social connections are less readily abandoned.[8] There are incentives for couples to resolve conflict when it could negatively impact other relationships. Their mutual friends and family members are more willing to nurture the relationship because they have a greater vested interest in seeing it thrive. Marriages that lack this social density become fragile because their success rests entirely on just two people. Merging social worlds can feel risky, but it makes marriages stronger.

Both Gen Z men and women have fears about what marriage will require of them and what they risk losing in the process. The cost-benefit analysis has subtly shifted. Marriage has evolved into a predominantly dyadic relationship, rather than embedding two people in a supportive community. The success of a marriage is judged by weighing the individual benefits it confers against the concessions it requires. In a culture that emphasizes the importance of individuality, the costs are not only lifestyle compromises, but identity: Can I be who I want to be? As habits become more entrenched and personal identity more established, hesitation grows. These concerns are not entirely symmetrical, and in one area in particular, young women are acutely sensitive to the disparity in domestic and emotional demands they may face in relationships with men.

Domestic Divisions

A generation of women who were raised to prioritize their education and professional pursuits have cast a warier eye on marriage. It's not necessarily because they believe marriage is irrelevant or no longer useful—Gallup has probed attitudes about marriage for decades and has reported little change in responses from young women. Rather, whether in practice or on purpose, most single women believe that though gender roles have evolved to various degrees over the past couple of decades, modern marriage is still structured to benefit men often at the expense of women. They feel that the weight of domestic duties will fall more heavily on their shoulders, regardless of their professional success—a fear that has been borne out by research showing that women who out-earn their husbands do not do less housework. Women still face more pressure to demonstrate basic domestic competency and to work harder at making a marriage successful, or even functional. But things have never been more equal—millennial husbands and fathers are doing more than ever. And the vast majority of married women report being satisfied with their marriages and their lives. So why do so many single women still believe marriage represents such a raw deal for them?

Many women experience this relationship dynamic. Sometimes it's taken on willingly as their partners shoulder more responsibilities outside the home, but other times the accumulation of domestic obligations occurs quietly without any acknowledgement. Regardless of their professional ambition, many young women believe that marriage will result in an unfair division of labor—necessitating vigilance and discernment in partner selection. We've seen proof of this sentiment emerge both in our in-person research and in viral online content. In my conversation with Abby, a student at Claremont McKenna College, she told me that one of her biggest concerns about getting married is whether or not she and her partner would prioritize balancing household responsibilities. It would be a problem, she said "if we're both working and then I'm doing all the extra emotional and physical work around the house." The concept of "mental load," the often invisible labor such as planning, organizing, and decision-making taken on disproportionately by women, gained widespread attention in 2017 after a cartoon depiction of it went viral. Although hardly new (the concept of "worry work" had been the subject of a number of academic articles), it was perfectly suited for social media.[9] On TikTok the concept really took off, with tens of thousands of videos about domestic labor and mental load springing up.[10] Whatever the source, the message was remarkably similar. One popular TikTok user put it like this: "The reality is that in most marriages, women get the short end of the stick, like women are the ones who have to sacrifice their careers, their health, their well-being, to take care of their husband and the children."[11] For driven, professionally ambitious women consuming this content, a husband was starting to become less of an asset to their lives and instead a potential liability.

The internet has latched onto a few buzz phrases that capture this sentiment well—one of them being a phenomenon known as *mankeeping*. Angelica Puzio Ferrara, a psychologist at the Clayman Institute for Gender Research at Stanford University, coined this term, and it went viral after being highlighted in a *New York Times* essay. Ferrara theorized that the decline in men's social networks required wives and partners to engage in a form of gendered labor where women take on the burdens of social and emotional support of their male partners.[12] The support covers a range of different behavior, including helping male partners to manage emotional distress, helping them articulate what they are feeling, or continually monitoring their emotional state for signs of problems. The term can also apply to more mundane social tasks, including keeping the family calendars, planning social activities, or assisting in the maintenance of their broader relational lives—such as providing reminders about family members' birthdays. Whatever form it takes, mankeeping behavior is defined as one-sided and extractive—it serves to benefit men while leaving women drained.

Undeniably, heterosexual women serve critical emotional support roles to heterosexual men as their romantic partners and spouses. A 2025 report from the American Institute for Boys and Men found that men are 13 percentage points more likely than women to rely on their spouse as their primary source of personal support.[13] Single men tend to fare the worst on most measures of social support, intimacy, and affection.

What is left out of these viral conversations is that successful relationships are built on incalculable acts of selflessness: the multitude of consideration, support, love, and affection we provide for each other. What we need from each other is not the same. The amount of emotional and social support that people require can vary considerably. Men get far less emotional support and validation from their friends than women do from theirs. In my own research, women are far more likely than men to have told a friend they loved them, to have received emotional support from friends, and to have shared personal feelings or problems with their friends.[14] While you might expect men to feel the effects of these dynamics, men with fewer close friends tend to be just as satisfied with the size of their social circle as women with comparably robust social connections. So what's needed here?

Clearly men should take responsibility for identifying how they are feeling and learn to express their emotions in constructive ways. Women should as well. But I'm wary of arguments that suggest women's emotionally expressive orientation should serve as the default mode or model. Not every feeling or emotional experience is equally deserving of expression, and there is a danger in being overly attentive to our varying emotional states as there is in repression. There are times when emotional restraint is necessary and beneficial—it's about achieving some sort of balance. There is more than one way to provide emotional support: It can be helping someone to identify and articulate how they are feeling, or providing a safe harbor for someone to process disorienting or difficult feelings.

It also means expanding one's range of social connections, which broadens opportunities for emotional and social engagement. Male friendships are a critical part of the equation, and while they will inevitably look different than female friendships, they need to meet the same needs of belonging, support, and affection that are non-negotiable requirements of healthy human existence. Throughout this book, I've argued that constructing a rich web of social connections is critical for men and women. It is the work of a lifetime. We have an obligation to encourage boys and men, girls and women, to nurture these formative relationships and maintain them. Our needs are too many for any single person to handle it all. Marriage is meant to serve as the foundation for community, but too often it falls short.

In the long run, Ferrara and her coauthor, Dylan Vergara, hope that men grow to become more attuned to the inequities of social and emotional labor and step in to ease the burden. "We look to a future where boys and men can create and sustain connection in ways that are unencumbered by rigid masculine norms, and where the meeting of men's social and emotional needs does not depend on women's unpaid and unequal care work," they write. But what are the more immediate implications of the mankeeping theory? The unfortunate conclusion spreading across some corners of social media is that women should do less. Eve Tilley-Colson, a lawyer with an active TikTok following, argued for this explicitly. She said: "We no longer depend on men financially, they need to not depend on us emotionally."[15]

This trend might explain why single women have become primed to believe that people should walk away earlier from unsatisfying marriages. More than three-quarters (77 percent) of single women believe that unhappy couples stay in bad marriages too long, a view shared by only 55 percent of single men.[16] Married Americans are far less inclined to believe that couples remain too long in unsatisfying relationships. Less than half of married men and women express this opinion. If the message from society is that marital relationships are to serve individual interests—rather than functioning as the cornerstone of family life—it makes sense that young women have become more sensitive to the individual demands and burdens they might have to bear.

Three-Quarters of Single Women Believe That Unhappy Couples Stay Married Too Long

Percentage of Americans who say that couples who are unhappy tend to stay in bad marriages for too long

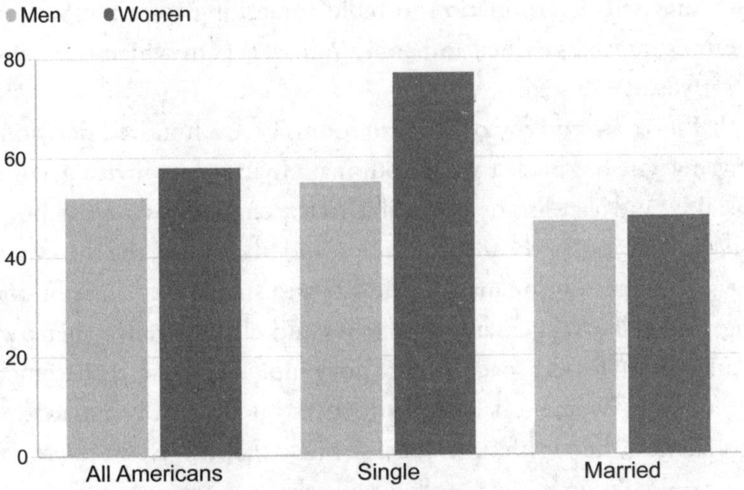

Note: "Single" refers to those who have never been married.
Source: Pew Research Center, American Trends Panel Wave 126, April 2023.

There has been a growing interest in studying the "costs of caring," especially for women.[17] An unequal burden of emotional and social labor is undoubtedly an unhealthy dynamic in any relationship. But the growing concern about what our social lives take from us ignores the fact that relationships are an investment. Their absence makes our lives smaller, meaner, and shorter. At a time of rising disconnection, we should prioritize social abundance by building out a variety of relationships. Men especially need to dedicate more time to fostering connection with the people in their lives, and our various institutions—schools, churches, workplaces—should recognize and rise to support this need. Investing more time and energy in the people around us will yield far better outcomes than restricting our care and consideration.

Domestic Equality

There is a paradox at the heart of every social arrangement we enter into willingly. We must freely give up some amount of personal freedom and self-determination to build something together. Success requires mutual sacrifice and compromise, acts in which trust and practice are essential.

If I look around my own living room, I see a hundred decisions that my wife has made to make our main living space inviting, comfortable, and as resistant as possible to the chaos of two active boys. All the decisions—the plant selection and placement, the throw pillows, the vases on the mantle, the size and shape of the mirror, the rug, and the arrangement of couches and chairs—reflect her particular vision for the space. But it's not simply her space, it's designed for all of us. While it has her distinctive touches, the room accommodates our hectic lifestyle. I feel strongly that this is not the room she would design if it was only for herself.

When it comes to childcare decisions, we engage in more rigorous back and forth, and as a result there are occasional disagreements. It was a difference of opinion over some childcare decision that resulted in one of the more memorable exchanges my wife and I had in over a decade of marriage. I forget how it started, but after several minutes of arguing, my frustration got the best of me. I told her: "You know, if you were not here things would be different!" Without missing a beat, she responded: "If you were not here, things would be exactly the same." That put an abrupt end to that discussion.

Of course, things are more complicated than that, as they are in most marriages. Having sat with that comment for a while, what insight I've managed is that in any couple raising children, individual decisions are regularly made without consultation, but enforcement must be carried out collectively. Big decisions are more easily coordinated, but small parenting decisions often require individual initiative and responsiveness. It's impossible to run the hundreds of decisions parents make every day through a committee. But they matter. Our daily lives are shaped mostly by the steady stream of small decisions. So what can we do? Articulate a shared set of values that can serve to guide individual decisions. But this requires that parents are prescriptive, identifying clearly the type of adult they want their child to be. It can feel anathema to modern child-directed parenting, but without it, families can struggle. If mothers feel overloaded by parenting demands, fathers can feel undermined and micromanaged. Marriage is a continuous conversation—a dynamic and evolving arrangement that thrives when two people maintain a singular focus on a shared goal. If we maintain a commitment to the same set of family values even when we differ or disagree, we are still assured that we're heading in the same direction.

Though women are seeing domestic labor as a risk with marriage, our research shows that dynamics of domestic and emotional labor in marriages are evolving rapidly. This is especially true when it comes to caring for children. Millennial husbands take on a far greater share of domestic responsibilities than their own fathers did. They are more involved parents too. Many millennial fathers accomplished this in the absence of helpful models. I grew up with media portrayals of emotionally immature, lazy, and incompetent fathers—*The Simpsons, Home Improvement, Married with Chil-*

dren, and *Family Guy*. Fatherhood was portrayed not so much as a vital part of child development, but as a source of comedic relief. It was a sideshow. Obviously, these were hardly the only portrayals of fathers found in popular media, but these shows were incredibly popular and, as a result, profoundly influential. Things are different now.

In our household, I make the school lunches. As the more morning-oriented parent, it's an easier assignment for me to take on. I feel a sense of accomplishment that even when we're running low on supplies, I can fix a balanced meal that the boys will (mostly) eat and enjoy. In any setting, and for any task, competency should be the requirement and the expectation. I once asked my oldest son whether he found any of his classmates' lunches better than his own. He said he always preferred what I packed him. You better believe that I take pride in it. There is nothing male or masculine about blundering your way through or shirking responsibilities you have to your family.

Research from the American Institute for Boys and Men shows that not only are fathers doing more today than they ever have, their interest in being attentive and engaged parents has risen as well.[18] Most dads say they want more time with their kids.[19] Another study found that many fathers are more likely than mothers to say workplace demands interfere with their capacity to spend time with their kids. Analysis of the Time Use Survey recorded a 30 percent increase in fathers' household responsibilities from 2019 to 2024. When the pandemic forced fathers to stay home from the office, they did not simply disappear into the study, they took on more household tasks.[20] Incredibly, there is no sign that fathers have reverted to pre-pandemic patterns, as the gap in domestic labor between mothers and fathers continues to shrink. I don't believe this has happened because millennial men were guilted into taking on more domestic responsibilities, but rather they willingly stepped into roles that obligated them to be engaged. It was a recognition rather than a requirement. And their lives are improved through every contribution that they make.

Questions of domestic inequality loom large in many marriages, but taking an accurate measure of individual contributions is complicated. There are many ways to compromise and contribute to a relationship. My wife handles far more of the logistical work in our household, but the nature of her work gives her far less flexibility to handle childcare emergencies during the workday. When the kids have sick days or snow days, I'm our first responder. As a researcher and writer, I control much more of my work schedule, while her days are frequently peppered with meetings and colleague check-ins. What matters more than the exact division of labor at any given moment is that we are full partners in initiating and carrying out the ordinary tasks associated with daily living. Maintaining a balance of labor, affection, and appreciation is always the goal. Marriage requires us to give up some part of our individual selves, to make concessions before they are asked, to deny selfish impulses, and to take on specific responsibilities. To me, the obligations of partnership are not a burden, but motivation—a reason to get up in the morning, to work, and to get better at the things that matter.

Marriage today offers less certainty but greater choice. It can be formed and reformed to fit any manner of preferences or lifestyle choices. Roles that were once clearly defined have to be continually negotiated. Arrangements maintain greater flexibility, but our obligations to each other can be less clear. When the parameters of relationships become too flexible, they lose their shape and no longer serve their formative purpose. Parenthood, marriage, and even friendship presuppose particular responsibilities; these relationships encourage intentionality by directing our actions and, yes, sometimes restraining our individualist impulses. Without a shared cultural understanding, relational roles can frequently fall victim to selfish tendencies or unequal power dynamics—the spouse who demands an open relationship, or the friend who never initiates plans. But unfortunately, this is where we find ourselves, and it heightens the sense of risk associated with entering a marriage. It also makes individuals feel more justified to engage in acts of selfishness and deceitful behavior when they're inside a marriage. Whether this has resulted in rising selfishness in relationships is unclear, but it has coincided with rising concerns about infidelity.

The Risk of Relationship Infidelity

Statistics on infidelity are difficult to come by for obvious reasons. Even survey respondents who are promised confidentiality may be hesitant to admit to engaging in behavior that Americans overwhelmingly condemn. Surveys that reliably track rates of marital infidelity have shown no signs that this behavior has become more prevalent, but this data is limited. Fewer Americans are getting married and even those who do are spending more time in long-term relationships beforehand. We have far less information about infidelity rates of non-marital relationships, but it would certainly not be surprising to find they are higher given that risk is lower; opportunities are greater for couples who don't live together and often have lower levels of investment in the relationship.

The most reliable statistics suggest that, in the era of online dating and social media, relationship infidelity is very common. A 2021 YouGov survey reveals that roughly one in three Americans *have cheated* on their partner—physically, emotionally, or both—while in a monogamous relationship.[21] An even greater share of Americans report having been in a committed relationship with a partner who was unfaithful. A 2023 survey found that four in ten Americans said they had a partner or spouse who had been unfaithful, including nearly half of women.[22] These are not small numbers.

But these statistics most likely underestimate the degree of infidelity due to the increasingly amorphous character of many relationships. When expectations are not well-articulated and the relationship status is unclear, it becomes incredibly difficult to make judgments about unacceptable behavior. Young adults have a well-documented aversion to labels and express more openness to flexible romantic arrangements. Bumble, for instance, introduced multiple new relationship categories like "intimacy, without commitment" and "ethical nonmonogamy," which allow people to skirt conversations about the obligations they have to each other.[23] It's not the only dating and social platform to include ambiguous relationship categories. Facebook now includes an "open relationship" option. The dating platform Hinge offers a diverse array of relationship goals that include "Life Partner," "Long-term relationship," "Long-term, open to short," "Short-term, open to long," "Short-term relationship," and "Figuring out my dating goals." It's difficult to see how this is any help to singles trying to decipher motives in potential dating partners. Dating is a situation in which well-defined labels and clearly specified objectives are extraordinarily helpful. They allow both parties to set clear expectations and boundaries, and, just as importantly, to identify when they have been violated. The problem with these labels is that though they give an illusion of clear expectations, they introduce considerable gray area around responsibility and intentions. They also place all relationship types on equal footing—an open relationship is as valid to pursue as a monogamous life partner. The labels also leave some of the most basic questions unanswered. What specific type of commitment would you like to exclude within your intimate relationships—regular dates, meeting each other's friends, watching their dog for them? How do you know what you owe each other? Romantic relationships thrive when roles and responsibilities are explicit. It's not that long-term monogamous commitment is without faults or flaws, but it tends to produce the greatest satisfaction over the longest period of time. We don't need greater flexibility in our relationships, we need more predictability. More labels are not the answer.

An informal courtship process blurs the boundaries of commitment, making transgressions more difficult to identify. Even when relationship commitments are clear, there is still considerable uncertainty about what types of behavior count as a violation. The issue has become more complicated as cheating has begun to take different forms in the era of social media and online communication. Relationship journalist Beth Ashley says "micro-cheating" has become a growing concern for many couples.[24] It's not perceived the same as having an affair; rather, she says, "It takes the form of engaging in inappropriate behaviors or interactions that teeter around the edges of intimacy or attempts facilitating intimacy with other people." There is no settled definition, but innumerable examples. One article identified a hundred different examples of micro-cheating: continuing to message with an ex-partner, flirting with someone in the comments of their online posts, maintaining an online dating profile or concealing your relationship status, and more.[25] It's a contested concept. Not everyone agrees about what constitutes micro-cheating, and research has found that young men and women often have very different definitions.

The problem lies with how seamless social media has made this type of activity—commenting on an image of an attractive woman or striking up a conversation with a stranger requires very little effort. It's also largely private. You can scroll through an endless catalogue of attractive strangers or flirt with another person when your partner is in the same room. Constant access to attention, validation, and alternative partners fosters the sense that commitment is provisional.

Taken individually, many of these behaviors are not particularly alarming—but engaged in regularly, they can undermine a sense of security in our partner. Whether it is inadvertent or purposeful, these activities allow people in committed relationships to maintain optionality—a virtual roster of potential romantic alternatives. Social media contributes to a dating culture that prioritizes connection without obligation.

Double Standard for Infidelity

Attitudes about sexual morality have changed dramatically over the past few decades. To varying degrees, Americans have become more accepting of premarital sex, homosexuality, and sex between consenting teenagers. Marital infidelity is a critical exception to this overall trend. Over the last couple of decades, Americans remain strongly committed to the idea that infidelity is morally objectionable. A 2025 Gallup poll found that nearly nine in ten (89 percent) Americans say it is morally wrong for a married man or woman to have an affair.[26] This number has fluctuated only slightly since it was first asked in 2001. Yet there are contextual caveats in how men and women view the morality of marital infidelity that are a disheartening consequence of the rising sense of vulnerability many young women feel and the tribal sensibilities that define so much of American social life.

A couple years ago I made the mistake of downloading TikTok. It was ostensibly to document various patterns of dating behavior being shared online, and especially on platforms attracting younger users. One of the things that struck me almost immediately was how tribal the conversations had become online—women and men accusing the opposite gender and excusing their own. I wondered if what was happening online was the emergence of a moral double standard. How would this trend stand up to more rigorous examination of gender differences in attitudes about sexual morality? Would moral objections to marital infidelity be different if it was committed by a man versus a woman? Our team set out to investigate these questions. We devised an experiment to determine whether men and women would make the same moral judgment about marital infidelity regardless of who was committing it. We divided our survey sample and asked one group of respondents to judge the morality of marital infidelity committed by men and the other group to judge infidelity committed by women. The results were eye-opening. Both men and women had similar views about the immorality of infidelity when committed by men, but women were less likely to judge other women by the same standard.[27] It might feel virtuous to make allowances for personal indiscretions—who are we to judge someone's individual situation? But it weakens the whole project when destructive behavior is given a pass. We cannot offer solutions if we cannot first identify the problem.

Overall, Americans judge men who commit adultery more harshly than women, but there is an important gender gap. Women are less likely to say it is "always morally wrong" when a woman has an affair than when a man does. Nearly three-quarters of young women say it is "always morally wrong" when married men have an affair, but only about half say the same when married women have an affair.[28] But the double standard evident in these responses was far more pronounced among younger women. There's a 22-point gap in evaluations of infidelity committed by married men and women, while for women age sixty-five or older the gap was less than half as large.

More Young Women Condemn Marital Infidelity When It Is Committed by Men

Percentage of women who say it is always morally wrong when . . .

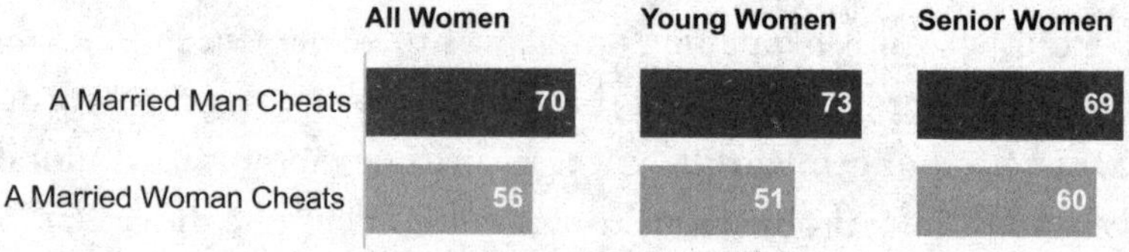

Note: "Young Women" refers to those age 18 to 29 and "Senior Women" refers to those age 65 and older.
Source: AEI Survey Center on American Life, Abortion and Religion Survey, August 2022.

There are many potential explanations for why young women might be uniquely disposed to apply different moral standards to women than men when it comes to infidelity. For instance, it could be heightened awareness about disparities of status and power that have traditionally advantaged men, or the fact that married men tend to be less faithful than women.[29] If young women believe that male infidelity is common, they may decide that women engage in this behavior for more justified reasons. As society has historically tended to judge women more harshly for displays of overt sexuality, many young women might feel less inclined to pile on to that judgment. Or perhaps it stems from the belief that men and women engage in adulterous activity for different reasons and in different ways.

It's impossible to separate these views from the personal sense of vulnerability that many young women feel about their place in society. There is a massive gap between married women and single women in how they feel women are faring in the United States. Single women increasingly believe the country has become a more hostile territory for women, and that men are largely responsible for it. In one survey, more than half of single women under forty said that men were responsible for "a great deal" of the problems that women face in American society.[30] Only 14 percent of single men under forty shared the belief that women are largely responsible for the challenges facing men.

Undoubtedly, these feelings reflect a growing tribal sensibility. The same study revealed that young women are far more likely than older women to report a greater sense of solidarity with other women living in the United States.[31] They feel connected by virtue of their shared experiences and challenges. In the wake of the Supreme Court's ruling in the *Dobbs v. Jackson Women's Health Organization* case, this feeling was sky-high among young women, especially single women. And young women who feel most threatened—that their rights and autonomy are at stake—are far more likely to apply different moral standards for men and women.

But a relationship culture that prioritizes a tribal mentality absolves people of their responsibility to others. The notion that people serve only as objects for our personal growth will only serve to justify selfish and self-indulgent behavior. And if we continue to tolerate this kind of behavior, people will come to expect it in relationships. It all leads to the same place: the further erosion of trust in marriage and long-term commitments. But the individual justifications people make for their behavior are less important than the collective consequences.

In his final column for *The New York Times,* columnist David Brooks offered a plaintive appeal for a moral consensus. "We told multiple generations to come up with their own individual values. This privatization of morality burdened people with a task they could not possibly do, leaving them morally inarticulate and unformed. It created a naked public square where there was no broad agreement about what was true, beautiful and good. Without shared standards of right and wrong, it's impossible to settle disputes; it's impossible to maintain social cohesion and trust."[32] On some level, we need to agree on what is right and what is wrong. What should be aspired to and what ought to be avoided. We should not refrain from passing judgment about things that we believe are wrong, but we should be as ready to offer forgiveness.

There is a path forward to instilling trust in marriage, in institutions, in romantic and platonic relationships between men and women—and it starts with admitting that we owe something to each other. Relationships are valuable because they ask something of us. As our research has shown, we are a happier and healthier society when we prioritize genuine connection. It benefits all of us to fight for this, and it's time that we start doing just that.

PART III

A PATH TO RECONCILIATION

WHAT happens when a culture encourages tit-for-tat responses, emphasizes pessimism more than problem-solving, and rewards avoidance over curiosity? We're living it. Our online lives have become infinite but empty, while our offline lives grow increasingly barren. Young men and women have internalized a mindset that they are unique, special, and unequivocally entitled to share their opinions with the world. They are preoccupied with what we can label, consume, and promote, leaving little time to focus on collective concerns and our shared social obligations.

If the preceding chapters were meant to instill a sense of urgency about the fraying of our relational lives, the final chapters are intended to inject a much-needed sense of optimism and agency. Even as we face a constellation of forces driving us apart, we are not powerless to resist them. From dating apps to pornography and social media, young adults are growing more aware of the pernicious effects of technology and a life adapted for performance. In this final section, I will provide a few tangible steps we can take to capitalize on this moment of wearying uncertainty to reaffirm shared values and rebuild relational experiences.

Getting offline is the first step. We need to reinvest in social spaces in the real world. We need a politics grounded in recognizing the unique challenges faced by men and women, and the will to address them. Lastly, we need to make the process of finding a partner less grueling and more joyful. Dating should not be solitary work, but a community-led endeavor. More than anything, we need to realize that hardship is universal, and that is why we need one another. If our first instinct is to express grace rather than grievance, we're one step closer to solving this crisis of connection.

CHAPTER 12

HOW WE COME TOGETHER: A BROADER VISION OF EQUALITY

The conflict between young men and young women is not primarily a clash of values, politics, or power. It is something quieter yet more destabilizing: It's a crisis of connection. The places that once brought young men and young women together in shared purpose now serve to affirm individual ambition and interests. Teenage girls are raised to believe that they are more vulnerable than ever, and that men face no accountability for even the worst offenses. Most teenage boys now feel that their schools routinely prioritize the interest of their female classmates, and their public behavior is subject to more criticism. More social interaction occurs in digital arenas that reward grievance and promote attention seeking. Dating has been privatized. Loneliness has been politicized. And everyone feels like a victim. So many young adults are exhausted.

How do we build solidarity when everything seems broken? If the previous chapters did not prompt a bit of pessimism, then I probably didn't do my job. Every generation inherits the problems created by the previous one as well as those of their own making. Even with all the challenges young people face, there is still a lot right in American society, and a hunger to find a better way forward. In the many conversations and interviews that have formed the basis for this book, I can still say that even the most dispiriting exchanges often yielded a more hopeful vision in the end. Almost no one I talked to said romantic partnership was a dead end, even if there was less certainty about how to attain it. None of us wants to live this way, and there is an urgency to make things better. But it will take more than individual initiative.

To outline how we can move forward, I will start with a broader vision of equality—one that recognizes not only persistent inequities but emerging challenges despite the progress we have achieved. We also need a renewed commitment to relational life that entails increased communal responsibility, courtship embedded in community, and identities rooted less in self-expression and more in mutual obligation.

Moving Beyond Zero-Sum Advocacy

One of the biggest obstacles to seeking a resolution to any problem is the belief that each side is sitting at opposite ends of a seesaw: When one side goes up, the other goes down. Research is increasingly finding that many Americans adopt zero-sum thinking when it comes to gender equality; advances for women are at the expense of men and advances for men are at the expense of women.[1] Harvard researchers found that zero-sum thinking is more common among younger adults, especially young men, who are more likely to believe that "women's wage gains have come at the expense of men's wages."[2] And a growing number of young men today reject the idea of a feminist label, because they no longer believe it stands for combating gender inequality and discrimination against women. Although more evident among men, zero-sum thinking can operate in both directions. Even acknowledging the specific problems men deal with can elicit concerns about how this might hamper efforts to address the enduring challenges facing women. In a recent article for *Nature* reviewing the challenges confronting boys and young men, the authors offered the caveat: "It is uncomfortable and sometimes controversial to talk about a male 'crisis' in the face of entrenched and often worsening discrimination against girls and women."[3] Young progressive women believe that "mediocre men" succeed in the workplace because of structural forces that keep women down, while young conservative men believe female progress is predicated on depressing male opportunity. It's a scarcity mindset that locks us in a state of victimhood, ensuring mutual hostility and shared misery and keeping us paralyzed to change.

The goal of gender equality is far more complicated than ensuring an equal fifty-fifty split between men and women. Faced with different biological imperatives, social incentives, and different interests and priorities, societal solutions for men and women must reflect this basic reality. We have to be strategic in delivering interventions where they are most needed. In this section, I'll outline how we move beyond zero-sum advocacy to better understand and address the distinctive pressures and problems faced by men and women. To do so, we need to understand how gender equality is widely perceived, how commitments to equality are pursued, and how this will help us bridge the growing empathy gap between men and women. Then we can take a look at shared goals that will help us move out of that gap.

On a large scale, both young men and young women believe their gender is a liability and that discrimination is more frequent and pernicious than it once was. A report by the Pew Research Center found that despite making demonstrable headway on gender equality, more Americans believe that men are better off than women in the United States today than did so a decade earlier. In 2019, a majority (57 percent) of Americans said men have a better life than women in the country today, an 18-point increase from 2010.[4] Young women remain pessimistic about the progress the country has made toward female equality, but young men simultaneously believe their gender is the one currently facing discrimination.

When progress is uneven, problems are more easily politicized, because it creates opportunities to push simple or politically expedient narratives. Motivated political actors can tell competing stories about which groups are most advantaged and who struggles. There is a fifty-one-point divide between Republicans and Democrats over whether the country still has work to do to ensure gender equality, and the gap is identical whether we're looking at women or men.[5] The political divide between young men and women is made worse by the way the country's political elites—elected officials, party leaders, political advocacy groups—tell divergent stories about the state of gender inequality, and the ongoing imperative to address it. It's happening on both sides.

During the 2010s, the systematic reduction of reproductive health access led Democrats to declare the existence of a "War on Women." The narrative around this war has been relentlessly pessimistic, coinciding with a dramatic curtailment of access to abortion and reproductive health services in many states. But whatever its efficacy as a political message, it flattened understanding about the nature of cultural and political change. Societal progress was reduced to winning or losing, moving forward or back. Actual progress is uneven, occurring in fits and starts, a combination of hard-fought success and setbacks. In 2015, the U.S. women's national soccer team's victory over Japan to win the World Cup became the most-watched soccer match in American history, drawing more than 26 million viewers.[6] Things were changing, but in ways that defied a simple characterization. For many left-leaning voters and activists, the rhetoric about women's rights left them feeling pessimistic about the lack of societal progress on gender equality. On any social problem, an accurate accounting of societal progress is a critical step toward solving it. Acknowledgment instills confidence in our collective ability to correct historic inequalities in our systems and institutions, even if progress occurs unevenly, imperfectly, or more slowly than we might wish.

If the Democratic Party sought advantage in framing policy disagreements as a frontal assault on female autonomy, the Republican Party in the Trump era grew comfortable belittling the personal choices women made regarding marriage and starting a family. Vice President J. D. Vance's infamous lament about the political influence of "childless cat ladies" reflects a reasonably widespread belief on the right that women were prioritizing the wrong things, namely professional success and financial security. Trump's denigration of accomplished women was well documented, but he also routinely communicated that male interests and achievements were more worthy of recognition. After the U.S. men's hockey team won the gold medal at the 2026 Winter Olympics, Trump called to congratulate them—something he failed to do when the women's team won their own gold medal three days earlier. During the call, he joked with the male players that he would be forced to honor the U.S. women's team or risk facing "impeachment," a comment that elicited laughter from some of the male players. Whether intentional or not, the message was clear: Women's accomplishments are less deserving of acknowledgment. It's hardly the worst thing Trump has done. We've become so accustomed to this type of callous behavior that it often fails to register, but sit with this for a minute: The men's national hockey team was honored at the White House; the women's team chose not to attend. This should bother all of us. It's a failure of leadership and of character and it makes things worse for everyone. Instead of a moment of solidarity, we are left with more division.

The political system rewards zero-sum thinking. Each side offers an overly simplified diagnosis of the problem and a one-sided solution to address it. Equality requires a collective effort, a shared recognition of ways society still falls short of this goal, and a commitment to addressing it. If we are to be successful, we need the ideological flexibility to identify how men and women are both subject to inequities, not necessarily in the same way or to the same degree, but in ways that meaningfully affect their lives.

Let's start with education. Removing educational obstacles that women have faced historically became a moral imperative and political priority. To great effect. Tremendous progress has been made in opening up opportunities for women. In many cases, young women are surpassing their male peers and outcompeting them. How do we think about equal opportunity for women in places such as higher education, where they are the numerical majority? This requires us to think about the distinctive social circumstances and cultural influences that affect boys and girls and appreciate how they differ. For instance, research has shown that boys are more susceptible to peer pressure when it comes to academic performance—a field experiment found that boys were less likely to register for a free SAT prep course after signees became public, while girls' interest was unaffected.[7] And findings from our 2026 survey of American teenagers reveal a substantial gender divide in higher educational intentions. About six in ten (59 percent) teen girls report that they are planning to attend a four-year college or university. For teen boys, the share is only 37 percent.[8] Does this mean we should stop supporting efforts to further educational opportunities for girls and young women? Of course not. Rather, I would argue that it requires us to recognize and address the specific obstacles boys face in education, and knock them down.

Part of the problem is that the goal of gender equality is not so easily quantified. Does equality imply that at every level, in every industry and profession, there are roughly equal numbers of women and men? Women have outnumbered men in law schools for nearly a decade. According to the American Bar Association, there were 65,754 women admitted to law schools in 2023, compared to 50,096 men.[9] The gender disparity in the composition of the law student body has grown every year since 2016, when there were roughly equal numbers of men and women seeking their JDs. The result of this imbalance of students is that firms now hire more women than men. In 2024, the National Association for Law Placement announced that, for the first time ever, women made up more than half of first-year associates at law firms. You could argue this is obvious equality, but it's not that simple. At the highest levels of the legal profession, women continue to be underrepresented, whether as general counsel positions at large corporations, as law school faculty, or as partners at prestigious law firms.

Another example is that women now account for 72 percent of workers employed in the field of psychology while men continue to be overrepresented in manual trades, such as plumbing and carpentry.[10] Do we need more male therapists and female electricians? Maybe, but we also have to consider stereotypical strengths that each gender has that might influence a disparity in certain careers. Do women tend to be more naturally empathetic and men physically stronger? Yes, and that isn't a bad thing. It doesn't mean that the opposite gender cannot also be emotionally attuned or physically talented. Different priorities and preferences may lead men and women to make different career decisions, though of course discrimination inarguably affects these outcomes as well. I don't think an equal number of men and women in every industry and at every level is an appropriate goal. I do think we have an obligation to aggressively upend obstacles that deny men and women opportunities to pursues their preferred educational or professional goals. We should also support choices that are freely made.

To truly move beyond the zero-sum mentality that separates men and women in America, we need to take a more expansive view of gender equality. One that not only tallies over- and underrepresentation but makes an attempt to understand both the source and significance. If gender equality is defined by the achievement of identical outcomes for men and women, then the goal will always be out of reach. Broadening our understanding of gender equality means adjusting the type of interventions that we champion—those that recognize our interconnectedness.

One place where we can begin is with gender-focused advocacy organizations. Policy-oriented organizations have historically focused on promoting autonomy, the exercise of political power and civic influence, and closing the gap between men's and women's health and economic opportunities. What if they widened the scope of their mission to advocate for strengthening our social and relational lives? If the goal of a women's group is to improve the overall welfare of women, it's difficult to see how that goal can be accomplished if men are failing. If the goal of a men's group is to, say, promote longevity, that can't be done without learning to develop trustworthy and genuine relationships with women in their lives. The problem defies a simple policy prescription, but interventions should prioritize in-person social experiences, repeated interactions, and collaborative engagement. They should also focus on young people.

Schools could also sponsor co-ed intramural sports teams to complement gender-segregated athletic programs. Health classes could talk about relational topics in the curricula beyond sex education—like how to communicate effectively, identify signs of romantic interest and disinterest, and the benefit of platonic relationships. Some classes already do. Regardless of the approach, social activities that encourage boys and girls to socialize and practice dating skills would serve as valuable opportunities to build comfort and confidence.

Lastly, our political leaders need to recommit to a message of economic optimism, one that resonates across gender, class, and racial divides. So much of the current resentment is aggravated by the practiced pessimism of political and cultural elites. We are encouraged to become well acquainted with our distinctive demographic disadvantages. When the most influential public figures keep telling us that things are terrible, we believe them. We begin to doubt our ability to improve our situation, and we feel less concerned about the welfare of others as we scramble to maintain our own footing. What if we had leaders who could encourage us to see our shared concerns, and offer a common agenda that men and women could rally around?

Addressing Social Disconnection

We are facing a crisis of connection. This fact should compel us toward a common purpose, but instead we treat the symptoms of loneliness differently for young men and women as if they originated from distinctive sources. The second key to understanding a broader sense of equality is recognizing that there isn't something inherently toxic about one gender or the other; the extremity of our division stems from the lack of interdependence.

On the occasion that I have told people about this book, I have often been asked about the Netflix show *Adolescence*. If you bought this book, there is a good chance you have heard of it. The four-episode British miniseries explores the reason a thirteen-year-old boy, Jamie, kills his female classmate. It's packed with social commentary, making explicit references to the manosphere, incels, pornography, and weighty discussions of masculinity and fatherhood. For a long time, I couldn't bring myself to watch it. I have two boys, and although they are growing rapidly, they are still little, or at least they are to me.

Eventually, I did watch, primarily out of a sense of obligation to this book. When it was released in early 2025, it became a major cultural event. Within the first three months of its release, the series garnered more than 141 million viewers, making it Netflix's second most popular English-language series of all time. It was a powerful, engrossing, and devastating viewing experience. The show spurred important conversations about masculinity, the manosphere, and male violence, but I also think it skipped too quickly past the problem of social disconnection, rather implying that the root problem was a manosphere and incel culture that trained young men to commit violence against women.

In creating the hit show, *Adolescence* creators Jack Thorne and Stephen Graham said they wanted to "look in the eye of male rage." Yet tracing a direct line from incel culture to acts of gender-based violence is difficult. The public perception around incels is that the places where they congregate encourage young men to blame their failures on women, and that things escalate to violence from there. However, studies by William Costello and David M. Buss, two leading researchers in this subject, have found that incels are actually less prone to violence than men overall. In fact, the authors speculate that online obsessions common to incels, such as pornography, not to mention gaming and gambling, may actually serve to pacify violent instincts and aggressive tendencies rather than inflame them. In their research, Costello and Buss have found that the online spaces incels inhabit actually tend to operate "as a fatalistic echo-chamber, where failure is celebrated, and individuals discourage each other from pursuing romantic success."[11] These young men are being encouraged to see the world as a hostile place and to see that they are permanently disadvantaged because of their own shortcomings. They are taught to hate themselves and a society that offers them nothing but scorn, and so they find a sense of fraternity in their "virtuous victimhood identity." The primary goal for many, if not most, of the men who wind up on these forums is not the denigration of women—although that language is distressingly common—but an appeal for recognition to feel, however fleetingly, a sense of belonging. It's also a trap. Incel membership is based on social and romantic failure—to find success is to be excommunicated.

The manosphere is also an inviting target for those who believe the problems between men and women stem from toxic masculinity or misogyny. Its potential influence is formidable. One study of adolescent and young men in the United Kingdom, Australia, and the United States found that nearly two-thirds of young men followed masculinity influencers online.[12] The platforms that manosphere personalities use to reach their audience, such as YouTube, are increasingly popular and are displacing traditional media. These platforms produce a variety of content, but two themes that arguably get the most attention are self-optimization and misogynistic commentary. But research shows that even when young men are exposed to sexist rants online, the influence of this type of content is difficult to quantify. Plenty of polls find that the vast majority of young men support gender equality, even if they do not identify as feminists. Young men today are more likely than previous generations to believe that working mothers can establish as secure a connection with their child as mothers who do not work. They express greater comfort with female leadership as well. Young men overwhelmingly reject the notion that men are better suited emotionally for politics than women.[13] So although these men are exposed to many instances of misogyny on various online forums, these ideas are not necessarily the reason so many are disconnected from women. Rather, so much male-oriented content perpetuates the notion that men need to relentlessly focus on improving themselves to be worthy of friendship and affection. This is a much deeper problem, because it advocates ignoring the critical importance of cultivating social connections.

As central as the manosphere is to Jamie's story in *Adolescence,* his relational challenges at school were arguably more consequential to his trajectory—he had only a couple of friends and very few social interactions with his female classmates. Jamie's sense of self was not only shaped by the toxic content he was consuming online, but by his lack of strong social connections in the real world and his struggles to develop a sense of belonging. He was not a strong athlete, and he viewed himself as ugly. These are concerns shared by many young men who get sucked into the manosphere. In fact, research indicates that incels generally overestimate the value of physical attractiveness and financial status in the dating market. Even if Jamie could not do much to alter his family's financial situation or his physical characteristics, stronger social ties might have helped him cultivate other appealing attributes, such as thoughtfulness, curiosity, and a sense of humor (characteristics often undervalued by incels in dating). The manosphere is not causing male loneliness and disconnection—it is simply a symptom of it.

The lack of a strong social connection is closely tied to feelings of grievance and unfairness, but only among men. Men with zero close friends are more than twice as likely as those with six or more close friends to believe that "society values you less because you're a man" (40 percent versus 19 percent, respectively).[14] There is a nearly identical pattern in perceptions of discrimination. Thirty-eight percent of men with no close friends believe that men face a lot of discrimination compared to 21 percent of men with at least six close friends.[15] These patterns are consistent regardless of race or ethnicity, class, and geography.

It's not clear if having fewer close friends leads men to feel more aggrieved, but more consistent social support can guard against the misfortunes of everyday life. Boys and young men are most attracted to the manosphere because it provides something lacking in their own lives: a sense of belonging. The collapse of male social

Socially Disconnected Men Feel More Disadvantaged

Percentage of men with the following number of friends who believe . . .

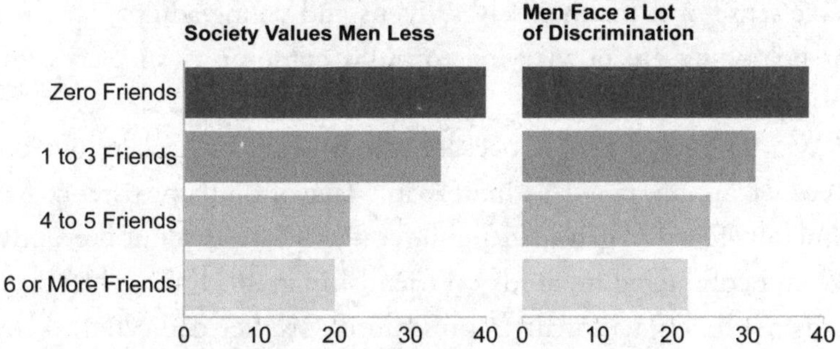

Note: Responses shown include those who "sometimes" or more often feel that society values men less. "Friends" refers to close friends, excluding relatives.
Source: AEI Survey Center on American Life, American Social Life Survey, 2025.

infrastructure—the fraternal organizations, the sports leagues, and the religious communities—has not diminished the need for these spaces. This does not mean we should refuse to condemn the type of misogyny trafficked on these online forums, but forceful denunciations and deplatforming fail to address the underlying problem. The manosphere is evidence not of an ideological problem but a social one.

The problem we face is not simply social disaffection and disconnection in the real world. It's an attention imbalance that has occurred both online and offline. Our online social world is too vast and our offline world too small, populated by a diminishing number of close connections. This imbalance is especially problematic for teenagers who are still in the process of building out their nascent web of social ties. Before the internet, the social lives of teenagers were far narrower than those of adults, in large part because they were restricted by the geography of their birth and their family ties. As we age, our social world typically expands, and our perspectives shift in response to new experiences and new people that come into our lives. The internet has destroyed this process of slowly widening our apertures. Now children and teenagers are fed a torrent of information—people, places, and ideas—before they can properly make sense of it for themselves. Teens and young adults searching for belonging are now trying to build community in places unequipped to provide it.

We don't need people because we are weak or broken, but because we are human. This inescapable fact of human existence has somehow failed to galvanize public concern—at least until recently. When I conducted my study on friendship in 2021, there had been vanishingly few nationally representative studies dedicated to the topic. It's a cultural blind spot. We once considered friendship, dating, and social connection as the inevitable by-products of growing up. It turns out they are not. They require tending and consistent cultivation throughout our lives. We are each responsible for building social bonds, but we have a collective obligation to provide well-lit pathways for boys and girls to follow. This is the lesson of the manosphere. The antidote to extremism is not ostracism.

Community-Oriented Courtship

Modern dating has been quietly privatized. Interactions once embedded in neighborhoods, congregations, workplaces, and extended friend groups now unfold in digital space largely invisible to public view. Online, we can be anything to anyone, and accountable to no one.

The consequences are by now familiar: more apathetic encounters and relational misfires, all leading to the creeping conviction that romantic failure is a personal deficiency rather than evidence of a structural problem. If you are lonely, you are told to optimize. If you are rejected, you are told to improve yourself. Rarely are we invited to question the system that has turned courtship into a marketplace and people into consumable products.

If we're going to restore connection between men and women, we need to reestablish the conditions that can foster genuine connection. This means restoring social norms and public etiquette so that expectations are clear, and we have to be willing to abide by rules even when they feel inconvenient. We need to treat dating as an extension of our social lives, rather than a wholly separate activity. Integrating it into existing social practices will lower the stakes and reduce anxiety around meeting a potential partner, which, at least for single men, can be the biggest hurdle. One of the ways dating apps have immiserated the process of finding a partner is by creating an entirely independent ecosystem that feels disconnected from the rest of our life. It feels artificial and awkward because it is.

I'm not suggesting a need for arranged marriages, chaperoned dates, or parental permission. It is something far more basic. Dating and courtship should be built around socially integrated activities—a process that mandates a steady progression of connecting to people. This new model would call for a recommitment to a more vigorous social life: attending events, joining clubs and organizations, and volunteering that expands our social and romantic reach.

In practice, this would mean entering someone's social world earlier and more deliberately. It could be accomplished in any number of ways: inviting a new partner to volunteer at a community garden, attend a sibling's soccer game, or go to a friend's birthday party. The aim is not to induce awkwardness but to see how a potential partner responds to the inconvenience and the small frictions of everyday life. How someone treats strangers, servers, or children says a lot more about who they are than how charming they can be across a candlelit table. It's not only about setting up a better vetting process, it's an opportunity for both men and women to demonstrate qualities such as patience, attentiveness, and consideration that are difficult to convey in an online profile.

Human beings reveal themselves most fully in community—in how they move through rooms, rather than in heavily scripted interactions and online encounters. If we allowed our social circles to overlap earlier, authenticity would surface sooner, for better or worse. Perhaps, in seeing one another as whole participants in a shared world rather than as isolated avatars in a competitive market, we might begin to repair the damage we have done to each other.

At one time, securing a partner was a communal affair, one that garnered the interest and attention of many different people. The interconnectedness of traditional social networks ensured a level of accountability that facilitated the development of trust and encouraged reciprocity. A culture that maximizes choice and prizes independence and autonomy has diminished this communal investment. The process of finding a partner is now a wholly individual endeavor. It has made the entire enterprise dispiriting, lonely, and exhausting. We now attribute failure to individual shortcomings.

Relationship progression should be tied to social integration. Rather than waiting for a certain number of dates before progressing a relationship further, what if the metric was meeting a certain number of their friends, colleagues, or family members? My wife and I met through mutual friends. On our very first official date, I dropped in on her office happy hour, and I ended up meeting about a half dozen of her colleagues. The invitation she extended and my willingness to join signaled that this was perhaps more than casual interest. At a time when online communication is a source of considerable ambiguity and uncertainty, these types of experiences can matter even more. Many years later, my wife informed me that my early emails and text messages to her betrayed a decidedly "flat affect" on my part. Fortunately for me, she was not inclined to consider this disqualifying, nor was she interested in sharing this information on social media to have strangers weigh in on whether this was a red flag. We could save this generation from so much hardship and heartache if singles did not feel compelled to date people they know so little about, or communicate with each other in terse, inscrutable ways online.

Socially integrated courtship is hardly a new concept. For most of our existence, it was the only option. You had to become part of someone's social world before you could become romantically involved with them. Dating apps and social media created socially disembodied experiences. But despite the convenience, few singles prefer it. Ask a young single person how they would prefer to meet a romantic partner and most will say through their existing social network of friends and family. This fact is not lost on dating app companies. Tinder recently launched a feature that allows a user's friends and families to play matchmaker.[16] A number of apps have also introduced double-date and group-date features to reintroduce a social component to the dating experience. It's not an innovation so much as a recognition that the basic premise is flawed. The more technology companies attempt to mimic offline interactions, the more apparent it will become that they are poor substitutes for the real thing.

The purpose of involving friends and family members is to build trust and discern compatibility. If you do not like any of your partner's friends, or they don't like you, social integration will become a lot more difficult. Online dating has reduced complex individuals to a list of personal experiences and physical attributes, when in reality it is the constellation of our social relationships that defines us.

To truly know someone is to know the people around them. What kind of relationship do they have with their parents or siblings? How do they treat their friends? What kind of relationship do they have with their work colleagues? These are hardly irrelevant questions when it comes to selecting a partner, and yet none of this information is available on dating app profiles. Instead, we've created an illusion of unrestricted possibility. Few singles are happier for it.

Whether we're willing to acknowledge it or not, we all have a stake in improving the odds and experiences of dating. Stable relationships are more likely to turn into stable marriages, which help create stable families, which build stable communities. This progression benefits everyone. In one study we conducted, we found that married parents, particularly those with college degrees, contributed to their communities at rates far higher than everyone else.[17] They were civic superheroes. Mothers were slightly more engaged than fathers, but both parents demonstrated a commitment far greater than the average American, whether it was volunteering, hosting neighbors, or attending a community meeting. These are the types of thankless activities that help address shared problems and enrich neighborhoods. So many of the societal problems we face are, at their root, relational problems.

Reinvesting in the Real World

There are reasons to be hopeful. Both men and women express an equal mix of exhaustion and frustration about the current culture. More young people are coming to reject technology-driven social experiences and the expedient, transactional culture it creates. It's hard to be nostalgic for a period of time you never lived through, yet many Gen Zers express an earnest longing for a time when physical spaces—alleys, driveways, parks, and cul-de-sacs—served as catalysts for creativity and the stage for romantic plots, youthful drama, and unscripted adventures. Who can blame them for wanting to live rather than perform, to spend their time in only one place at one time—unsupervised experiences that were shared by an intimate few. It's a loss that is recoverable. The physical world has not disappeared, it just needs to be reclaimed.

In my own neighborhood, Tin Can phones have become increasingly popular. They are landline phones that offer kids an opportunity to connect with their friends without the digital distraction produced by smartphones. The beauty of these phones is they are built for a single purpose: to help kids find each other in the real world. After a few false starts—talking into the wrong end of the receiver—my boys use their phone to call their friends, and most recently to coordinate a meetup at the large mulch pile in our local park. In a little over a year, the company reported that use of their landline phones increased one-hundred-fold.[18] These throwback technologies are becoming popular for a reason.

Teenagers are starting to recognize the pernicious effect that social media has on their social lives. In 2022, the Pew Research Center found that less than one in three (32 percent) U.S. teens said that social media was having a "mostly negative" impact on people their age.[19] Only two years later, roughly half (48 percent) of teens said social media's impact on people their age was primarily negative. The number of teens who felt that social media was a positive force in the lives of people their age was more than halved. That's a dramatic change over an incredibly short period of time. It's not only their views that are changing; there are signs that their behavior is as well. In our own survey of teenagers, we found that more than four in ten had attempted to reduce their use of social media at some point in the last twelve months. That number was even higher among teenage girls, whose social media use tends to be greater. There has been an explosion of apps, devices, and embedded utilities designed to help users practice "appstinence," and the growth for some of them is staggering. Brick, a small gray cube that requires users to physically tap the phone against it to unlock preselected apps, has experienced a 600 percent increase in downloads of its associated app.[20]

More Teens Say Social Media Is Having a Negative Influence on Their Generation

Percentage of teenagers (age 13 to 17) who believe the impact social media has had on people their age has been . . .

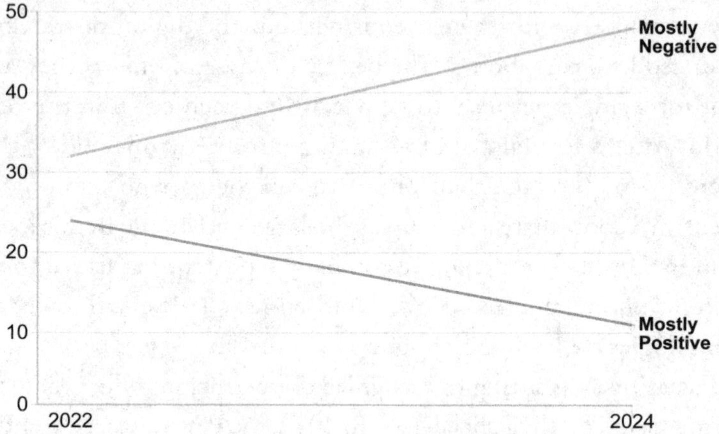

Source: Pew Research Center, Teens Survey, May 2022; Pew Research Center, Teens Survey, October 2024.

This is hardly the only change that is starting to emerge in public opinion data relating to the impact of the internet. Among young men, there is a growing realization that the ubiquity of pornography has also come at a significant cost. Historically, young men have consistently expressed few reservations about the morality of pornography.[21] Even today, young men are divided over whether it is ethical to consume pornographic material. In the last five years, however, there has been a remarkable turnabout in support for restrictions on internet pornography. Nearly two-thirds (64 percent) of young men ages eighteen to twenty-four are in favor of restricting access to pornographic content online.[22] This represents an increase of over 20 points since 2021, when less than half (43 percent) supported restrictions. And significantly, it's this cohort of the youngest men who are among the most supportive of pornography restrictions. Less than half of men ages twenty-five to fifty-four share their views. It's likely that young men's exposure to extreme and explicit content online has led to a reexamination of the way it warps their sense of intimacy and dulls interest in pursuing romantic experiences.

Young Men Grow More Supportive of Restrictions on Pornography

Percentage of young men (age 18 to 24) who favor or oppose making it more difficult to access online pornography

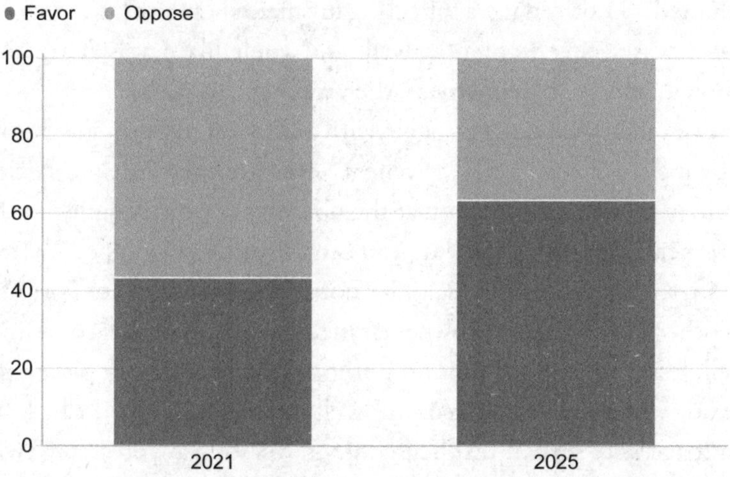

Source: AEI Survey Center on American Life, American National Family Survey, 2021; AEI Survey Center on American Life, American Social Life Survey, 2025.

Although nearly all young people have been exposed to video pornography at some point in their lives, they are not the heaviest consumers of it—this status belongs to men in their thirties and forties. It is young men, however, who report the highest levels of *problematic* pornography use. Nearly one in five (17 percent) young men report that they have had a "problem with pornography use" at some point in their lives. Compulsive pornography use, sometimes referred to as "porn addiction," is not recognized as an official diagnosis by the American Psychiatric Association. Yet, in conversations with young men, we have found that it weighs on them heavily. In our Raleigh focus groups, more than one young man admitted to struggling with a pornography addiction. For one participant, Jackson, the addiction got so out of hand that it started interfering with his real-life relationship: "I know it's not an addiction for everybody. For me, it was, and so I needed to remove that for my life, especially when I started getting into a committed relationship." Another young man, Ben, talked about the mental toll his addiction inflicted: "I noticed it was affecting my mental [health]. Kind of the way I was seeing women as well, and I felt like I wasn't treating women, or wasn't seeing them, the way they should be."

Even men who don't struggle with addiction to pornography are growing weary of its pervasiveness. Jesse, another Raleigh participant, expressed exasperation at the ubiquity of pornography on the internet. "You can't escape it. You can't go on Instagram or Twitter or anything anymore," he said. It's not simply a problem of Pornhub or other pornography sites; social media is awash in this content as well. Jesse argued that bans on pornographic websites in places like Texas, where he once lived, are well-intentioned but do little to limit access to sexually explicit content. "As soon as you go on Twitter, there is full-on porn there. And if you linger on it too long, guess what's coming three posts down? Even more hardcore porn." This feeling was widely shared among other men in the group, reflecting their own experiences. For some men, the widespread availability of sexually explicit and provocative content is the reason they spend less time on social media. It's about more than seeking to avoid provocative material; a growing number of young men are now acknowledging that early and easy access to pornography might harm their ability to form meaningful relationships with women.

Pornography use isn't the only digital activity that has drawn increased scrutiny. More than any previous technology, the internet revolutionized humanity's capacity to meet and interact with strangers. Within a decade of their launches, online dating sites and their companion apps completely transformed the dating marketplace. Social stigma surrounding dating apps quickly evaporated as their use increased. American singles became so heavily reliant on the new technology that it quickly surpassed all other ways of meeting romantic partners. Research found that, by 2017, meeting online through dating apps, social media, and online forums had become the most common way couples meet.[23]

The initial appeal of dating apps and of meeting people through social media was obvious. It requires so little effort while avoiding the worst sting of rejection. It even serves as a source of validation to some (mostly female users and successful men) who are inundated with match requests and, in theory, provides nearly limitless options. The early success of these platforms is not difficult to understand. However, the decline was also predictable. Singles have grown to hate dating apps and what they stand for. In our Raleigh focus groups, not one member of our groups of single women or single men spoke up in defense of online dating. As one participant, Audra, noted, "Men were not supposed to see this many women in their lifetime."

The digital dating era has dramatically increased efficiency but produced manifestly inferior experiences with predictable results. More singles have grown disillusioned with online dating, spending less time and money on dating apps. Paid subscriptions and downloads of popular dating apps, such as Tinder and Bumble, have decreased significantly over the past few years. Since 2021, Bumble has lost more than $40 billion in market value.[24] One estimate suggests that average time on the apps dropped by nearly half in less than a decade, from one hundred minutes a day to fifty-one minutes a day.[25] At the same time, in-person dating events have seen explosive growth.

I'm encouraged by the fact that young singles are ditching the dating apps in favor of real-world meetups, and prioritizing using their friend groups to find romantic partners. Half of young women who are currently in a committed relationship or married report that they were friends with their partner before they started dating.[26] Finding a romantic partner in one's own friend group remains the most preferred way of meeting. Researcher Michael Rosenfeld and his colleagues found that, in the decades after World War II and prior to the takeoff of social media, "the most popular way heterosexual Americans met their romantic partners was through the intermediation of friends."[27] Though the internet has largely displaced friendship as a method of finding a partner, there are signs that this trend may be reversing. Our immediate social connections—friends, family, and colleagues—are starting to reassert their role in the dating marketplace. Still, not everyone can leverage a robust network of social connections to facilitate the task.

Although it's taken time, it's heartening to see young adults become more discerning users of these technologies, and clear-eyed about what these platforms are costing them. Our lumbering institutions are being successfully prodded into action as well. Support for technological restrictions is gaining traction. School districts across the country have introduced substantial restrictions or outright bans on phone use during the school day. As of writing this book, eleven states have passed legislation that curbs phone use in public schools, and seventeen more state legislatures have introduced bills to limit their use.[28] Many summer sleepaway camps now advertise phoneless experiences, freeing young campers to unplug from their devices for their duration. In 2025, the first phone-free bar opened in Washington, D.C., requiring patrons to place their cellphones in magnetically sealed pouches that can only be unlocked when they leave.[29] In New York City, campaign posters of the newly launched AI companion, Friend, were aggressively graffitied.[30] The ads, many of which implied AI offered a superior model of companionship—"I'll never bail on our dinner plans; I'll never leave dirty dishes in the sink"—provoked a variety of negative responses, including:

"Human connection is sacred."

"Befriend something alive."

"AI wouldn't care if you lived or died."

I don't anticipate a coming Luddite revolution, nor do I believe this would be in any way desirable. Social technologies may have transformed our personal behavior in ways that were unimaginable only a few years ago, but they have not erased our fundamental human need for connection and belonging. Young adults still want unmediated social interactions with their peers and the opportunity to forge authentic connections. Human companionship, affection, and attention are still valued far more than their synthetic alternatives. Even if young people are less comfortable talking to strangers, they appreciate the importance of having someone's complete and undivided attention without the threat of screen-based interruptions. Too often, our devices serve as an impediment to creating authentic connection by constantly clamoring for our attention. The world is vast, complex, and, yes, it can be a scary place. We need to shrink it back down to a manageable size. More of our attention and time needs to be spent in our own communities with the people who live and work there. To accomplish this, it's imperative that we reinvest in our social infrastructure—the public pools, parks, coffee shops, and movie theaters—that serve as a way for young men and women to find each other.

Grace and Understanding

Everything leads to this: Both men and women are exhausted by fear, they are wary of each other, and they want to be understood.

The path forward requires men and women to develop an abiding interest in the welfare of people whose experiences, inclinations, and interests are often different from their own. We have to learn to acknowledge our differences without letting them distance us from each other.

In the fall of 2024, I conducted a series of focus groups with young men and women that alluded to this point. The ninety-minute conversations touched on a variety of topics, including relationships, dating, infidelity, the 2024 election, and pornography. At the end of each session, we posed a single question to our male participants and had them write down a response: "What do you wish young women understood about what it's like to be a young man today?" We posed the same question to female participants about what they wished young men understood.

Most of the women cited the issue of safety in their responses. They mentioned that the steps they took to avoid danger were a major part of their lives—something they were forced to think about often, and an experience they felt many men knew little or nothing about. The issue of sexual violence came up often.

A young woman named Shannon said, "I wish men understood the harassment that women go through on a daily basis. Most women can't even leave the house without getting catcalled or even get to dress a certain way. If men could walk in the shoes of a woman just once, maybe they'll change their mindset and ways."

Amanda, a thirty-two-year-old woman in the focus groups, reflected on how this omnipresent fear dictated so much of her everyday routines. "As a young woman today, we don't feel safe, heard, or understood," she said. "Simple, mundane acts like getting dressed, exercising, walking home, and ordering food at home or an Uber need to be thoroughly analyzed, dissected, and planned so that we don't end up in compromising situations."

One woman expressed that even when simply being out in the world, men treat women "like they are prey."

These feelings are so raw, punctuated by a sense of anger. Yet, comments like this reflect an abiding appeal to be seen and supported. Many single young women living in large cities feel vulnerable in ways that are simply foreign to their male friends, co-workers, and peers. The exhaustion expressed in these conversations is not entirely due to the fear they feel, but the knowledge that they carry the burdens of vigilance alone. They are left to fend for themselves in a dangerous world.

The conversations I had with men were different, but few felt that they were any better off. Greg, a twenty-seven-year-old, expressed a view that was fairly common: "There is still that expectation that men get, both from men and women, that men will just shoulder whatever's going on," he said. "We'll just carry on with life. And I think that's why we kill ourselves at much higher rates. I think it's why we smoke and overdose and drink ourselves to death at much higher rates." Men too often feel they have been left to make their way without aid.

In different rooms and at different times, I heard from single men and women about the challenges of dating, and relationships, and the sometimes harsh realities of modern life. Their experiences varied dramatically, but in one way they are both seeking the same thing: Men and women asked for greater understanding and patience.

One young man named Connor said, "We are trying very, very hard to meet your needs. But we need a chance. Give us patience, grace, and understanding and we will grow. Society is changing, and so are we, but we need your help."

Elise had a similar request of young men: "Give more grace! Women can't just show up as themselves in this world. We constantly have to adjust and present as 'acceptable' in this world. So please just extend grace and truly consider what it's like to be a woman today."

Conditioned by social media, we have come to expect the very worst of each other. We have become so quick to judge behavior that we don't fully understand. Modern life has rapidly accelerated the pace of social interaction and reduced the contextual clues available to us, leaving us more prone to misjudging someone's intentions. What if we simply slowed it down? Led with curiosity rather than criticism.

What emerged most clearly from these conversations is a sense of mutual frustration: Both young women and young men feel misunderstood. Both young men and young women feel there is neither any room for error nor any interest in giving people the benefit of the doubt. Women describe a world that too often minimizes their fears, while men feel discouraged from expressing their own fears, much less asking for help.

Across these exchanges, there was an often-unstated plea for a culture that recognizes their distinct experiences, acknowledges the hardships they face, and fosters a sense of mutual obligation, trust, and respect.

On our second date, over appetizers at a small restaurant in Washington, D.C.'s Adams Morgan neighborhood, my now wife asked me a question that I could not hear over the din of crowded conversation. Instead of asking her to repeat it, I breezily informed her that "I only listen to about three-quarters of what you say." My recollection is hazy, but it's hard to believe this was anything other than a moment of pure insanity. Fortunately for me, my wife perceived correctly that it was an ill attempt at humor, the result of nervous energy. Over the course of our early dating lives, she made her share of miscues too, but we both benefited from not having every mistake, impetuous action, and intemperate remark digitally catalogued and broadcast, offered up as an embarrassing highlight reel. Our words and deeds matter, but they should live for a time, die, and be buried. The half-life of our mistakes has become too long. Too many young adults live in perpetual fear that their misdeeds will follow them forever. The internet doesn't forget. This makes it all the more necessary that we practice forgiveness of the small slights, the oversights, and the misjudgments.

CHAPTER 13

BUILDING SOMETHING TOGETHER: A RENEWED COMMITMENT TO RELATIONAL LIFE

Renewing a Sense of Belonging

Reactions to the TV show *Adolescence* varied, but for me it was watching the unfolding of a slow-moving nightmare. No parent wants to believe their child is capable of causing so much grief and pain in others. Individual pain does not stay self-contained, it radiates outward, traveling along all our social ties. There's a popular saying that a parent is only as happy as their least happy child. It's an acknowledgment that our life satisfaction is not entirely of our own making but depends greatly on the welfare of the people closest to us. Research has demonstrated that children are also affected by the well-being of their parents; it's not unidirectional. One of the powerful and painful lessons of *Adolescence* is that our fate is intertwined with others and not something that is easily cast off. For better or worse, this is how it should be.

In the final moments of the series, the family debates whether they should move away from the town and escape their family's tarnished reputation. It's a proposition that Jamie's sister, Lisa, firmly rejects. She argues that wherever they would go, someone would eventually learn about what Jamie did, and the family would be put through a fresh round of hell. For me, the most powerful moment of the entire series comes when Lisa refuses to put any distance between Jamie and the rest of the family, even as they still struggle with what he did. "He is ours," she says. It is not a grand gesture, but a simple statement of fact. Jamie belongs to all of them. And they belong to him.

It's a profound realization. So often, our social relationships are measured against their capacity to serve our self-interest—embraced when they do and abandoned when they do not. At a time when the bonds of family and friendship are sometimes considered transactional, an unbreakable bond feels revelatory. It's a socio-centric perspective on relationships—we exist as part of a larger social structure that shapes our character and understanding of ourselves. It's an understanding that is increasingly disputed. Yuval Levin warns that "we have gradually come to treat the intense and nearly universal desire for family life more as a longing for recognition than as a hunger for order and structure."[1] He's right that although family ties can be a source of immeasurable joy, they can also cause irreparable harm. But they still serve to give us a sense of the world and a sense of ourselves. The point is that our most important relationships are not easily set aside, even when they become personally inconvenient.

Every generation of young adults has had to figure out their place in the world and find their people. Yet we have made it harder for them to do so. The rise of single-parent households, the collapse of religious communities, and the primacy of an ethic of individualism have weakened our sense of belonging. Young adults raised by unmarried parents who are not living together are twice as likely as those with married parents to report feeling that "there is nowhere you really belong."[2] Secular young adults face a similar deficit of belonging compared to their religious peers. The United States has the highest rates of single-parent households, and one of the lowest rates of community belonging.[3,4] Young people have become less rooted in physical spaces and connected with the people who occupy them, instead operating more as free agents moving through an impermanent mélange of social environments. More young people feel unclaimed—that there is not a community of people who are responsible for them or care what happens to them. And in turn, there are few people they feel responsible for.

A feeling of belonging not only provides young people with a sense of security and serves as a source of identity; it also constrains their worst impulses. Understanding that our behavior reflects well or poorly on our families or communities is a powerful restraint. Without the sense of responsibility to the people in our lives, it is easier to engage in self-serving and self-destructive behavior. If our actions no longer reflect negatively (or positively) on our friends, colleagues, or family members, we become disinhibited. It becomes easier to separate our actions from their consequences.

Individual decisions have social consequences. Our fates are linked. A single act of violence can destroy many lives, but only in a community can someone who was lost become found. It's possible for many lives to be blown apart in a single moment, but it takes incremental effort and regular engagement to repair them. Our social structures, culture, and family arrangements should reflect this fundamental fact.

We're Not That Different and You're Not That Special

If your parents ever told you how special, unique, or talented you were they probably meant it. In a broader sense, it's not exactly true—in all likelihood you're not that special. And that's okay. Your value is not derived from your unique voice, or personal accomplishments, but rather in how the distinctive contours of your life fit in with others'. Life is a collaborative enterprise. Unfortunately, we often fail to appreciate the contributions of our coauthors. A culture that prizes performative individualism and provides an overabundance of autonomy warps our understanding of ourselves and our relationships to others. Fortunately, the instinct to establish social connections is incredibly strong.

Today's culture has trained young people to treat uniqueness as a commodity, an effective way to attract attention and demonstrate their value. But the truth is that long-lasting fulfillment lies in connection with other people. The more time we spend looking for what we have in common, the more opportunities we will have to create a society of interdependence, where we can be known, supported, and challenged.

Adopting this mindset may take unlearning the lessons of childhood. It's definitely going to take getting honest about the gravity of the situation and the obstacles in front of us. More than half (52 percent) of young adults still report feeling "like there is something special about them." Among seniors, only 36 percent said the same.[5] That's a big gap, and society doesn't make it easy for us to change. In almost every part of modern life, we are incentivized to demonstrate our uniqueness and individuality. In interviews, we're asked about what separates us from our competition. In relationships, we're taught to learn our "love languages" so that our partners can personalize their romantic approach. There are a growing number of identity labels young adults can adopt to express their individuality: astrological signs, sexual and gender identities, political orientations, personality types (introvert or extrovert), attachment styles (anxious, avoidant), and mental health statuses (neurodivergent, ADHD)—to name only a few. And to make matters more complicated, our identities can change at any point for any reason. They are intersectional, gaining particular salience under certain conditions or in certain contexts.

We have gained unprecedented autonomy in our self-presentation, but we have made it so much more difficult to relate to other people. We're starting to see the consequences of that. More than half of Americans report that no one knows them well.[6] This feeling is even more pronounced among America's youngest and most diverse generation—68 percent of Gen Z believe that no one really knows them. Chasing uniqueness keeps us lonely.

It's time to face the hard truth: Not only are you likely not so different from your co-workers, neighbors, and family members; you're probably not more interesting, generous, or intelligent than they are either. Chances are, you are fairly unexceptional in most ways and you live in a standard American neighborhood in an unassuming house or a modest apartment. If you have children, they will likely be no better than average in most of the things that they attempt.

Even if you believe yourself to be above average, there is a strong likelihood that your aspirations are not so unique. Despite our differences, when you ask people about their life goals or personal priorities, people say a lot of the same things. When we asked the young singles in our focus groups what an ideal life looks like, there was remarkable consistency in their responses. Nearly everyone mentioned financial stability, health, and companionship of some type. They had different educational and racial backgrounds, unique perspectives on politics, and different sexual orientations and genders. Yet, the aspirations they had were similar.

The answer of how to come together probably lies more in sociology than psychology. How do co-workers build bridges of collegiality if they come from different walks of life? They are encouraged to spend time together, to learn about what they care about, and to find opportunities to collaborate. How do neighbors develop a sense of belonging and trust? They work together to address a shared concern. How do couples build trust, even if they have different communication styles? By spending time together, listening, and generously giving their most valuable resource: attention.

The principle of homophily recognizes a central human tendency: It turns out we prefer to spend time with people like ourselves. We are less apt to feel apprehension when dealing with the familiar. Put simply: "Similarity breeds connections."[7] When we are incentivized to showcase our distinct identities or opinions, we make it more difficult to forge social connections. The good news is that we have a lot more in common with one another than we think. Even our ideological adversaries are not as hateful, ignorant, or bigoted as our imaginations make them out to be.[8]

It's not enough to gather people together in a room. That has been tried, and although the results were promising, it doesn't scale.[9] What we need is a shared purpose—a reason to work together, to toil, and, yes—to sacrifice. Religious and spiritual communities operate on this implicit understanding of human nature—individuals are flawed, frightened, and occasionally hostile, but capable of accomplishing incredible acts of heroism and generosity when working for something greater than themselves. We've lost sight of that fact. The act of attending to the needs, questions, and problems of others focuses our gaze outward. Any parent can tell you about a time when they had an awful day at work only to have their problems immediately melt away when they arrived home to the wild laughter of their kids. It's something I've experienced myself. It's not simply a distraction from self-doubt and insecurity; it's an unavoidable reminder of who we are and how we matter. And it's an experience accessible to everyone, not only a fortunate few.

Too often, society feels like a lottery. There are a few massive winners, but most of us walk away with nothing. We need a culture that acknowledges that most of us are unexceptional; we have reasonable levels of intelligence, ability, and ambition. Yet, it is possible for us to live extraordinary lives because of the people in them.

Seeking Relational Identities

When we look at what it takes to move forward, after we recognize a shared purpose, we need to reclaim the shared identities that tie us together as a society. Parent. Partner. Friend. Neighbor. Mentor. Sister. Brother. These are identities that connect us. When we start to think of ourselves in these roles, we realize that identity isn't only who we are, it's also who we are to one another. These identities are based on our relationship to the people in our lives and the obligations we have to them. They can foster an appreciation for someone's point of view by acknowledging our shared relationship experiences, responsibilities, and challenges. And they even have the added benefit of avoiding divisive tribal allegiances; in most cases they are politically and culturally neutral.

I often hear people complain about uncomfortable conversations they have with people they do not know well. The purpose of small talk is not to interrupt your peace, but rather to identify commonalities between strangers. These superficial conversations can reveal shared experiences that can serve as the jumping-off point for deeper and more personal topics. People complain about the weather not because it's interesting, but because it offers one of the best ways to create a shared experience—most of us do not like when it rains, or when it is too hot or too cold.

Relational identities also instill a sense of duty and obligation. In my role as a parent, neighbor, friend, or partner, what are my social responsibilities—what do I owe others? These identities challenge us to improve ourselves, to be a better parent, colleague, or neighbor. They are not status markers—lots of people are neighbors and co-workers—but signifiers of our place in a community and our collective responsibility.

Robert Bellah recognized the problem posed to a society when there are few limits on individual autonomy. In *Habits of the Heart,* Bellah and his colleagues argued that " 'finding oneself' is not something one does alone. The quest for personal growth and self-fulfillment is supposed to lead one into relationships with others."[10] Of course, our relationships are meant to fulfill personal needs, but they are also meant to shape us. Relational identities clarify our commitments to others and to ourselves. We find our way in the world not through self-actualization, but through the bonds we build. When a society actively prioritizes personal expression above all else without regard to the consequences, it weakens social bonds, civic engagement, and shared commitments. When the highest priority is revealing our true self to the world, it makes compatibility more difficult and compromise less attractive.

When relationships are optional and commitments perpetually negotiable, who we are and what we are supposed to do becomes unstable. Meaningful identities are not simply an indicator of personal preference but a statement about our priorities. This is an acknowledgment of what we owe, and what we are owed. Daily acts of obligation to people and communities provide purpose and direction; they ground our decisions. This isn't regression, it's maturity. And it's the only way forward.

Cultivating a Culture of Kindness

How readily would you blast someone on social media if you were going to see them in church, sit next to them in class, or run into them at the office the next day? Contemplating the social consequences might lead us to pause, reflect, and consider an alternative way to vent our frustrations. We've become addicted to expressing our self-righteous indignation. And every mean-spirited social media post, degrading meme, and caustic public remark delivered by our political leaders coarsens our culture. Those nasty remarks serve as a model of public engagement. In 2024, nearly two-thirds of voters said Trump was "mean-spirited," but that was hardly a politically disqualifying attribute.[11] Four in ten of Trump's own supporters described him that way.

We live in an era of artificiality, so, naturally, we prize authenticity in our social interactions, personal experiences, news sources, and even politicians. The Pew Research Center found that 82 percent of Americans valued authenticity in the people they get their news from.[12] More young adults have come to deride small talk as fake, and social grace and generosity as evidence of phoniness. Our culture has so thoroughly embraced an individualistic mentality that some prosocial behavior is viewed with inherent suspicion. Supposedly, altruistic behavior masks a hidden agenda or is performative. Men attempting to signal an embrace of feminist values are accused of engaging in "performative male" behavior. As *The New York Times* put it, "The Performative Male curates his aesthetic in a way that he thinks might render him more likable to progressive women."[13] Young women, in turn, have faced a barrage of criticism for having platonic relationships with young men who are interested in them—keeping them in the "friend zone"—as a perverse method of validation.

In all three of his presidential campaigns, Donald Trump benefited tremendously from the perception that he was not a typical politician—his offensive behavior proved his authenticity.[14] Supporters would consistently remark that, while they don't always approve of the way he communicates, they appreciate that he says what he thinks. In America, to be rude is to be real. And it is a quality that is not only celebrated but rewarded.

Authenticity and indignation are not the same thing, and they should no longer be treated as such. Courtesy is costless, but so often we believe that individual expression is stifled by acts of consideration. The freedom we have to say what we want is an unequivocal gift, but we must take seriously the obligations that come with it. The sheer volume of our online communication can rob an individual act of its meaning: Who cares if I made a snide remark on social media? But they represent our contribution to a culture, one that can serve others, that seeks kindness, or that serves our own selfish interests. Every word we type matters.

Cultivating Mutual Curiosity

We've effectively privatized the provision of care and consideration, freeing us of the obligation to look out for one another. Women and men have adopted hyper-vigilant postures in different ways and for different reasons. Each side is fearful that their vulnerabilities will be exploited by the other. The institutions, such as schools and churches, that once brought us together and instilled a sense of civic mindedness, are now more likely to inspire scorn and skepticism instead. Fear has become an organizing principle and animating force of our public life. And that has made intimacy, connection, and cooperation feel risky. And so, abstention has become the default.

The solution to the self-vigilance culture isn't another app, self-help session, or self-defense strategy. It's a shift in mindset. Life is too often treated as a spectator sport, when it requires our full participation. Algorithms may effectively predict what we want to see, but not how any particular social interaction will play out. We cannot optimize our way out of this mess, so we need to get comfortable with a certain amount of ambiguity and friction.

One unfortunate result of this heightened state of anxiety is that so much of the advice on how to avoid putting yourself in harm's way encourages an antisocial approach. Do not make eye contact or smile. Better yet: Scowl at other human beings to fend off conversation. Walk quickly or walk with a dangerous-looking dog. It's sort of like being in the Matrix—every unknown man is potentially dangerous, so the only expedient solution is to treat them all that way. For men, even a modest gesture or innocuous comment can leave them exposed to viral takedown from women who interpret these acts as evidence of hostility. But the more we protect ourselves from one another, the less we see one another as human.

Young men should understand that intimidation and threatening behavior are not anomalous experiences for many young women, and they should be unafraid to ask about them. In social interactions, differences in physicality matter. There is a growing chorus urging young men to be bold in their romantic interactions. This is good advice, but young men should be aware that being fifty pounds heavier and six inches taller than the woman they are talking to has an impact on how their actions and words are interpreted. Expressions of male anger are different than female anger, especially when directed at women. It's not the same and leads to very different consequences.

Even having a social media presence can make young women feel especially vulnerable. If you think women are overly sensitive, I invite you to reach out to any prominent female figure online and politely ask her to share the feedback she's gotten. Plenty of research has documented online harassment, but statistics fail to adequately convey the feeling of receiving a rape threat for the simple act of expressing an opinion. The catalogue of vicious threats and dehumanizing comments is often invisible. The asymmetry of this experience is difficult to convey. A message that threatens a woman with bodily harm can stay with her for weeks or months and be expediently forgotten by its author. The internet makes delivery seamless and creates the illusion that these acts are victimless.

But curiosity also needs to flow in both directions. When men remain silent, it does not mean they are free of worry, but that they believe society is less willing to abide or acknowledge their pain. Young men take less care of their physical and mental health—they are far less likely to access routine checkups and preventative care—not because they are waiting for a woman to take care of them, but because many have learned along the way that they are disposable. When we become separated from one another, these experiences can seem unimaginable. The less time we spend together, the fewer opportunities we have to learn not only how we differ, but how we can step in to make a difference.

Reimagining Chivalry: A Prosocial Proposal

An unrelenting emphasis on ourselves has led us to neglect our social responsibilities. But even if we agree on the necessity of recommitting to our interpersonal obligations, the question remains as to how this is accomplished. One solution doesn't require a radical reimagining of public responsibilities, but instead recognizes men's unique contributions to civility in public spaces. Call it a reimagined chivalry. It is encouraging men to look out for others, not out of a misplaced sense of entitlement, but out of a sense of duty. The goal is not to diminish women, but to recover a model of masculinity that benefited society: an ethic of attentiveness.

For most of human history, the greater size, strength, and speed that men possessed afforded them a physical advantage over women and played a critical role in perpetuating societal inequalities. Cultural norms have changed, however, and technological advancements have diminished the importance of physical labor. The rising importance of education and social skills in the labor market has eroded some benefits of physical strength. But not all of them.

Size differences still matter in social interactions between men and women. But young people are increasingly taught to disregard them since, in the simple act of acknowledging biological reality, we are somehow accused of treating women as less capable and less equal. But ignoring our differences doesn't make the world fairer; it just makes it harder to talk about how they shape our lived experience.

Feminist author Melinda Wenner Moyer argues that teaching boys to be chivalrous reinforces female dependency. "Chivalry does more than merely reinforce the idea that women are the weaker sex—it also celebrates and rewards certain kinds of women, and certain kinds of behaviors, at the expense of others. In a culture shaped by benevolent sexism, men are rewarded for their power and strength (including caring for women), while women are rewarded for their warmth and docility (including allowing men to serve as their protectors)."[15]

Narratives like this have taught men to not extend special consideration to women in social settings because doing so perpetuates a belief that men and women are unequal. This is emblematic of how many modern conversations about gender equality proceed; girls and young women learn that they are just as capable as men but must overcome institutional obstacles—obstacles that benefit men and make women's lives more difficult.

In many cases, young men learn they should not intercede on behalf of women. In the absence of a shared ethic that men should look out for women, the likelihood that they intervene on behalf of someone they do not know is greatly reduced. In a meta-study covering eighty-five published research articles on the "bystander effect" in sexual assault or harassment situations, researchers found that social expectations played a significant role in predicting whether people intervene.[16] If young men believe their efforts to intervene on behalf of women will result in condemnation, they are far less likely to do so.

In interviews with young people, I posed the question of chivalry. Many young women were highly supportive of a culture in which people looked out for each other, where those who are more vulnerable were provided extra consideration. However, very few of the women I talked to were eager for strange men to intervene directly in their affairs. In an emergency, many young women hoped that men would step in to help, but there was not a great deal of confidence that they would.

For the most part, chivalry can work without grand gestures or heroic acts. Instead, it can operate as an antidote to a culture that fosters aggression online and ambivalence in the real world. Men can and should take an outsize role in enforcing social norms in public spaces—the work of acknowledging others in public spaces with respect. Men once did this with a simple gesture—tipping their hat.

I'm not arguing that American society needs to return to traditional forms of chivalry, which in many ways are outmoded. Girls and boys want to be the heroes and heroines of their story. But all heroes rely on others at some point. The assistance that men and women can offer is not always the same, but both can serve individual and social interests. The challenge arises when any form of intervention on behalf of women is ruled out of hand as benevolent sexism that perpetuates the idea that women are weaker, incapable of protecting themselves, and in need of male assistance.

The growth of online harassment makes this a more complicated task. In the real world, chivalrous norms can help to avoid harmful behavior before it happens, but online, those norms often require a response to abuse. One study found that "digital bystanders" were disinclined to intervene unless the harassment was obvious and they knew the victim well.[17] The study also found that bystanders were worried that getting involved could escalate the situation, making it worse. Private reporting was often the preferred approach, but this was often viewed as ineffectual and doing nothing to change the culture of behavior online.

I'm not going to pretend there is an easy answer here, but this should not stop us from acting. First, we need to address and change the misbelief that online harassment is not the serious offense it is. Second, men should establish norms of expressive solidarity with women who have experienced abuse—publicly acknowledging that the abusive behavior is weird, gross, or creepy. Acts of harassment and abuse should be well publicized. Finally, authority figures—parents, educators, elected officials, and religious leaders—must set a higher standard for public online discourse. How can we possibly teach young people appropriate ways to act if we cannot commit ourselves to a higher level of decency in how we engage in romantic, social, and political conversations online? It's not inevitable that algorithms promote the most abusive and vitriolic posts. We can put public pressure on social media companies to change, abstain from using the worst platforms, or strategically ignore posts meant to bait us into response. If young people are more regularly exposed to examples of respectful behavior on social media, they are more likely to adopt it themselves. They would see a new model of norms and etiquette. It doesn't need to be perfect to be better than it is now.

Reformed chivalry provides one of the few prosocial models for men that encourages them to be vigilant and to act in service to others. Young men can play a unique role in ensuring public spaces are safe for others. Taking on this responsibility also requires an acknowledgement that men are frequently the reason these spaces are dangerous to begin with. In the rush to end patriarchal privileges and demonstrate a commitment to gender equality, we have avoided the most critical aspect of human existence: that we need to rely on each other.

There is a prosocial alternative available. Young men should learn to exercise greater situational awareness—the type most women develop early in their lives and deploy unceasingly. How difficult would it be for young men to engage this way? Some men already do. A friend of mine says if he's walking at night and there is a woman walking alone ahead of him, he will often cross to the other side of the street so she knows he is not a threat. Or he'll take a moment to tie his shoe to give her time to get well ahead of him. It can be engaging someone in conversation at the bus stop or the bar to offer a distraction or create an exit for a woman in distress. Sometimes, the act of naming what is happening is enough to attract public attention to effectively serve as a deterrent. The important point is that it rarely requires physical confrontation. It's not about dramatic displays—in fact, many such acts are probably so discreet as to go unnoticed—but rather about making modest changes in how men act in public. It does, however, require acknowledgment that men and women require different types of accommodation to feel comfortable in certain public spaces.

The debate about safety reveals a fundamental tension in what it means to need help from others. This is part of a larger societal shift toward the personalization of societal problems. Social problems no longer catalyze collective response, but are foisted on individuals to solve or manage. Technological innovations provide new tools, techniques, and strategies to make us more self-sufficient. There are over nine thousand items sold by Amazon under the category of "Women's Personal Safety Products," such as personal GPS systems, mace key chains, drink covers, portable door locks, door jambs, and alarms. We harness America's consumerist culture and information environment to figure out things for ourselves instead of relying on a shared ethic of responsibility to keep public spaces safe. Young people, raised online, are increasingly taught to manage these challenges on their own. But they shouldn't have to.

Could this model possibly work? There is some evidence that it already has. A review of research on prosocial helping behavior conducted in the mid-1980s found that men were more likely to lend a hand than women.[18] The explanation for the discrepancy in helping behavior was attributed to notions of chivalry and heroism embedded in traditional norms of masculinity. We should strive to create a society that prioritizes solicitousness in general, but the size and strength advantage men have creates additional opportunities for them to be uniquely helpful in certain circumstances. I don't think it benefits anyone if men no longer feel an obligation to render help to those who need it.

A reimagined chivalry does not require acts of heroism, but of attention and accommodation. It requires that men and women take a more active role in enforcing social norms and attending to violations of them. The act of simply noticing aggressive or antisocial behavior in public and expressing public disapproval rather than ignoring it can alter the way people act. It requires that we take our headphones out and put our phones away at least while we inhabit shared public space. Acknowledging that people are more vulnerable does not require thinking less of them. Giving up a seat on the train for a pregnant passenger or an elderly rider is not denigrating or demeaning. It communicates first that we see each other, and that we appreciate the additional hardship that some people face in simply moving through the world. Safety isn't something we can buy or outsource—it's a practice we have to perform together.

What We Owe One Another

Social media is awash in terrible relationship advice. In one recent post on X, a young woman shared her experience of breaking off a relationship with the boyfriend who wanted to marry her because she was still infatuated with another guy who was only interested in sex. The responses—mostly from women—largely supported her decision. More than a few posters argued that her ex-boyfriend was not entitled to anything from her. "You don't owe him anything."

This has become a reflexive comment used to shield ourselves against any sense of responsibility to other people. And it is nearly always wrong. We don't owe every person everything, but we owe them something. It might be acknowledging someone's perspective, giving someone our full attention, or offering respect. Perhaps it's much more than that. We show each other kindness, respect, and decency not because people are worthy of these expressions, but because we are capable of providing them. A culture of obligation is built piece by piece, with small gestures, simple acts of compassion, and a consistent regard for others.

I tend to believe that the insistence that we don't owe much of anything to anyone is not only about maintaining independence in our lives; more Americans have become increasingly uncomfortable with expressions of devotion, especially acts of service to romantic partners. Manosphere influencers castigate men who prioritize their wife's career or put her professional needs ahead of their own. Young women ponder publicly whether even wanting a boyfriend is cringe. A *Vogue* article titled, "Is Having a Boyfriend Embarrassing Now?" set off a firestorm about the state of dating.[19] On Instagram, a torrent of comments from young women expressed support for the argument.

"The value of having a boyfriend has depreciated."

"Having a bf is a PR disaster."

"It's a humiliation ritual."

"It just doesn't fit my brand."

"Every boyfriend I've ever had has embarrassed me."

There are hundreds more. It's incredibly bleak.

We live in a culture that no longer celebrates relational accomplishments. Being in a healthy marriage is an accomplishment. Being an active parent and raising kids who can be constructive and kind is praiseworthy. Many young Americans scoff at the notion of dedicating their lives to public service only because it has become more difficult to imagine engaging in this behavior in their private lives. Our romantic relationships have become transactional rather than transformational.

Admitting that we owe something to one another doesn't require grand gestures or sweeping sacrifices, but rather a recognition that none of us can make it on our own. It means caring about how our actions impact those around us and appreciating how technology degrades our capacity to connect. When someone seeks support, affection, or attention, both the giver and the receiver are benefited—it is this need that creates bonds of trust and reciprocity. Whether in public spaces or in private moments, men and women have a role in rebuilding our sense of trust. Simply because it has become easier to survive on our own does not mean men and women do not need one another.

My wife and I will often get up a bit earlier than our kids, at least on school days. After making her tea in the morning, we'll sit together in our living room. Sometimes we sit in silence as we take on the requisite amount of caffeine and prepare for the day. Most days, we'll have our phones out, or occasionally a laptop. When we talk to each other we do so through the dense attention fog these technologies produce. As a result, I do not always listen as closely as I should, sense the tenseness in her question as she wrestles with a challenging work problem, or remember all the details of our conversation a few hours later.

One morning, I decided to put the distractions away. The phone. The laptop. The tablet. She asked me a question and I looked her in the eyes, thought for a minute about what she was asking, and replied. I don't know whether it made any difference to her, but it made a difference to me.

ACKNOWLEDGMENTS

In the life of any book, there are a few people who see it grow from a tangle of disparate ideas into a cohesive narrative. My Penguin Random House editor, Leita Williams, not only fought for this book from the earliest days, but she also patiently guided it through various stages of development. She has been both an unrelenting advocate and a conscientious critic for it. I'm indebted to her efforts. I owe a debt of gratitude to the research team at the Survey Center on American Life, a collection of remarkable people: Jae Grace, Avery Shields, and Kelsey Eyre Hammond. For the last year and a half, they have supported this book in nearly every conceivable way, from assisting with research, qualitative contributions, and providing editorial feedback. As I write this, they are working assiduously to verify every claim and data point that appears in the book. No small task.

The original polling and qualitative research, which serves as the foundation for this book, would not have been possible without the institutional support of the American Enterprise Institute. I'm grateful to AEI President Robert Doar for his steady leadership and unwavering support for the Survey Center and its central mission to produce rigorous and intellectually honest research. I'm equally grateful to my AEI colleagues: Yuval Levin, for his continual encouragement and guidance, and Nicole Penn, for her patient advocacy and steady presence through the entire process. This book's existence would not have been possible if not for Karlyn Bowman, whose long and remarkable career as a scholar of public opinion paved the way for my work at AEI. And to Ryan Streeter, who brought me to AEI seven years ago and was instrumental in the creation of the Survey Center.

I want to express appreciation to Christine Rosen for her careful and thoughtful comments on an early manuscript, and to Amelia Thomson-Deveaux for her help in thinking through its structure. I am grateful to Mallory Newall at Ipsos for her support with much of the qualitative research we conducted for this book. And of course, my literary agent Christopher Combemale, who first approached me about writing a book based on my research and who played a critical role helping me transform these early ideas into a compelling book proposal.

If you finished the book and are not skipping ahead to read the Acknowledgements, it will have been abundantly clear that my wife, Stephanie, and our two boys were profoundly important in shaping my thoughts about romantic relationships, parenting, family commitments, and civic obligations. These are not abstract concepts, but deeply personal experiences that pushed me to engage with the empirical evidence with greater empathy, humility, and understanding. It was not my intent to share so much of my own story in this book, but at some point in the writing process it felt necessary. If polling research spurred my early interest in this topic, some of the most important insights and observations were drawn from my experience as a husband, a father, a friend, and a neighbor. This book is a product of both.

ABOUT THE AUTHOR

Daniel A. Cox is the founder and director of the Survey Center on American Life and a senior fellow in polling and public opinion at the American Enterprise Institute (AEI). He received his PhD in Government from Georgetown University and has worked in the field of public opinion research for two decades. He began his polling career at the Pew Research Center. Since joining AEI in 2019, his work has focused on Gen Z politics, religious changes in the United States, dating and romantic relationships, friendship, and social disconnection. His research has been cited in hundreds of news stories from major outlets, including *The New York Times, The Wall Street Journal, The Washington Post,* and CNN. He currently writes *American Storylines* on Substack, a biweekly newsletter providing polling-based commentary on the experiences, challenges, and aspirations of everyday Americans. He lives in Washington, D.C., with his wife and two sons. He is an unwavering supporter of Chelsea F.C.

NOTES

Introduction

1. Pfeifer, Valeria A., and Matthias R. Mehl. "Sliding Into Silence? We Are Speaking 300 Daily Words Fewer Every Year." *Perspectives on Psychological Science,* 2026. https://doi.org/10.1177/17456916261425131.

Chapter 1

1. Evans, Jonathan, Kirsten Lesage, Manolo Corichi et al. "In 25-Country Survey, Americans Especially Likely to View Fellow Citizens as Morally Bad." Pew Research Center. March 5, 2026. https://www.pewresearch.org/religion/2026/03/05/in-25-country-survey-americans-especially-likely-to-view-fellow-citizens-as-morally-bad/?utm_source=twitter&utm_medium=social&utm_campaign=fedica-Main.
2. Kand, Cecilia, Ryan Mac, and Eli Tan. "Meta and YouTube Found Negligent in Landmark Social Media Addiction Case," *The New York Times*, March 25, 2026. https://www.nytimes.com/2026/03/25/technology/social-media-trial-verdict.html.
3. Nicas, Jack. "The Internet's Final Frontier: Remote Amazon Tribes." *The New York Times.* May 23, 2025. https://www.nytimes.com/2024/06/02/world/americas/starlink-internet-elon-musk-brazil-amazon.html.
4. Perrin, Andrew. "Social Media Usage: 2005-2015." Pew Research Center, October 8, 2015. https://www.pewresearch.org/internet

/2015/10/08/social-networking-usage-2005-2015/?cb_viewport=tablet.

5. Pew Research Center. "American Trends Panel Wave 168." Data file. April 14–20, 2025, https://www.pewresearch.org/wp-content/uploads/sites/20/2025/07/PI_2025.07.31_Scams_TOPLINE.pdf.
6. Zuckerberg, Mark. "Mark Zuckerberg's Post." Facebook. January 11, 2018. https://www.facebook.com/zuck/posts/one-of-our-big-focus-areas-for-2018-is-making-sure-the-time-we-all-spend-on-face/10104413015393571.
7. "Social Media and Youth Mental Health." *National Library of Medicine*. 2023. https://www.ncbi.nlm.nih.gov/books/NBK594759/#:~:text=Social%20media1%20use%20by,8%E2%80%9312%20use%20social%20media.
8. Anderson, Monica, and Michelle Faverio. "Teens, Social Media and Technology 2022." Pew Research Center, August 10, 2022. https://www.pewresearch.org/internet/2022/08/10/teens-social-media-and-technology-2022.
9. Cox, Daniel A., and Kelsey Eyre Hammond. "The Politics of Progress and Privilege: How America's Gender Gap Is Reshaping the 2024 Election." AEI Survey Center on American Life. September 24, 2024.
10. Cox and Hammond, "The Politics of Progress and Privilege."
11. Haidt, Jonathan. *The Anxious Generation: How the Great Rewiring of Childhood Is Causing an Epidemic of Mental Illness*. Penguin Press. 2024.
12. Rothwell, Jonathan. "Teens Spend Average of 4.8 Hours on Social Media per Day." Gallup. October 13, 2023. https://news.gallup.com/poll/512576/teens-spend-average-hours-social-media-per-day.aspx.
13. Cox, Daniel A., Kelsey Eyre Hammond, and Kyle Gray. "Generation Z and the Transformation of American Adolescence: How Gen Z's Formative Experiences Shape Its Politics, Priorities, and Future." AEI Survey Center on American Life. November 9, 2023. https://www.americansurveycenter.org/research/generation-z-and-the-transformation-of-american-adolescence-how-gen-zs-formative-experiences-shape-its-politics-priorities-and-future.

14. Cox, Hammond, and Gray, "Generation Z and the Transformation of American Adolescence."
15. "Differences in How Democrats and Republicans Behave on Twitter." Pew Research Center. October 15, 2020. https://www.pewresearch.org/politics/2020/10/15/differences-in-how-democrats-and-republicans-behave-on-twitter.
16. Bestvater, Samuel. "How U.S. Adults Use TikTok." Pew Research Center. February 22, 2024. https://www.pewresearch.org/internet/2024/02/22/how-u-s-adults-use-tiktok.
17. Gottfried, Jeffrey and Eugenie Park. "Americans' Social Media Use 2025." Pew Research Center, November 20, 2025. https://www.pewresearch.org/internet/2025/11/20/americans-social-media-use-2025/#large-age-gaps-in-use-of-many-platforms.
18. Cox, Hammond, and Gray, "Generation Z and the Transformation of American Adolescence."
19. Anderson, Monica, Emily A. Vogels, Andrew Perrin, and Lee Rainie. "What Teens Post on Social Media." Pew Research Center. November 16, 2022. https://www.pewresearch.org/internet/2022/11/16/1-what-teens-post-on-social-media.
20. Cox, Daniel A., Kelsey Eyre Hammond, and Jae Grace. "How Social Media Made Us Less Social." American Storylines. April 3, 2025. https://www.americanstorylines.com/p/how-social-media-made-us-less-social.
21. Putnam, Robert D. "Tuning In, Tuning Out: The Strange Disappearance of Social Capital in America." *PS, Political Science & Politics* 28, no. 4 (1995): 664–683. https://doi.org/10.2307/420517.
22. Winn, Marie. "What Became of Childhood Innocence?" *The New York Times*, January 25, 1981. https://www.nytimes.com/1981/01/25/magazine/what-became-of-childhood-innocence.html.
23. "This Gen X Mess." *New York Times*. May 14, 2019. https://www.nytimes.com/interactive/2019/05/14/style/generation-xers.html.
24. "When You Are in Public Spaces, How Often Do You Wear Earbuds or Headphones?" YouGov. May 4, 2025. https://yougov.com/en-us/daily-results/20250504-e9c20-1.
25. McClain, Colleen, Monica Anderson, Olivia Sidoti, and William Bishop. "What Parents Say About Their Teen's AI Use." Pew Re-

search Center. February 24, 2026. https://www.pewresearch.org/internet/2026/02/24/what-parents-say-about-their-teens-ai-use.

26. Horwitz, Jeff. "Meta's AI Rules Have Let Bots Hold 'Sensual' Chats with Kids, Offer False Medical Info." Reuters. August 14, 2025. https://www.reuters.com/investigates/special-report/meta-ai-chatbot-guidelines.
27. Tiku, Nitasha, and Leo Sands. "Judge Rejects Claim Chatbots Have Free Speech in Suit over Teen's Death." *Washington Post*. May 22, 2025. https://www.washingtonpost.com/nation/2025/05/22/sewell-setzer-suicide-ai-character-court-lawsuit.
28. "Aura Releases New 2025 State of the Youth Report." Aura. December 16, 2025. https://www.aura.com/reports/state-of-the-youth-2025.
29. Mastroianni, Adam. Interview by Daniel A. Cox. Zoom, August 22, 2025.
30. Epley, Nicholas, and Juliana Schroeder. "Mistakenly Seeking Solitude." *Journal of Experimental Psychology. General* 143, no. 5 (2014): 1980–1999. https://doi.org/10.1037/a0037323.
31. Sandstrom, Gillian M., and Elizabeth W. Dunn. "Is Efficiency Overrated? Minimal Social Interactions Lead to Belonging and Positive Affect." *Social Psychological and Personality Science* 5, no. 4 (2014): 437–442. https://doi.org/10.1177/1948550613502990.
32. Kennedy, Brian, Eileen Yam, Emma Kikuchi, Isabelle Pula, and Javier Fuentes. "Americans on the Risks, Benefits of AI—in Their Own Words." Pew Research Center. September 17, 2025. https://www.pewresearch.org/science/2025/09/17/americans-on-the-risks-benefits-of-ai-in-their-own-words.
33. Perez, Sarah. "AI Companion Apps on Track to Pull in $120M in 2025." *TechCrunch*. August 12, 2025. https://techcrunch.com/2025/08/12/ai-companion-apps-on-track-to-pull-in-120m-in-2025.
34. "What Type of Social Content Creators Do Global Audiences Follow?" YouGov. January 17, 2023. https://yougov.com/articles/46113-what-types-of-social-content-creators-do-global-audiences-follow.
35. Merrill, Jeremy B., Joe Fox, and Leslie Shapiro. "Are you in TikTok's cat niche? What 121,000 videos reveal." *The Washington Post*, De-

cember 10, 2025. https://www.washingtonpost.com/technology/interactive/2025/tiktok-algorithm-video-map-interests.

36. Robb, Michael B., and Supreet Mann. "Boys in the Digital Wild: Online Culture, Identity, and Well-Being." Common Sense Media, 2025. https://www.commonsensemedia.org/sites/default/files/research/report/2025-boys-in-the-digital-wild-report_for-web.pdf.
37. Robertson, Claire E., Kareena S. del Rosario, and Jay J. Van Bavel. "Inside the Funhouse Mirror Factory: How Social Media Distorts Perceptions of Norms." *Current Opinion in Psychology* 60 (December 2024): 101918. https://doi.org/10.1016/j.copsyc.2024.101918.
38. Habib, Hussam, and Rishab Nithyanand. "YouTube Recommendations Reinforce Negative Emotions: Auditing Algorithmic Bias with Emotionally-Agentic Sock Puppets." *arXiv [Cs.SI].* http://arxiv.org/abs/2501.15048.
39. Kates, Naama. "Investigating the Incel Community." *Modern Wisdom* podcast #363 August 26, 2021. https://modernwisdom.libsyn.com/363-naama-kates-investigating-the-incel-community.
40. Silva, Christianna. "Freemasons Say They're Needed Now More than Ever. So Why Are Their Ranks Dwindling?" NPR, November 28, 2020. https://www.npr.org/2020/11/28/937228086/freemasons-say-theyre-needed-now-more-than-ever-so-why-are-their-ranks-dwindling.
41. Barber, Kristen. "The Gentrification of the Barbershop." *The New Republic*, August 8, 2016. https://newrepublic.com/article/135907/gentrification-barbershop.
42. "Majorities Say All-Female and All-Male Social Groups Have a Positive Impact on Women's and Men's Overall Well-Being." Pew Research Center. January 10, 2025. https://www.pewresearch.org/2025/01/16/the-impact-of-all-male-and-all-female-social-groups/st_2025-1-16_social-connections_3-01.
43. Way, Niobe. *Deep Secrets: Boys' Friendships and the Crisis of Connection.* Cambridge: Harvard University Press, 2013.
44. Cox, Daniel A. "The State of American Friendship: Change, Challenges, and Loss." Survey Center on American Life, June 8, 2021. https://www.americansurveycenter.org/research/the-state-of-american-friendship-change-challenges-and-loss.

Chapter 2

1. Cox, Daniel A. and Kelsey Eyre Hammond. "Individuality and Moral Behavior: A Generational Divide in Moral Judgements and Self-Expression." Survey Center on American Life, November 20, 2025. https://www.americansurveycenter.org/research/individuality-and-moral-behavior-a-generational-divide-in-moral-judgments-and-self-expression.
2. Cox, Daniel A. "Emerging Trends and Enduring Patterns in American Family Life." Survey Center on American Life, February 9, 2022. https://www.americansurveycenter.org/research/emerging-trends-and-enduring-patterns-in-american-family-life.
3. Cooperman, Alan. "Most U.S. Parents Pass Along Their Religion and Politics to Their Children." Pew Research Center. May 10, 2023. https://www.pewresearch.org/short-reads/2023/05/10/most-us-parents-pass-along-their-religion-and-politics-to-their-children.
4. Gopnik, Alison. *The Gardener and the Carpenter: What the New Science of Child Development Tells Us About the Relationship Between Parents and Children*. (New York: Farrar, Straus and Giroux, 2016), 47.
5. Wurzburger, Andrea. "Everything Charlize Theron Has Said About Motherhood." *People,* August 7, 2022. https://people.com/parents/charlize-theron-motherhood-quotes.
6. Fivush, Robyn, Marshall Duke, and Jennifer Bojanek. "Do You Know . . . The Power of Family History in Adolescent Identity and Well-Being." *Journal of Family Life,* 2010. https://ncph.org/wp-content/uploads/2013/12/The-power-of-family-history-in-adolesce.
7. Cohen, Philip N. *Enduring Bonds: Inequality, Marriage, Parenting, and Everything Else That Makes Families Great and Terrible.* University of California Press. 2018. https://doi.org/10.1525/9780520965959.
8. Pinsker, Joe. "The Age of the Unique Baby Name." *The Atlantic.* February 4, 2022. https://www.theatlantic.com/family/archive/2022/02/most-popular-baby-names-unique/621491.
9. Learning Heroes and Gallup. "B-flation: How Good Grades Can Sideline Parents." Fact sheet. Learning Heroes, Fall 2023. https://bealearninghero.org/wp-content/uploads/2023/11/Learning-Heroes-Gallup-research_fact-sheet.pdf.

10. Horowitch, Rose. "Accommodation Nation." *The Atlantic*. January 2026. https://www.theatlantic.com/magazine/2026/01/elite-university-student-accommodation/684946.
11. Bialek, Kristen. "Middle Children Have Become Rarer, but a Growing Share of Americans Now Say Three or More Kids Are 'Ideal.'" Pew Research Center. August 9, 2018. https://www.pewresearch.org/short-reads/2018/08/09/middle-children-have-become-rarer-but-a-growing-share-of-americans-now-say-three-or-more-kids-are-ideal.
12. Cox, "Emerging Trends and Enduring Patterns."
13. Cox and Hammond, "Individuality and Moral Behavior."
14. Brummelman, Eddie, Sander Thomaes, Stefanie A. Nelemans, Bram Orobio de Castro, Geertjan Overbeek, and Brad J. Bushman. "Origins of Narcissism in Children." *Proceedings of the National Academy of Sciences of the United States of America* 112, no. 12 (2015): 3659–3662. https://doi.org/10.1073/pnas.1420870112.
15. "Is Gen Z the Most Success-Oriented Generation?" Barna Group. June 6, 2018. https://www.barna.com/research/is-gen-z-the-most-success-oriented-generation.
16. Schaeffer, Katherine and Shradha Dinesh. "32% of Americans have a tattoo, including 22% who have more than one." Pew Research Center, August 15, 2023. https://www.pewresearch.org/short-reads/2023/08/15/32-of-americans-have-a-tattoo-including-22-who-have-more-than-one.
17. Children's Hospital of Philadelphia. "Talking to Kids about Gender and Sexual Orientation." Health Tip. June 24, 2020. https://www.chop.edu/news/health-tip/talking-to-kids-about-gender-and-sexual-orientation.
18. Cox, Hammond, and Gray, "Generation Z and the Transformation of American Adolescence."
19. Minkin, Rachel, Juliana Menasce Horowitz, Luona Lin, and Dana Baraga. "Experiences with Coming Out as Gay, Lesbian, Bisexual or Transgender." Pew Research Center. May 29, 2025. https://www.pewresearch.org/social-trends/2025/05/29/experiences-with-coming-out-as-gay-lesbian-bisexual-or-transgender.
20. Cox, Daniel A., Jae Grace, and Avery Shields. "What's Behind the Rapid Rise in LGBTQ Identity? Nearly One in Three Young Women

Are LGBTQ." *American Storylines*. March 6, 2025. https://www.americanstorylines.com/p/whats-behind-the-rapid-rise-in-lgbtq.

21. Morandini, James S., Liam Dacosta, and Ilan Dar-Nimrod. "Exposure to Continuous or Fluid Theories of Sexual Orientation Leads Some Heterosexuals to Embrace Less-Exclusive Heterosexual Orientations." *Scientific Reports* 11 (2021). https://www.nature.com/articles/s41598-021-94479-9.
22. Cox, Grace, and Shields, "What's Behind the Rapid Rise in LGBTQ Identity?"
23. al-Gharbi, Musa. "Queer Elites Are Still Elites." *Queer Majority,* June 15, 2025. https://www.queermajority.com/essays-all/queer-elites-are-still-elites.
24. al-Gharbi, Musa. *We Have Never Been Woke: The Cultural Contradictions of a New Elite.* (Princeton: Princeton University Press, 2024), 70.
25. Cox, Hammond, and Gray, "Generation Z and the Transformation of American Adolescence."
26. Knoester, Chris, and Chris Bjork. "The Rise of Private Club and Travel Teams in the U.S.: Generational Changes in Youth Sports Participation and Associations with Socioeconomic Statuses and Family and Community Sport Cultures." *Journal of Sport and Social Issues* 49, no. 6 (2025). https://journals.sagepub.com/doi/10.1177/01937235251377472.
27. Cox, "Emerging Trends and Enduring Patterns."
28. Minkin, Rachel, Juliana Menasce Horowitz, and Carolina Aragão. "Perceived Pros and Cons of Not Having Children." Pew Research Center. July 25, 2024. https://www.pewresearch.org/social-trends/2024/07/25/perceived-pros-and-cons-of-not-having-children.
29. Jamil, Jameela. "I Don't Want Children. I Don't Want Children. I Don't Want Children. I Don't Want Children." *A Low Desire to Please with Jameela Jamil.* December 28, 2025. https://jameelajamil.substack.com/p/i-dont-want-children-i-dont-want.
30. Levin, Yuval. *A Time to Build: From Family and Community to Congress and the Campus, How Recommitting to Our Institutions Can Revive the American Dream*. Basic Books. 2020.
31. Levin, *A Time to Build.*

32. Coleman, Joshua. Interview by Daniel A. Cox. Zoom, July 22, 2025.
33. Trampe, Debra, Jordi Quoidbach, and Maxime Taquet. "Emotions in Everyday Life." *PloS One* 10, no. 12 (2015): e0145450. https://doi.org/10.1371/journal.pone.0145450.
34. Cox, Hammond, and Gray, "Generation Z and the Transformation of American Adolescence."
35. Shrier, Abigail. *Bad Therapy: Why the Kids Aren't Growing Up*. (New York: Sentinel, 2024), 238.
36. Volpe, Allie. "'Protecting Your Peace' Can Kill Your Friendships." *Vox*. February 5, 2025. https://www.vox.com/even-better/390576/protecting-your-peace-relationships-conflict-avoidance-individualism.
37. @fraudfemme. X. December 3, 2024. https://x.com/fraudfemme/status/1863859295038722453.

Chapter 3

1. Haidt, *The Anxious Generation,* 9.
2. Petri, Alexandra E. "'Everyone's in Sync': Phone Ban on NYX Dance Floors Is Getting Rave Reviews." *The New York Times,* November 21, 2025. https://www.nytimes.com/2025/11/21/nyregion/nyc-nightlife-no-phones.html.
3. Meisel, Jordan. Quoted in Klein, Elana. "The Biggest Dating App Faux Pas for Gen Z? Being Cringe." *Wired*. May 12, 2025. https://www.wired.com/story/biggest-dating-app-faux-pas-for-gen-z-being-cringe/?_sp=0c46af1d-a45d-45eb-8f4c-223c14dab042.1767896275333.
4. Rudy, Lisa Jo. "How Many People Drive in the U.S.? 2026." ConsumerAffairs. January 21, 2026. https://www.consumeraffairs.com/automotive/number-of-drivers-in-us.html.
5. Zhou, Youyou. "Want more time with friends? It's the ordinary things that matter." *The Washington Post,* December 23, 2024. https://www.washingtonpost.com/opinions/interactive/2024/friends-loneliness-solitude-friendships.
6. Cox, Hammond, and Gray, "Generation Z and the Transformation of American Adolescence."
7. Cox, Daniel A. "Generation Z and the Future of Faith in America."

Survey Center on American Life, March 24, 2022. https://www.americansurveycenter.org/research/generation-z-future-of-faith.

8. Campbell, David E. and Robert D. Putnam. *American Grace: How Religion Divides and Unites Us.* New York: Simon & Schuster, 2010.
9. Haidt, *The Anxious Generation*, 9.
10. Elting, Liz. "Managers Don't Want To Hire Gen-Z Workers, Citing A Lack Of Soft Skills—Survey Says." Forbes, December 23, 2024. https://www.forbes.com/sites/lizelting/2024/12/23/managers-dont-want-to-hire-gen-z-workers-citing-a-lack-of-soft-skills-survey-says.
11. Thier, Jane. "Managers' latest complaints about Gen Z: They lack soft skills and have unrealistic workplace expectations." Fortune, January 23, 2024. https://fortune.com/2024/01/23/gen-z-lacks-soft-skills-unrealistic-workplace-expectations.
12. Orrell, Brent, Daniel A. Cox, and Jessie Wall. "The Social Workplace: Social Capital, Human Dignity, and Work in America." Survey Center on American Life, October 25, 2022. https://www.americansurveycenter.org/research/the-social-workplace-social-capital-human-dignity-and-work-in-america.
13. "Why Are US Homes Getting Bigger While Households Shrink?" USAFacts. September 8, 2023. https://usafacts.org/articles/why-are-us-homes-getting-bigger-while-households-shrink.
14. Guzzo, Karen Benjamin, and Jaden Loo. "Number of Children Ever Born to Women Aged 40–44, 1980–2022." *Family Profiles,* FP-23-29. Bowling Green, OH: National Center for Family & Marriage Research, Bowling Green State University, 2023. https://doi.org/10.25035/ncfmr/fp-23-29.
15. Waters, Michael. "A Subtle Shift Shaking Up Sibling Relationships." *The Atlantic.* March 8, 2024. https://www.theatlantic.com/family/archive/2024/03/sibling-age-gap-child-benefit/677676.
16. Mandel, Bethany. "You Can't Hover Over Nine Kids . . . and That's a Good Thing." *Mom Wars.* https://themomwars.substack.com/p/you-cant-hover-over-nine-kids-and.
17. Robb, Michael B., and Supreet Mann. "The Common Sense Census: Media Use by Kids Zero to Eight." Common Sense Media, 2025.

https://www.commonsensemedia.org/sites/default/files/research/report/2025-common-sense-census-web-2.pdf.

18. Murthy, Vivek H. "Our Epidemic of Loneliness and Isolation." Office of the U.S. Surgeon General. 2023. https://www.hhs.gov/sites/default/files/surgeon-general-social-connection-advisory.pdf.
19. Atherton, Annie Midori. "Why Do So Many Parents Think Kids Need Their Own Bedroom?" *The Atlantic*, May 13, 2024. https://www.theatlantic.com/family/archive/2024/05/children-home-solo-bedroom/678354.
20. Hill, Faith. "How Much Alone Time Do Kids Need?" *The Atlantic*. November 22, 2022. https://www.theatlantic.com/family/archive/2022/11/kids-need-alone-time-benefits/672209.
21. Klinenberg, Eric. *Going Solo: The Extraordinary Rise and Surprising Appeal of Living Alone*. (New York: Penguin Books, 2013), 58.
22. Mueller, Paige, and Jeffrey Havsy. "The U.S. Student Housing Market: On-Campus, Student Housing and Student-Competitive Properties." NMHC Research Foundation. January 2020. https://www.nmhc.org/globalassets/research—insight/research-reports/student-housing/student-housing-research-report-final.pdf.
23. Collisson, Brian, Eliana Saunders, and Chloe Yin. "The Ick: Disgust Sensitivity, Narcissism, and Perfectionism in Mate Choice Thresholds." *Personality and Individual Differences* 238 (May 2025): 113086. https://www.sciencedirect.com/science/article/pii/S0191886925000480.

Chapter 4

1. Gilbert, Elizabeth. *Eat Pray Love: One Woman's Search for Everything*. (New York: Riverhead Books, 2007), xvii.
2. Lenz, Lyz. *This American Ex-Wife: How I Ended My Marriage and Started My Life*. (New York: Crown, 2024), 249.
3. Burge, Ryan. "Is Divorce the Next Front in the Culture War?" *Graphs About Religion*. August 7, 2025. https://www.graphsaboutreligion.com/p/is-divorce-the-next-front-in-the.
4. Dugan, Andrew. "U.S. Divorce Rate Dips, but Moral Acceptability Hits New High." Gallup. July 7, 2017. https://news.gallup.com/poll/213677/divorce-rate-dips-moral-acceptability-hits-new-high.aspx.

5. Davern, Michael, René Bautista, Jeremy Freese, Pamela Herd, and Stephen L. Morgan. General Social Survey, 1972–2024. NORC at the University of Chicago, 2025. Sponsored by the National Science Foundation. Machine-readable data file, 1 data file (75,699 logical records) and 1 codebook (500 pp.).
6. Campbell, David E. and Robert D. Putnam. *American Grace: How Religion Divides and Unites Us.* New York: Simon & Schuster, 2010.
7. Cox, "Emerging Trends and Enduring Patterns."
8. Cox and Hammond, "Individuality and Moral Behavior."
9. Smith, Gregory A., Alan Cooperman, Becka A. Alper, Besheer Mohamed, Chip Rotolo, Patricia Tevington, Justin Nortey, Asta Kallo, Jeff Diamant, and Dalia Fahmy. "Decline of Christianity in the U.S. Has Slowed, May Have Leveled Off." Pew Research Center, February 26, 2025. https://www.pewresearch.org/religion/2025/02/26/decline-of-christianity-in-the-us-has-slowed-may-have-leveled-off.
10. "Religious Landscape Study." Pew Research Center. February 26, 2025. https://www.pewresearch.org/religious-landscape-study.
11. Alper, Becka A., Chip Rotolo, Patricia Tevington, Justin Nortey, and Asta Kallo. "Spiritual Practices." Pew Research Center. December 7, 2023. https://www.pewresearch.org/religion/2023/12/07/spiritual-practices.
12. "Religious Landscape Study."
13. Toh, Justine. "Eastern Philosophy and Western Indulgence." ABC News, October 18, 2010. https://www.abc.net.au/religion/eastern-philosophy-and-western-indulgence/10101952.
14. Alper, Becka A., Chip Rotolo, Patricia Tevington, Justin Nortey, and Asta Kallo. "Measuring Spirituality." Pew Research Center, December 7, 2023. https://www.pewresearch.org/religion/2023/12/07/measuring-spirituality.
15. Cox and Hammond, "Individuality and Moral Behavior."
16. Cox, Daniel A., Ryan Streeter, Samuel J. Abrams, Beatrice Lee, and Dana Popky. "Public Places and Commercial Spaces: How Neighborhood Amenities Foster Trust and Connection in American Communities." Survey Center on American Life, American Enterprise Institute, October 20, 2021. https://www.americansurveycenter.org/research/public-places-and-commercial-spaces-how-neighborhood-amenities-foster-trust-and-connection-in-american-communities.

17. Haidt, *The Anxious Generation,* 86.
18. Minkin, Rachel, Kim Parker, Juliana Menasce Horowitz, and Carolina Aragão. "5. Parents' Relationship with Their Young Adult Children." Pew Research Center. January 25, 2024. https://www.pewresearch.org/social-trends/2024/01/25/parents-relationship-with-their-young-adult-children.
19. Minkin, Rachel, Kim Parker, Juliana Menasce Horowitz, and Carolina Aragão. "2. Financial Help and Independence in Young Adulthood." Pew Research Center. January 25, 2024. https://www.pewresearch.org/social-trends/2024/01/25/financial-help-and-independence-in-young-adulthood.
20. Cox, "The State of American Friendship."
21. "CDC Museum COVID-19 Timeline." Centers for Disease Control and Prevention. January 31, 2025. https://www.cdc.gov/museum/timeline/covid19.html.
22. Morris, Eric A., Samuel Speroni, and Brian D. Taylor. "Going Nowhere Faster: Did the Covid-19 Pandemic Accelerate the Trend Toward Staying Home?" *Journal of the American Planning Association* 91, no. 3 (2024): 361–379. https://doi.org/10.1080/01944363.2024.2385327.
23. Korducki, Kelli María. "The Unfriendly Skies." *Business Insider.* April 25, 2025. https://www.businessinsider.com/travel-chaos-flight-attendants-plane-passengers-freaked-out-flying-2025-4.
24. Schaeffer, Katherine, and Beshay Sakla. "Almost Half of Americans Say People Have Gotten Ruder Since the COVID-19 Pandemic." Pew Research Center. March 12, 2025. https://www.pewresearch.org/short-reads/2025/03/12/almost-half-of-americans-say-people-have-gotten-ruder-since-the-covid-19-pandemic.
25. "Youth sports referee shortage grows amid aggression from parents, coaches." *CBS News.* May 21, 2023. https://www.cbsnews.com/philadelphia/news/youth-sports-referee-shortage-grows-amid-aggression-from-parents-coaches.
26. Parti, Katalin, Cheryl E. Sanders, and Elizabeth K. Englander. "Sexting at an Early Age: Patterns and Poor Health-Related Consequences of Pressured Sexting in Middle and High School." *Journal of School Health* 93, no. 1 (2023): 73–81. https://doi.org/10.1111/josh.13258.
27. Sherman, Carter, *The Second Coming: Sex and the Next Generation's Fight Over Its Future.* (New York: Gallery Books, 2025), 175.

28. Emba, Christine. *Rethinking Sex: A Provocation.* (New York: Sentinel, 2022), 143.
29. Yudkin, Daniel Alexander, Geoffrey Philip Goodwin, Andrew Reece, Kurt Gray, and Sudeep Bhatia. "A Large-Scale Investigation of Everyday Moral Dilemmas." *PNAS Nexus* 4, no. 5 (May 2025): pgaf119. https://doi.org/10.1093/pnasnexus/pgaf119.
30. Yudkin, Daniel. Interview by Daniel A. Cox. Zoom, August 5, 2025.
31. Yudkin, interview by Cox.
32. Sutin, Angelina R., Yannick Stephan, Martina Luchetti et al. "Differential Personality Change Earlier and Later in the Coronavirus Pandemic in a Longitudinal Sample of Adults in the United States." *PloS One* 17, no. 9 (2022): e0274542. https://doi.org/10.1371/journal.pone.0274542.
33. Burn-Murdoch, John. "The Troubling Decline in Conscientiousness." *Financial Times.* August 8, 2025. https://www.ft.com/content/5cd77ef0-b546-4105-8946-36db3f84dc43.
34. GeorgeDaGreat 123. "I Analyzed 15 Years of Commentson R/relationship_Advice." Reddit. 2025. https://www.reddit.com/r/dataisbeautiful/comments/1o87cy4/oc_i_analyzed_15_years_of_comments_on.

Chapter 5

1. Jones, Jeffrey M. "New High of 45% in U.S. Identify as Political Independents." Gallup. January 12, 2026. https://news.gallup.com/poll/700499/new-high-identify-political-independents.aspx.
2. Jones, Robert P., and Maxine Najle. "American Democracy in Crisis: The Fate of Pluralism in a Divided Nation." *PRRI,* February 22, 2019. https://prri.org/research/american-democracy-in-crisis-the-fate-of-pluralism-in-a-divided-nation.
3. Associated Press. "AP VoteCast 2024 Presidential Election Survey," data file, 2024, distributed by Associated Press/NORC Center for Public Affairs Research.
4. "The Youth Vote in 2024." Center for Information & Research on Civic Learning and Engagement. Tufts. n.d. https://circle.tufts.edu/2024-election.

5. Cox, Daniel A. "The Political Gender Gap is Exploding." *American Storylines.* Newsletter. June 9, 2022. https://www.americanstorylines.com/p/the-political-gender-gap-is-exploding.
6. Gallup, Inc. *Gallup Poll Social Series, 2024.* Washington, DC: Gallup, Inc., 2024. Dataset.
7. Jones, Jeffrey M. "Democrats Regain Advantage in Party Affiliation." Gallup. July 31, 2025. https://news.gallup.com/poll/692978/democrats-regain-advantage-party-affiliation.aspx.
8. CIRCLE (Center for Information and Research on Civic Learning and Engagement). "Election Night 2016: 24 Million Youth Voted, Most Rejected Trump." Tufts University. November 9, 2016. https://circle.tufts.edu/latest-research/election-night-2016-24-million-youth-voted-most-rejected-trump.
9. "Donald Trump: Favorable Rating." Civiqs. August 28, 2025. https://civiqs.com/results/favorable_donald_trump?annotations=true&uncertainty=true&zoomIn=true&net=false.
10. Hopkins, Dan, and Hans Noel. "How Trump Has Redefined Conservatism." FiveThirtyEight. June 24, 2021. https://fivethirtyeight.com/features/how-trump-has-redefined-conservatism.
11. Associated Press, "AP VoteCast 2024."
12. Jones, Robert P. and Daniel A. Cox. "Financial Misconduct Worse Than Sexual Misconduct for Public Officials." *PRRI.* June 22, 2011. https://www.prri.org/research/more-americans-say-financial-misconduct-by-elected-officials-is-a-very-serious-moral-problem-than-say-sexual-misconduct.
13. Cox, Hammond, and Gray, "Generation Z and the Transformation of American Adolescence."
14. "Americans' Dismal Views of the Nation's Politics." Pew Research Center. September 19, 2023. https://www.pewresearch.org/politics/2023/09/19/americans-dismal-views-of-the-nations-politics.
15. "1. Views of Trump: Personal Traits, Confidence on Issues, Ideology." Pew Research Center. November 22, 2024. https://www.pewresearch.org/politics/2024/11/22/views-of-trump-personal-traits-confidence-on-issues-ideology.
16. Kessler, Glenn. "Trump Made 30,573 False or Misleading Claims as President. Nearly Half Came in His Final Year." *Washington Post.*

January 23, 2021. https://www.washingtonpost.com/politics/how-fact-checker-tracked-trump-claims/2021/01/23/ad04b69a-5c1d-11eb-a976-bad6431e03e2_story.html.

17. Healy, Patrick, Frank Luntz, and Adrian J. Rivera. 2024. "These 14 Undecided Young Voters Are Starting to Change Their Minds." *New York Times,* September 17, 2024. https://www.nytimes.com/interactive/2024/09/17/opinion/politics/17focus-group-persuadable-voters-2.html.
18. Cox and Hammond, "The Politics of Progress and Privilege."
19. Scher, Avichai. "#MeToo Is Making Colleges Teach Toxic Masculinity 101." *The Daily Beast,* September 27, 2018. https://www.thedailybeast.com/metoo-is-making-colleges-teach-toxic-masculinity-101.
20. Pew Research Center. "American Trends Panel Wave 53." Data file. September 3–15, 2019. https://www.pewresearch.org/politics/dataset/american-trends-panel-wave-53.
21. Pew Research Center. "American Trends Panel Wave 167." Data file. April 7–13, 2025. https://www.pewresearch.org/dataset/american-trends-panel-wave-167.
22. Alter, Charlotte. "A Year Ago, They Marched. Now a Record Number of Women Are Running for Office." *Time*. January 18, 2018. https://time.com/5107499/record-number-of-women-are-running-for-office.
23. Gallup. "Party Affiliation." Gallup Historical Trends. Accessed May 1, 2026. https://news.gallup.com/poll/15370/party-affiliation.aspx.
24. Gallup, "Party Affiliation."
25. Cohn, Nate. "How Educational Differences Are Widening America's Political Rift." *New York Times.* September 8, 2021. https://www.nytimes.com/2021/09/08/us/politics/how-college-graduates-vote.html.
26. Cox, Daniel A. "Have Democrats Given Up on Men?" *American Storylines*. May 2, 2024. https://www.americanstorylines.com/p/have-democrats-given-up-on-men.
27. King, Jordan. "Jasmine Crockett Mocks 'Mediocre White Boys' Complaining About DEI." *Newsweek,* February 4, 2025. https://

www.newsweek.com/jasmine-crockett-dei-donald-trump-politics-2025745.

28. Lilla, Mark. *The Once and Future Liberal: After Identity Politics.* Harper. 2017.
29. Bolies, Corbin. "The 'Hotties for Harris' Planning a Sexy Party at the DNC." *The Daily Beast,* August 15, 2024. https://www.thedailybeast.com/the-hotties-for-harris-planning-a-sexy-party-at-the-dnc.
30. Cox, Daniel A., Kelsey Eyre Hammond, and Kyle Gray. "An Unsettled Electorate: How Uncertainty and Apathy Are Shaping the 2024 Election." AEI Survey Center on American Life. May 28, 2024. https://www.americansurveycenter.org/research/an-unsettled-electorate-how-uncertainty-and-apathy-are-shaping-the-2024-election.
31. Peters, Jeremy W., Ruth Igielnik, and Lisa Lerer. "Many Americans Say the Democratic Party Does Not Share Their Priorities." *New York Times.* February 2, 2025. https://www.nytimes.com/2025/02/02/us/democrats-ipsos-poll-abortion-lgbt.html.
32. Schaeffer, Katherine. "The Data on Women Leaders." Pew Research Center. September 27, 2023. https://www.pewresearch.org/social-trends/fact-sheet/the-data-on-women-leaders.
33. "Women in the Legal Profession." American Bar Association. November 18, 2024. https://www.americanbar.org/news/profile-legal-profession/women.
34. Cox, Hammond, and Gray, "An Unsettled Electorate."
35. Flegenheimer, Matt, Rebecca R. Ruiz, and Nellie Bowles. "Bernie Sanders and His Internet Army." *New York Times.* January 27, 2020. https://www.nytimes.com/2020/01/27/us/politics/bernie-sanders-internet-supporters-2020.html.
36. Stephens, Bret. "Bernie's Angry Bros." *New York Times.* January 31, 2020. https://www.nytimes.com/2020/01/31/opinion/sanders-bernie-bros.html?smid=tw-nytopinion&smtyp=cur.
37. Stein, Jeff. "The Bernie voters who defected to Trump, explained by a political scientist" *Vox*, August 24, 2017. https://www.vox.com/policy-and-politics/2017/8/24/16194086/bernie-trump-voters-study.
38. Chapman, Tim. Quoted in Miller, Claire Cain. "How Some Voters

Moved from Bernie Sanders to Donald Trump." *New York Times*. December 9, 2024. https://www.nytimes.com/2024/12/09/upshot/voters-trump-bernie-sanders.html.

39. One study identified more than 45,000 news stories that linked Trump to anti-PC rhetoric. Schwarz, Ori. "Why Did Trump Call Prayers Politically Correct? The Coevolution of the PC Notion, the Authenticity Ethic, and the Role of the Sacred in Public Life." *Theory and Society* 52 (2023): 771–804. https://pubmed.ncbi.nlm.nih.gov/37362149.
40. Forman-Katz, Naomi, Michael Lipka, Katerina Eva Matsa, Kaitlyn Radde, Chris Baronavski, and Justine Coleman. "Young Adults and the Future of News." Pew Research Center. December 3, 2025. https://www.pewresearch.org/journalism/2025/12/03/young-adults-and-the-future-of-news.
41. Analyzing twenty-three million headlines from forty-seven news media outlets in the United States, the authors find a growth in headlines that convey anger, fear, disgust, and sadness from 2000 to 2019. Rozado, David, Ruth Hughes, and Jamin Halberstadt. "Longitudinal Analysis of Sentiment and Emotion in News Media Headlines Using Automated Labelling with Transformer Language Models." *PLOS One* 17, no. 10 (2022): e0276367. https://journals.plos.org/plosone/article?id=10.1371/journal.pone.0276367#references.
42. McClain, Colleen, and Risa Gelles-Watnick. "From Looking for Love to Swiping the Field: Online Dating in the U.S." Pew Research Center. February 2, 2023. https://www.pewresearch.org/internet/2023/02/02/from-looking-for-love-to-swiping-the-field-online-dating-in-the-u-s.
43. Cox, Daniel. "Are Political Differences Behind America's Dating Woes?" Institute for Family Studies. February 14, 2025. https://ifstudies.org/blog/are-political-differences-behind-americas-dating-woes.
44. Cox, Daniel A. "America's Cultural Crossroads: Enduring Discontent, Rising Disconnection, and an Uncertain Future." Survey Center on American Life. July 2, 2025. https://www.americansurveycenter.org/research/a-cultural-crossroads-americas-uncertain-future-amidst-enduring-discontent-and-rising-disconnection.

Chapter 6

1. Acharya, Rohit, and Rhett Morris. "Why Did U.S. Homicides Spike in 2020 and Then Decline Rapidly in 2023 and 2024?" *Brookings.* December 16, 2024. https://www.brookings.edu/articles/why-did-u-s-homicides-spike-in-2020-and-then-decline-rapidly-in-2023-and-2024.
2. "UCR Summary of Crime in the Nation, 2023." U.S. Department of Justice. 2024. https://elements.visualcapitalist.com/wp-content/uploads/2024/09/UCR_Summary_of_Crime_in_-Nation_2023.pdf.
3. Babbie Center for Survey Research. "Chapman Survey of American Fears 2024: Key Findings." Chapman University. 2024. https://www.chapman.edu/wilkinson/research-centers/babbie-center/_files/2024-csaf-key-findings-final.pdf.
4. Duggan, Maeve. "Online Harassment 2017." Pew Research Center. July 11, 2017. https://www.pewresearch.org/internet/2017/07/11/online-harassment-2017.
5. Vogels, Emily A. "1. Personal Experiences with Online Harassment." Pew Research Center. January 13, 2021. https://www.pewresearch.org/internet/2021/01/13/personal-experiences-with-online-harassment/#:~:text=Women%20are%20more%20likely%20than,3.
6. Modrek, Sepideh, and Bozhidar Chakalov. "The #MeToo Movement in the United States: Text Analysis of Early Twitter Conversations." *Journal of Medical Internet Research* 21, no. 9 (2019): e13837. https://doi.org/10.2196/13837.
7. How Things Work (@HowThingsWork_). "One Method to Reduce Drinks Being Spiked." X. August 8, 2025. https://x.com/HowThingsWork_/status/1953963686369894634.
8. Jones, Leslie. Post on X. https://x.com/Lesdoggg/status/1778646238222799002.
9. "'Nobody Has More Respect for Women Than Donald Trump.' We Disagree." ACLU Massachusetts. December 6, 2017. https://www.aclum.org/publications/nobody-has-more-respect-women-donald-trump-we-disagree.
10. Brenan, Megan. "Record-Low 46% of Women Pleased with Society's Treatment." Gallup. January 17, 2019. https://news.gallup.com/poll/246056/record-low-women-pleased-society-treatment.aspx.

11. Noveck, Jocelyn. "After Trump's Victory, Shock and Despair for Women Who Supported Clinton." PBS News. November 9, 2016. https://www.pbs.org/newshour/politics/trumps-victory-shock-despair-women-supported-clinton.
12. Anderson, Monica, and Skye Toor. "How Social Media Users Have Discussed Sexual Harassment Since #MeToo Went Viral." Pew Research Center. October 11, 2018. https://www.pewresearch.org/short-reads/2018/10/11/how-social-media-users-have-discussed-sexual-harassment-since-metoo-went-viral/?.
13. Melnick, R. Shep. "Analyzing the Department of Education's Final Title IX Rules on Sexual Misconduct." Brookings Institution. June 11, 2020. https://www.brookings.edu/articles/analyzing-the-department-of-educations-final-title-ix-rules-on-sexual-misconduct.
14. Yoffe, Emily. "The College Rape Overcorrection." *Slate*. December 7, 2014. https://www.slate.com/articles/double_x/doublex/2014/12/college_rape_campus_sexual_assault_is_a_serious_problem_but_the_efforts.html?wpsrc=sh_all_dt_tw_bot.
15. Bartholet, Elizabeth, et al. "Rethink Harvard's Sexual Harassment Policy." *Boston Globe*, October 15, 2014. https://www.bostonglobe.com/opinion/2014/10/14/rethink-harvard-sexual-harassment-policy/HFDDiZN7nU2UwuUuWMnqbM/story.html.
16. Brown, Anna. "More Than Twice as Many Americans Support Than Oppose the #MeToo Movement." Pew Research Center. September 29, 2022. https://www.pewresearch.org/social-trends/2022/09/29/more-than-twice-as-many-americans-support-than-oppose-the-metoo-movement.
17. Cox and Hammond, "The Politics of Progress and Privilege."
18. Kearney, Melissa S., and Phillip B. Levine. "Media Influences on Social Outcomes: The Impact of MTV's 16 and Pregnant on Teen Childbearing." NBER Working Paper No. 19795. Cambridge, MA: National Bureau of Economic Research, 2015. https://www.nber.org/system/files/working_papers/w19795/w19795.pdf.
19. Kearney, Melissa S., and Phillip Levine. "Media Influences on Social Outcomes: The Impact of MTV's '16 and Pregnant' on Teen Childbearing." Brookings Institution. January 15, 2014. https://www

.brookings.edu/articles/media-influences-on-social-outcomes-the-impact-of-mtvs-16-and-pregnant-on-teen-childbearing.
20. Sullivan, Sean. "The Rapid Surge of Abortion Restrictions—in One Chart." *Washington Post*. January 2, 2014. https://www.washingtonpost.com/news/the-fix/wp/2014/01/02/the-rapid-surge-of-state-abortion-restrictions-in-one-chart.
21. Lewin, Tamar. "#ShoutYourAbortion Gets Angry Shouts Back." *New York Times,* October 2, 2015. https://www.nytimes.com/2015/10/02/us/hashtag-campaign-twitter-abortion.html?smid=fb-nytimes&smtyp=cur.
22. Blank, Christopher. "Billboards Supporting Women Seeking Abortions Are Popping Up Along I-55 Heading North." NPR, October 11, 2023. https://www.npr.org/2023/10/11/1202456541/billboards-supporting-women-seeking-abortions-are-popping-up-along-i-55-heading-.
23. Saad, Lydia. "Gender Gaps on Abortion Reach Historic Highs." Gallup. June 9, 2025. https://news.gallup.com/poll/691370/gender-gaps-abortion-reach-historic-highs.aspx.
24. Korecki, Natasha. "A Timeline of Trump's Many, Many Positions on Abortion." NBC News. April 8, 2024. https://www.nbcnews.com/politics/donald-trump/trumps-many-abortion-positions-timeline-rcna146601.
25. Bowman, Karlyn, and Daniel A. Cox. "Gender, Generation and Abortion: Shifting Politics and Perspectives After Roe." AEI Survey Center on American Life. October 4, 2022. https://www.americansurveycenter.org/research/gender-generation-and-abortion-shifting-politics-and-perspectives-after-roe.
26. Saad, "Gender Gaps on Abortion Reach Historic Highs."
27. Evans, Jonathan, and Manolo Corichi. "What Do Americans Consider Immoral?" Pew Research Center, March 19, 2026. https://www.pewresearch.org/religion/2026/03/19/what-do-americans-consider-immoral.
28. Jones, Robert P., Daniel A. Cox, and Rachel Laser. "Committed to Availability, Conflicted about Morality: What the Millennial Generation Tells Us about the Future of the Abortion Debate and the Culture Wars." *PRRI.* 2011. http://www.prri.org/research/committed

-to-availability-conflicted-about-morality-what-the-millennial-generation-tells-us-about-the-future-of-the-abortion-debate-and-the-culture-wars.

29. "President Bill Clinton's Signing of Executive Orders Defining Abortion Rights." January 22, 1993. C-SPAN, 3:09. https://www.c-span.org/clip/white-house-event/user-clip-bill-clinton-1221993-safe-llegal-and-rare/5164229.
30. Cox, Daniel A. "American Social Life Survey." Data file. March 10–28, 2025. https://www.americansurveycenter.org/wp-content/uploads/2025/07/American-Social-Life-Survey-Topline-Questionnaire-2.pdf.

Chapter 7

1. Gallup, Inc. *Gallup Poll Social Series, 2024*. Washington, DC: Gallup, Inc., 2024. Dataset.
2. Downen, Robert, Lise Olsen, and John Tedesco. "20 Years, 700 Victims: Southern Baptist Sexual Abuse Spreads as Leaders Resist Reforms." *Houston Chronicle*. January 31, 2022. https://www.houstonchronicle.com/news/investigations/article/Southern-Baptist-sexual-abuse-spreads-as-leaders-13588038.php.
3. Graham, Ruth, and Elizabeth Dias. "Southern Baptist Sex Abuse Report Stuns, from Pulpit to Pews." *New York Times*. May 23, 2022. https://www.nytimes.com/2022/05/23/us/southern-baptist-sex-abuse-report.html.
4. Kahlon, Suchait. "Police Failure to Investigate Sexual Assault Is Endemic. Where Is DOJ?" *Slate*. February 26, 2024. https://slate.com/news-and-politics/2024/02/doj-police-failures-sexual-assault-cases.html.
5. Lorenz, Katherine, Anne Kirkner, and Sarah E. Ullman. "A Qualitative Study of Sexual Assault Survivors' Post-Assault Legal System Experiences." *Journal of Trauma & Dissociation* 20, no. 3 (2019): 263–287. https://doi.org/10.1080/15299732.2019.1592643.
6. Cox, "America's Cultural Crossroads."
7. Brenan, Megan. "Crime Fears Rebound in U.S. After Lull During 2020 Lockdowns." Gallup. November 10, 2021. https://news.gallup.com/poll/357116/crime-fears-rebound-lull-during-2020-lockdowns.aspx.

8. Chokrane, Boutayna. "Which Safety App Should You Trust for Personal Protection?" *Wired.* November 7, 2024. https://www.wired.com/gallery/which-personal-safety-app-is-best-for-me.
9. Baumgartner, Frank R., and Sarah McAdon. "There's Been a Big Change in How the News Media Covers Sexual Assault." *Washington Post.* May 11, 2017. https://www.washingtonpost.com/news/monkey-cage/wp/2017/05/11/theres-been-a-big-change-in-how-the-news-media-cover-sexual-assault/?next_url=https://www.washingtonpost.com/news/monkey-cage/wp/2017/05/11/theres-been-a-big-change-in-how-the-news-media-cover-sexual-assault.
10. Creswell, Julie, and Tiffany Hsu. "Women's Whisper Network Raises Its Voice." *The New York Times,* November 4, 2017. https://www.nytimes.com/2017/11/04/business/sexual-harassment-whisper-network.html.
11. Savchenko, Anna. "Man Sues 27 Women in an 'Are We Dating the Same Guy' Facebook Group." WUNC News. April 5, 2024. https://www.wunc.org/2024-04-05/man-sues-27-women-in-an-are-we-dating-the-same-guy-facebook-group.
12. "Debate Rage Quit/She Is Suing?! 150 IQ Ivy League Feminist vs. Andrew Wilson." *Whatever.* 2025. https://www.youtube.com/watch?v=NoarNmUMbh4.
13. United States Sentencing Commission. "Quick Facts: Sexual Abuse Offenses." Fiscal Year 2024. Washington, DC: United States Sentencing Commission, 2024. https://www.ussc.gov/sites/default/files/pdf/research-and-publications/quick-facts/Sexual_Abuse_FY24.pdf.
14. Lamont, Ellen. "If You Want a Marriage of Equals, Then Date as Equals." *The Atlantic.* February 14, 2020. https://www.theatlantic.com/ideas/archive/2020/02/if-you-want-marriage-equals-then-date-equals/606568.
15. Cox, Daniel A., and Kelsey Eyre Hammond. "Romantic Recession: How Politics, Pessimism, and Anxiety Shape American Courtship." Survey Center on American Life. January 29, 2025. https://www.americansurveycenter.org/research/the-state-of-american-romance-how-politics-and-pessimism-influence-dating-experiences.
16. Nadeau, Miranda. Quoted in Oliver, David. "Dating Horror Story Videos Are Taking Over TikTok. Why?" *USA Today.* February 27,

2023. https://www.usatoday.com/story/life/health-wellness/2023/02/27/dating-horror-stories-tiktok-bad-dates/11316459002.

17. Caddick, Nick, Cassandra Phoenix, and Brett Smith. "Collective Stories and Well-Being: Using a Dialogical Narrative Approach to Understand Peer Relationships Among Combat Veterans Experiencing Post-Traumatic Stress Disorder." *Journal of Health Psychology* 20, no. 3 (March 2015): 286–299. https://doi.org/10.1177/1359105313511839.
18. Relihan, Daniel P., Nickolas M. Jones, E. Alison Holman, and Roxane Cohen Silver. "Shared Social Identity and Media Transmission of Trauma." *Scientific Reports* 13, no. 1 (2023): 11609. https://doi.org/10.1038/s41598-023-33898-2.

Chapter 8

1. Cox, Daniel A. "American Gender and Society Survey." Dataset. Survey Center on American Life, August 16–26, 2024. https://www.americansurveycenter.org/download/american-gender-and-society-survey.
2. Stone, Lyman. "1-In-3: A Record Share of Young Adults Will Never Marry." Institute for Family Studies. February 26, 2024. https://ifstudies.org/blog/1-in-3-a-record-share-of-young-adults-will-never-marry.
3. "Rise of the SHEconomy." Morgan Stanley. August 22, 2019. https://www.morganstanley.com/ideas/womens-impact-on-the-economy.
4. Vera Cruz, Germano, Elias Aboujaoude, Lucien Rochat, and Francesco Bianchi-Demichelli. "Finding Intimacy Online: A Machine Learning Analysis of Predictors of Success." *Cyberpsychology, Behavior, and Social Networking* 26, no. 6 (2023): 437–444. https://doi.org/10.1089/cyber.2022.0367.
5. Cox, Daniel A. "Gen Z's Romance Gap: Why Nearly Half of Young Men Aren't Dating." American Institute for Boys and Men. February 8, 2024. https://aibm.org/commentary/gen-zs-romance-gap-why-nearly-half-of-young-men-arent-dating.
6. Cox, Daniel A. "January 2023 American Perspectives Survey." https://www.americansurveycenter.org/download/january-2023-american-perspectives-survey.

7. D'Angelo, Jonathan D., and Catalina L. Toma. "There Are Plenty of Fish in the Sea: The Effects of Choice Overload and Reversibility on Online Daters' Satisfaction with Selected Partners." *Media Psychology* 20, no. 1 (2017): 1–27. https://doi.org/10.1080/15213269.2015.1121827.
8. Brown, Anna. "Nearly Half of U.S. Adults Say Dating Has Gotten Harder for Most People in the Last 10 Years." Pew Research Center. August 20, 2020. https://pewsocialtrends.org/wp-content/uploads/sites/3/2020/08/PSDT_08.20.20.dating-relationships.final_.pdf.
9. Bergström, Marie. *The New Laws of Love: Online Dating and the Privatization of Intimacy*. Polity. 2022.
10. Bergström, *The New Laws of Love*.
11. Fetters, Ashley. "The Five Years That Changed Dating." *The Atlantic*. December 21, 2018. https://www.theatlantic.com/family/archive/2018/12/tinder-changed-dating/578698.
12. DeChant, Kayla. "My Boyfriend Is Always Going on TikTok Watching Other Girls Dance and Social Media. It Drives Me Nuts." Quora. 2023. https://qr.ae/pC8LDQ.
13. Cox and Hammond, "Romantic Recession."
14. "Detectives." *Saturday Night Live*. NBC. 2024. https://www.youtube.com/watch?v=nzh727t944k.
15. Vogels, Emily A., and Monica Anderson. "Dating and Relationships in the Digital Age." Pew Research Center. May 8, 2020. https://www.pewresearch.org/internet/2020/05/08/dating-and-relationships-in-the-digital-age.
16. Sosnick, Charlie. "Why Are Men Obsessed with YouTube?" *GQ*, January 15, 2026. https://www.gq.com/story/why-are-men-obsessed-with-youtube.
17. Tolentino, Daysia. "'Who TF Did I Marry?' TikToker says she hopes people finish watching her saga." NBC News, February 22, 2024. https://www.nbcnews.com/news/who-tf-did-i-marry-tiktoker-shares-reaction-whats-next-rcna139811.
18. Cox, "American Gender and Society Survey."
19. SheraSeven. "How To Get Him to Spend His Money On You." YouTube. October 18, 2023. https://www.youtube.com/watch?v=ka5OgfD5YLs.

20. Braga, Dana. "12th Grade Girls Are Less Likely Than Boys to Say They Want to Get Married Someday." Pew Research Center. November 14, 2025. https://www.pewresearch.org/short-reads/2025/11/14/12th-grade-girls-are-less-likely-than-boys-to-say-they-want-to-get-married-someday.
21. Appiah, Kwame Anthony. "I Let My Wife Have an Affair. Do I Have to Console Her Now That It's Over?" *New York Times*. January 25, 2026. https://www.nytimes.com/2026/01/24/magazine/wife-affair-ethics.html.
22. Lippert, Jordan, and Janell Feterolf. "Best Age to Get Married, Have a Child, Buy a Home and Retire? Here's What Americans Say." Pew Research Center. March 19, 2025. https://www.pewresearch.org/short-reads/2025/03/19/best-age-to-get-married-have-a-child-buy-a-home-and-retire-heres-what-americans-say.
23. Sibley, D. Scott. "What Ever Happened to Dating? The Rise of 'Just Talking' Relationships." Institute for Family Studies, August 13, 2024. https://ifstudies.org/blog/what-ever-happened-to-dating-the-rise-of-just-talking-relationships.
24. Cox and Hammond, "The Politics of Progress and Privilege."
25. Horowitz, Juliana Menasce, Nikki Graf, and Gretchen Livingston. "Marriage and Cohabitation in the U.S." Pew Research Center. November 6, 2019. https://www.pewresearch.org/social-trends/2019/11/06/marriage-and-cohabitation-in-the-u-s.
26. Kraus, M. W. "Voice-Only Communication Enhances Empathic Accuracy." *American Psychologist* 72, no. 7 (2017): 644–654. https://psycnet.apa.org/record/2017-43854-002.

Chapter 9

1. Cox, Hammond, and Gray, "Generation Z and the Transformation of American Adolescence."
2. Sharkey, Patrick. "Homebound: The Long-Term Rise in Time Spent at Home Among U.S. Adults." *Sociological Science* 11, no. 20 (2024). https://sociologicalscience.com/articles-v11-20-553.
3. "American Time Use Survey Summary." U.S. Bureau of Labor Statistics. June 26, 2025. https://www.bls.gov/news.release/atus.nr0.htm.
4. Cox, "America's Cultural Crossroads."
5. Cox, Daniel A. "American Men Suffer a Friendship Recession." *Na-*

tional Review. July 6, 2021. https://www.nationalreview.com/2021/07/american-men-suffer-a-friendship-recession.

6. Kalenkoski, Charlene Marie, and Sabrina Wulff Pabilonia. "Teen Social Interactions and Well-Being During the COVID-19 Pandemic." Working Paper 566. May 1, 2024. U.S. Department of Labor, U.S. Bureau of Labor Statistics, Office of Productivity and Technology. https://www.bls.gov/osmr/research-papers/2023/pdf/ec230060.pdf.
7. Miller, Claire Cain, and Amy Fan. "How Video Games Are Shaping a Generation of Boys, for Better and Worse." *The New York Times,* October 3, 2025. https://www.nytimes.com/2025/10/03/upshot/video-games-boys-young-men.html.
8. Radhakrishnan, Lakshmi, Rebecca T. Leeb, Rebecca H. Bitsko et al. "Pediatric Emergency Department Visits Associated with Mental Health Conditions Before and During the COVID-19 Pandemic—United States, January 2019–January 2022." *Morbidity and Mortality Weekly Report* 71, no. 8 (2022): 319–324. https://doi.org/10.15585/mmwr.mm7108e2.
9. Anderson, Monica, Michelle Faverio, and Colleen McClain. "How Teens Navigate School During COVID-19." Pew Research Center. June 2, 2022. https://www.pewresearch.org/internet/2022/06/02/how-teens-navigate-school-during-covid-19.
10. Tan, Huileng. "World's Largest Condom-Maker Says Condom Sales Precipitously Slumped During the Pandemic." *Business Insider.* January 11, 2022. https://www.businessinsider.com/people-had-less-sex-with-condoms-covid-pandemic-closed-hotels-2022-1.
11. "OnlyFans—Statistics & Facts." n.d. Statista. https://www.statista.com/topics/10083/onlyfans.
12. Cox and Hammond, "Individuality and Moral Behavior."
13. Harrington, Mary. "Female Celebrities Are Making Millions on OnlyFans. Will They Regret It?" *Wall Street Journal.* March 13, 2025. https://www.wsj.com/lifestyle/female-celebrities-are-making-millions-on-onlyfans-will-they-regret-it-f35a560c?mod=hp_trendingnow_article_pos2.
14. "OnlyFans Monthly Traffic Distribution by Gender 2025." n.d. Statista. https://www.statista.com/statistics/1563226/onlyfans-audience-by-gender.

15. Elson, Ed. "Company of the Year." *Simply Put.* January 5, 2026. https://edwardelson.substack.com/p/company-of-the-year?utm_campaign=post-expanded-share&utm_medium=post%20viewer&triedRedirect=true.
16. Koerner, Brendan I. "I Went Undercover as a Secret OnlyFans Chatter. It Wasn't Pretty." *Wired.* May 15, 2024. https://www.wired.com/story/i-went-undercover-secret-onlyfans-chatter-wasnt-pretty.
17. Thomas, Daniel. "OnlyFans Hands Record $701mn Dividend to Owner Ahead of Sale." *Financial Times.* August 22, 2025. https://www.ft.com/content/7d936956-f1b9-4fe4-b3de-feaddac79953.
18. Cox and Hammond, "Individuality and Moral Behavior."
19. Cox, Daniel A. "Yes, Having More Friends Is Better." Survey Center on American Life. August 9, 2021. https://www.americansurveycenter.org/yes-having-more-friends-is-better.
20. Tiku, Nitasha. "AI friendships claim to cure loneliness. Some are ending in suicide." *The Washington Post.* December 6, 2024. https://www.washingtonpost.com/technology/2024/12/06/ai-companion-chai-research-character-ai.
21. Cox, Daniel A. "From Swiping to Sexting: The Enduring Gender Divide in American Dating and Relationships." Survey Center on American Life, February 9, 2023. https://www.americansurveycenter.org/research/from-swiping-to-sexting-the-enduring-gender-divide-in-american-dating-and-relationships.
22. Orrell, Cox, and Wall, "The Social Workplace."
23. Emba, *Rethinking Sex,* 127.
24. Cox and Hammond, "The Politics of Progress and "Privilege."
25. Orth, Taylor. "How Often Do Americans Go on Dates? Not as Often as They'd Like." YouGov. February 4, 2025. https://today.yougov.com/society/articles/51519-how-often-do-americans-go-on-dates.
26. Cox, "America's Cultural Crossroads."
27. Allen, Joseph P., Rachel K. Narr, Jessica Kansky, and David E. Szwedo. "Adolescent Peer Relationship Qualities as Predictors of Long-Term Romantic Life Satisfaction." *Child Development* 91, no. 1 (2020): 327–340. https://doi.org/10.1111/cdev.13193.
28. Helliwell, John F., and Haifang Huang. "Comparing the Happiness

Effects of Real and On-Line Friends." *PLOS One* 8, no. 9 (2013): e72754. https://doi.org/10.1371/journal.pone.0072754.

29. Rosen, Christine. *The Extinction of Experience: Being Human in a Disembodied World.* W.W. Norton. 2024.
30. Kumar, Amit, and Nicholas Epley. "It's Surprisingly Nice to Hear You: Misunderstanding the Impact of Communication Media Can Lead to Suboptimal Choices of How to Connect with Others." *Journal of Experimental Psychology* 150, no. 3 (2021): 595–607. https://doi.org/10.1037/xge0000962.
31. Montooth, Amelia [@ameliamontooth]. "It's okay to ask your friends for favors." TikTok, March 28, 2024. https://www.tiktok.com/@ameliamontooth/video/7351557773450022186.

Chapter 10

1. Cox, "From Swiping to Sexting."
2. Anderson, Monica, Emily A. Vogels, and Erica Turner. "The Virtues and Downsides of Online Dating." Pew Research Center, February 6, 2020. https://www.pewresearch.org/internet/2020/02/06/the-virtues-and-downsides-of-online-dating.
3. Parker, Kim, Juliana Menasce Horowitz, and Renee Stepler. "On Gender Differences, No Consensus on Nature vs. Nurture." Pew Research Center, December 5, 2017. https://www.pewresearch.org/social-trends/2017/12/05/on-gender-differences-no-consensus-on-nature-vs-nurture.
4. Hurst, Kiley, Nick Zanetti, John Carlo Mandapat, and Reem Nadeem. "How Do U.S. Men and Women Spend Their Time?" Pew Research Center. March 17, 2026. https://www.pewresearch.org/social-trends/feature/how-do-u-s-men-and-women-spend-their-time.
5. Vogels, Emily A., and Colleen McClain. "Key Findings About Online Dating in the U.S." Pew Research Center. February 2, 2023. https://www.pewresearch.org/short-reads/2023/02/02/key-findings-about-online-dating-in-the-u-s.
6. Wu, Hao, Shanhong Luo, Annelise Klettner, Tyler White, and Kate Albritton. "Gender Roles in the Millennium: Who Pays and Is Expected to Pay for Romantic Dates?" *Psychological Reports* 126, no. 2 (2023): 791–811. https://doi.org/10.1177/00332941211057144.

7. Nova, Annie, and Ana Teresa Solá. "People Are Spending Hundreds a Month on Dating Apps as Free Versions Turn 'Borderline Unusable.'" CNBC. December 9, 2023. https://www.cnbc.com/2023/12/09/why-dating-apps-can-now-cost-users-hundreds-of-dollars-a-month.html.
8. Orrell, Cox, and Wall, "The Social Workplace."
9. Cox, "From Swiping to Sexting."
10. Townsend, J. M., and T. Wasserman. "The Perception of Sexual Attractiveness: Sex Differences in Variability." *Archives of Sexual Behavior* 26, no. 3 (1997): 243–268. https://doi.org/10.1023/a:1024570814293.
11. Cox, "From Swiping to Sexting."
12. Anderson, Vogels, and Turner, "The Virtues and Downsides of Online Dating."
13. Harper, Christopher R., Patricia J. Dittus, Jami S. Leichliter, and Sevgi O. Aral. "Changes in the Distribution of Sex Partners in the United States: 2002 to 2011-2013." *Sexually Transmitted Diseases* 44, no. 2 (2017): 96–100. https://doi.org/10.1097/OLQ.0000000000000554.
14. Cox, "American Gender and Society Survey."
15. Uecker, Jeremy E., and Mark D. Regnerus. "Bare Market: Campus Sex Ratios, Romantic Relationships, and Sexual Behavior." *Sociological Quarterly* 51, no. 3 (2010): 408–435. https://pmc.ncbi.nlm.nih.gov/articles/PMC3130599.
16. Costello, William. Interview by Daniel A. Cox 2025.
17. Cox, "From Swiping to Sexting."
18. Fry, Richard. "A Record-High Share of 40-Year-Olds in the U.S. Have Never Been Married." Pew Research Center. June 28, 2023. https://www.pewresearch.org/short-reads/2023/06/28/a-record-high-share-of-40-year-olds-in-the-us-have-never-been-married.
19. Cappelen, Alexander W., Ranveig Falch, and Bertil Tungodden. "Experimental Evidence on the Acceptance of Males Falling Behind." *Journal of the European Economic Association* 23, no. 6 (2025): 2212–2240. https://academic.oup.com/jeea/article/23/6/2212/8112864.

Chapter 11

1. Braga, Dana. "12th Grade Girls Are Less Likely Than Boys to Say They Want to Get Married Someday." Pew Research Center. November 14, 2025. https://www.pewresearch.org/short-reads/2025/11/14/12th-grade-girls-are-less-likely-than-boys-to-say-they-want-to-get-married-someday.
2. The Knot Research & Insights Team. "The Knot Real Weddings Study: Data Read-Out (2023)." The Knot, February 26, 2025. https://www.theknot.com/content/wedding-data-insights/weddings-in-2023.
3. Blumberg, Perri Ormont. "Why Some Couples Are Turning Their Weddings into Trivia Night." *New York Times*. February 7, 2026. https://www.nytimes.com/2026/02/07/fashion/weddings/wedding-receptions-games-trivia-night.html?smid=nytcore-ios-share.
4. Cox, "Emerging Trends and Enduring Patterns."
5. "More Couples Are Signing Prenups Before Saying 'I Do.'" The Harris Poll. July 12, 2022. https://theharrispoll.com/briefs/popularity-of-prenups-rising-2022.
6. Cox, "American Gender and Society Survey."
7. Olsen, Jenny G., Scott I. Rick, Deborah A. Small, and Eli J. Finkel. "Common Cents: Bank Account Structure and Couples' Relationship Dynamics." *Journal of Consumer Research* 50, no. 4 (2023): 704–721. https://academic.oup.com/jcr/article-abstract/50/4/704/7077142?redirectedFrom=fulltext.
8. Fischer, Claude S. 1982. *To Dwell Among Friends: Personal Networks in Town and City*. Chicago: University of Chicago Press.
9. Grose, Jessica. "A Modest Proposal for Equalizing the Mental Load." *New York Times*. June 11, 2019. https://www.nytimes.com/2019/06/11/parenting/mental-load.html.
10. #mentalload. TikTok. n.d. https://www.tiktok.com/tag/mentalload.
11. Wilshere, Meredith. "Woman Declares 'Marriage Is a Bad Decision' for Women Today. Why She Thinks It Only Leads to 'Pain and Heartbreak.'" *People*. May 10, 2025. https://people.com/woman-believes-women-should-not-get-married-and-it-is-a-bad-decision-11698520.
12. Ferrara, Angelica P., and Dylan Vergara. "Theorizing Mankeeping: The Male Friendship Recession and Women's Associated Labor as a

Structural Component of Gender Inequality." *Psychology of Men & Masculinities* 25, no. 4 (2024): 391–401. https://doi.org/10.1037/men0000494.

13. Bledsoe, Isaac, and Ben Smith. "Male Loneliness and Isolation: What the Data Shows." American Institute for Boys and Men, August 20, 2025. https://aibm.org/research/male-loneliness-and-isolation-what-the-data-shows/.
14. Cox, "The State of American Friendship."
15. Tilley-Coulson, Eve. "Male Loneliness Epidemic." TikTok. 2025. https://www.tiktok.com/@ebtilley/video/7473147693649382699.
16. Pew Research Center, "American Trends Panel Wave 126." Data file. April 10–16, 2023. https://www.pewresearch.org/social-trends/wp-content/uploads/sites/3/2023/09/ST_2023.09.14_Modern-Family_Topline.pdf.
17. Kessler, Ronald C., Jane D. McLeod, and Elaine Wethington. "The Costs of Caring: A Perspective on the Relationship Between Sex and Psychological Distress." In Social Support: Theory, Research and Applications, edited by Irwin G. Sarason and Barbara R. Sarason, 491–506. NATO ASI Series, vol. 24. Springer, Dordrecht. https://doi.org/10.1007/978-94-009-5115-0_25.
18. Smith, Ben, Sarah Schoppe-Sullivan, and Jay Fagan. "Dads Rock: The Evidence." American Institute for Boys and Men. June 13, 2024. https://aibm.org/research/dads-rock-the-evidence.
19. Livingston, Gretchen. "Most dads say they spend too little time with their children; about a quarter live apart from them." Pew Research Center, January 8, 2018. https://www.pewresearch.org/short-reads/2018/01/08/most-dads-say-they-spend-too-little-time-with-their-children-about-a-quarter-live-apart-from-them.
20. "Millennials Spend More Time Than Past Generations with Their Children." *The Economist*. January 9, 2026. https://www.economist.com/graphic-detail/2026/01/09/millennials-spend-more-time-than-past-generations-with-their-children.
21. Dumitru, Oana. "How Many Americans Have Cheated on Their Partners in Monogamous Relationships?" YouGov. October 4, 2022. https://today.yougov.com/society/articles/43605-how-many-americans-have-cheated-their-partner-poll.

22. Cox, "From Swiping to Sexting."
23. "A New Era of Bumble." Bumble.com. 2024. https://bumble.com/en-us/the-buzz/bumble-new-era.
24. Ashley, Beth. "Is Your Partner 'Micro-Cheating' on You?" *Mashable.* August 11, 2023. https://mashable.com/article/micro-cheating-what-is-it.
25. Allykaymoms. "100 Signs Micro-Cheating Online." *Medium.* December 5, 2023. https://medium.com/@allykaymoms/100-examples-of-micro-cheating-behaviors-online-1a259c0de7c6.
26. Brenan, Megan. "Adultery, Cloning Still Seen as Most Immoral Behaviors." Gallup. July 22, 2025. https://news.gallup.com/poll/692801/adultery-cloning-seen-immoral-behaviors.aspx.
27. Cox, "August 2022 Abortion and Religion Survey."
28. Cox, "August 2022 Abortion and Religion Survey."
29. Wang, Wendy. "Who Cheats More? The Demographics of Infidelity in America." Institute for Family Studies. January 10, 2018. https://ifstudies.org/blog/who-cheats-more-the-demographics-of-cheating-in-america.
30. Cox and Hammond, "Individuality and Moral Behavior."
31. Cox, "August 2022 Abortion and Religion Survey."
32. Brooks, David. "Time to Say Goodbye." *New York Times*. January 30, 2026. https://www.nytimes.com/2026/01/30/opinion/david-brooks-leaving-columnist.html.

Chapter 12

1. Chinoy, Sahil, Nathan Nunn, Sandra Sequeira, and Stefanie Stantcheva. "Zero-Sum Thinking and the Roots of U.S. Political Differences." *American Economic Review* 116, no. 1 (2026): 1052–1096. https://socialeconomicslab.org/wp-content/uploads/2024/05/zero_sum_political_divides.pdf.
2. Stantcheva, Stefanie. "Beyond Zero-Sum Thinking on Gender." American Institute for Boys and Men. December 16, 2024. https://aibm.org/commentary/beyond-zero-sum-thinking-on-gender/#:~:text=Third%2C%C2%A0younger%20generations,chart%20below%20suggests.
3. Pearson, Helen. "Are boys really in crisis? What the science says in

the age of the manosphere." *Nature* 652 (March 21, 2026): 22-25. https://doi.org/10.1038/d41586-026-00968-0.

4. Horowitz, Juliana Menasce, and Janell Fetterolf. "Worldwide Optimism About Future of Gender Equality, Even as Many See Advantages for Men." Pew Research Center. April 30, 2020. https://www.pewresearch.org/social-trends/2020/04/30/worldwide-optimism-about-future-of-gender-equality-even-as-many-see-advantages-for-men.
5. Cox and Hammond, "The Politics of Progress."
6. Sandomir, Richard, "Women's World Cup Final Was Most-Watched Soccer Game in United States History." *The New York Times,* July 6, 2015. https://www.nytimes.com/2015/07/07/sports/soccer/womens-world-cup-final-was-most-watched-soccer-game-in-united-states-history.html.
7. Bertrand, Marianne, Ariel Kalil, and Noah Liu. " 'School's Not Cool': How Peer Pressure Can Hurt Boys' Education." American Institute for Boys and Men. February 11, 2026. https://aibm.org/research/schools-not-cool-how-peer-pressure-can-hurt-boys-education.
8. Cox, "American Teenagers Survey."
9. "Women in the Legal Profession." American Bar Association. 2024. https://www.americanbar.org/news/profile-legal-profession/women.
10. Nuzzo, James L. "Sex of Psychologists in the U.S., 2007–2023." *The Nuzzo Letter*. February 23, 2026. https://jameslnuzzo.substack.com/p/sex-of-psychologists-in-the-us-2007.
11. Buss, David M, and William Costello. "Why Isn't There More Incel Violence?" *Adaptive Human Behavior and Physiology* 9, no. 3 (2023): 252–259. https://doi.org/10.1007/s40750-023-00220-3.
12. Fisher, Krista, Simon Rice, and Zac Seidler. "Young Men's Health in a Digital World." n.d. Movember.com. https://ex.movember.com/movember-institute/masculinities-report.
13. Downey, Allen, and Richard Reeves. "No, Young Men Are Not Turning Away from Gender Equality." American Institute for Boys and Men. July 24, 2024. https://aibm.org/commentary/no-young-men-are-not-turning-away-from-gender-equality.
14. Cox, "America's Cultural Crossroads."

15. Cox, "America's Cultural Crossroads."
16. Weatherbed, Jess. "Tinder Now Lets Mom Pick Your Next Date." The Verge. October 23, 2023. https://www.theverge.com/2023/10/23/23928363/tinder-matchmaker-dating-app-feature-recommendations.
17. Cox, Daniel A. and Sam Pressler. "Disconnected: The Growing Class Divide in American Civic Life." Survey Center on American Life, August 22, 2024. https://www.americansurveycenter.org/research/disconnected-places-and-spaces.
18. Sherry, Allison. "Can 'Tin Can' Be the Answer to Delaying Smartphone Use? Some Colorado Families Are Giving It a Try." *CPR News.* February 4, 2026. https://www.cpr.org/2026/02/04/tin-can-kids-landline-cellphone-alternative.
19. Faverio, Michelle. "Teens, Social Media and Mental Health." Pew Research Center. April 22, 2025. https://www.pewresearch.org/internet/2025/04/22/teens-social-media-and-mental-health.
20. "Addicted to Your Phone? Try 'Bricking' It." *The Economist.* February 15, 2026. https://www.economist.com/culture/2026/02/15/addicted-to-your-phone-try-bricking-it.
21. Dugan, Andrew. "More Americans Say Pornography Is Morally Acceptable." Gallup, June 5, 2018. https://news.gallup.com/poll/235280/americans-say-pornography-morally-acceptable.aspx.
22. Cox, "America's Cultural Crossroads."
23. Rosenfeld, Michael J., Reuben J. Thomas, and Sonia Hausen. "Disintermediating Your Friends: How Online Dating in the United States Displaces Other Ways of Meeting." *Proceedings of the National Academy of Sciences of the United States of America* 116, no. 36 (2019): 17753–17758. https://doi.org/10.1073/pnas.1908630116.
24. Pearson, Catherine. "A New Way to Date: The Old-Fashioned Way." *New York Times.* June 6, 2025. https://www.nytimes.com/2025/06/06/well/dating-irl-analog-online.html.
25. Roman, Daniel. "The Incredible Shrinking Dating App." *Wired.* February 13, 2025. https://www.wired.com/story/dating-apps-by-the-numbers.
26. Cox, "From Swiping to Sexting."
27. Rosenfeld, Thomas, and Hausen, "Disintermediating Your Friends."

28. Panchal, Nirmita, and Sasha Zitter. "A Look at State Efforts to Ban Cellphones in Schools and Implications for Youth Mental Health." KFF. September 5, 2024. https://www.kff.org/affordable-care-act/a-look-at-state-efforts-to-ban-cellphones-in-schools-and-implications-for-youth-mental-health.
29. Shammas, Brittany. "D.C.'s First Phone-Free Bar Brings Surprise, Delight and Lots of Polaroids." *The Washington Post,* September 15, 2025. https://www.washingtonpost.com/dc-md-va/2025/09/13/hush-harbor-phone-free-bar-dc.
30. Montali, Stefano. "A Debate About A.I. Plays Out on the Subway Walls." *New York Times*. October 7, 2025. https://www.nytimes.com/2025/10/07/style/friend-ai-subway-ads-new-york.html.

Chapter 13

1. Levin, *A Time to Build.*
2. Cox and Pressler, "Disconnected: The Growing Class Divide in American Civic Life."
3. Fetterolf, Janell, and Stephanie Kramer. "Americans Are Less Likely Than Others Around the World to Feel Close to People in Their Country or Community." Pew Research Center. May 8, 2024. https://www.pewresearch.org/short-reads/2024/05/08/americans-are-less-likely-than-others-around-the-world-to-feel-close-to-people-in-their-country-or-community.
4. Kramer, Stephanie. "U.S. Has World's Highest Rate of Children Living in Single-Parent Households." Pew Research Center, December 12, 2019. https://www.pewresearch.org/short-reads/2019/12/12/u-s-children-more-likely-than-children-in-other-countries-to-live-with-just-one-parent.
5. Cox and Hammond, "Individuality and Moral Behavior."
6. Ballard, Negar. "Over Half of Americans Report Feeling Like No One Knows Them Well." *Ipsos.* May 1, 2018. https://www.ipsos.com/en-us/news-polls/us-loneliness-index-report.
7. McPherson, Miller, Lynn Smith-Lovin, and James M. Cook. "Birds of a Feather: Homophily in Social Networks." *Annual Review of Sociology* 27, no. 1 (2001): 415–444. https://doi.org/10.1146/annurev.soc.27.1.415.

8. "The Perception Gap." More in Common. https://perceptiongap.us.
9. "America in One Room." Stanford Deliberative Democracy Lab. n.d. https://deliberation.stanford.edu/america-one-room.
10. Bellah, Robert N., Richard Madsen, William M. Sullivan, Ann Swidler, and Steven M. Tipton. *Habits of the Heart: Individualism and Commitment in American Life.* Berkeley: University of California Press, 1985.
11. Nadeem, Reem. "Biden's and Trump's Personal Qualities and Handling of Issues." Pew Research Center. July 11, 2024. https://www.pewresearch.org/politics/2024/07/11/biden-and-trumps-personal-qualities-and-handling-of-issues.
12. Eddy, Kirsten. "How Americans View Journalists in the Digital Age." Pew Research Center. August 20, 2025. https://www.pewresearch.org/journalism/2025/08/20/how-americans-view-journalists-in-the-digital-age.
13. Haridasani Gupta, Alisha, and Nicole Stock. "How Do You Spot a 'Performative' Male? Look for a Tote Bag." *New York Times.* August 14, 2025. https://www.nytimes.com/2025/08/14/style/performative-men.html.
14. Kenny, John, Sofia Breitenstein, and Michael S. Lewis-Beck. "Political Authenticity: Cases and Consequences." *Polity* 57, no. 2 (2025): 189–197. https://doi.org/10.1086/734784.
15. Wenner Moyer, Melinda. "Why I Won't Teach My Son Chivalry." *Now What*, October 25, 2022, https://melindawmoyer.substack.com/p/why-i-wont-teach-my-son-chivalry.
16. Mainwaring, C., F. Gabbert, and A.J. Scott. "A Systematic Review Exploring Variables Related to Bystander Intervention in Sexual Violence Contexts." *Trauma, Violence, & Abuse* 24, no. 3 (July 2023): 1727–1742. https://doi.org/10.1177/15248380221079660.
17. Davidovic, Anna, Catherine Talbot, Catherine Hamilton-Giachritsis, and Adam Joinson. "To Intervene or Not to Intervene: Young Adults' Views on When and How to Intervene in Online Harassment." *Journal of Computer-Mediated Communication* 28, no. 5 (2023): zmad027. https://academic.oup.com/jcmc/article/28/5/zmad027/7237464?login=false.
18. Crowley, Maureen, and Alice H. Eagly. "Gender and Helping Behav-

ior: A Meta-Analytic Review of the Social Psychological Literature." *Psychological Bulletin* 100, no. 3 (1986): 283–308. https://doi.org/10.1037/0033-2909.100.3.283.

19. Joseph, Chanté. "Is Having a Boyfriend Embarrassing Now?" *Vogue,* October 29, 2025. https://www.vogue.com/article/is-having-a-boyfriend-embarrassing-now.

"Daniel Cox is one of the nation's preeminent experts in polling and public opinion. In *Generation Uncoupled,* he shows he is also an indispensable social critic. Weaving together new survey data, extensive interviews, and thoughtful analysis of cultural trends, including dating, marriage, family formation, and civic engagement, Cox describes the alarming crisis of connection faced by young Americans. Thanks to this urgent and important work, we will all be better prepared to help Gen Z repair and rebuild their trust in our institutions—and in each other."

—Christine Rosen, author of *The Extinction of Experience* and senior fellow at the American Enterprise Institute

Praise for *Generation Uncoupled*

"With a wealth of data and the deft touch of a highly trained social scientist, Daniel Cox describes in careful detail the social atomization of modern America. But beyond that he also offers a pathway forward, that focuses on curiosity, kindness, and a real desire to cultivate community again. *Generation Uncoupled* is essential reading to understand how we got in this mess and what it will take to get us out of it."

—Ryan Burge, Professor of Practice, John C. Danforth Center on Religion and Politics at Washington University

"The history of humanity has been one of people coming together, creating families, and shaping the next generation. How did we get to a place where young people are turning away from that project? From the political divides disrupting dating lives, the cultural expectations weighing on parents, and the technologies warping our sense of reality, Daniel Cox examines how we arrived here and what it might take to fix it."

—Kristen Soltis Anderson, founding partner of Echelon Insights and author of *The Selfie Vote*

"This beautifully written book helped me to understand my divided generation, and reminded me that the bravest, most countercultural step we can take is to come together."

—Freya India, author of *GIRLS*®